READING
the RIVER

READING the RIVER

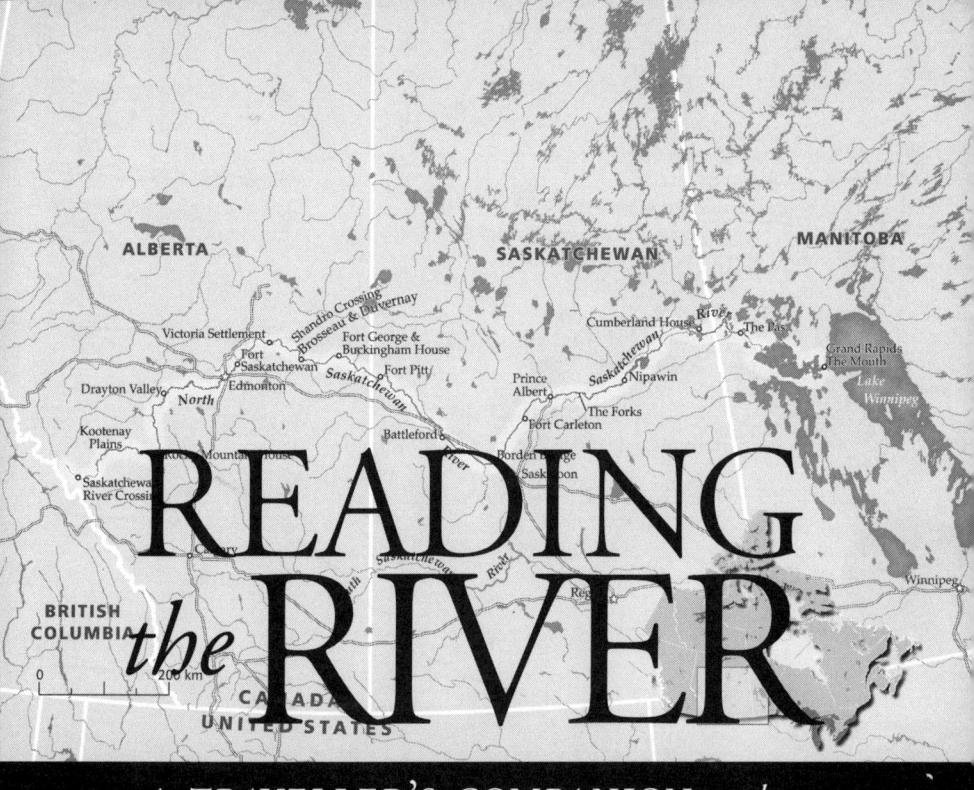

A TRAVELLER'S COMPANION *to the* NORTH SASKATCHEWAN RIVER

MYRNA KOSTASH
with DUANE BURTON

COTEAU BOOKS

© Myrna Kostash, 2005. First US edition, 2006.

All rights reserved. No part of this publication may be reproduced, stored in a retrieval system, or transmitted, in any form or by any means, without the prior written consent of the publisher or a licence from The Canadian Copyright Licensing Agency (Access Copyright). For an Access Copyright licence, visit www.accesscopyright.ca or call toll-free to 1-800-893-5777.

Edited by Roberta Mitchell Coulter.
Cover image: "Kootenay Plains and North Saskatchewan River Alberta, Canada."
© Daryl Benson / Masterfile.
Interior maps by Jeff Wielki.
Cover and book design by Duncan Campbell.
Printed and bound in Canada by Marquis Book Printing Inc.

Library and Archives Canada Cataloguing in Publication

Reading the river : a traveller's companion to the North Saskatchewan River / edited by Myrna Kostash with Duane Burton.

Includes bibliographical references.
ISBN 1-55050-317-0

1. North Saskatchewan River (Alta. and Sask.)—Description and travel.
2. North Saskatchewan River (Alta. and Sask.)—History.
3. North Saskatchewan River Region (Alta. and Sask.)—Description and travel.
4. North Saskatchewan River Region (Alta. and Sask.)—History.
I. Kostash, Myrna II. Burton, Duane

FC3544.4.R42 2005   971.23'3   C2005-906573-7

10 9 8 7 6 5 4 3 2 1

COTEAU BOOKS
2517 Victoria Avenue
Regina, Saskatchewan
Canada S4P 0T2

Available in Canada & the US from
Fitzhenry & Whiteside
195 Allstate Parkway
Markham, ON, Canada L3R 4T8

The publisher gratefully acknowledges the financial support of its publishing program by: the Saskatchewan Arts Board; the Canada Council for the Arts; the Government of Canada through the Book Publishing Industry Development Program (BPIDP); the City of Regina Arts Commission; the Saskatchewan Cultural Industries Development Fund of Saskatchewan Culture Youth and Recreation; SaskCulture Inc.; the Saskatchewan Heritage Foundation; and Saskatchewan Centennial 2005.

RIVERS
(for Myrna)

The river flows one way
and in its passing, swift
or slow, you feel
the weight of time,
the lunar pull, the turn
of seasons. Go with
the current and it takes
you where all things
come at last together.

But there is another way –
turn against the flow
and brunt the mystery
leading you where things
begin, where a river is
just a notion wrought
from sun and ice and stone.
The river flows one way,
but in the wonder of its
passing, we choose.

Glen Sorestad

Contents

Preface: *An Essential River* – 1

Opening: *A Gift of the Gods* – 7

Saskatchewan River Crossing: *The Heart of an Untouched Land* – 21

Kootenay Plains: *Meadow of the Winds*, by Duane Burton – 33

Rocky Mountain House: *The Fur Trade* – 49

Drayton Valley: *The Great Secret of the River* – 75

Edmonton: *The Watery Highway* – 87

Fort Saskatchewan: *Mountain Trout and Roasted Beaver* – 137

Victoria Settlement: *The Great Valley* – 149

Shandro Crossing/Brosseau/Duvernay: *Blessed Water* – 169

Fort George & Buckingham House: *The Region of Plenty* – 177

Fort Pitt: *Mistahimaskwa: Big Bear* – 189

Battleford: *Untold Stories* – 205

Borden Bridge: *Gracing the Space* – 217

Fort Carlton: *The Fertile Belt* – 223

Prince Albert: *Gateway to the North* – 241

The Forks: *What a Highway!* – 253

Nipawin: *Between Farmland and Forest* – 263

Cumberland House: *A Strategic Location* – 271

The Pas: *Where the River Narrows* – 291

Grand Rapids/The Mouth: *The Great Marsh* – 311

Conclusion: *What Is a River For?* – 327

Biographies – 335
Author Acknowledgements – 344
Text Acknowledgements – 344
Photograph Acknowledgements – 349

ALBERTA

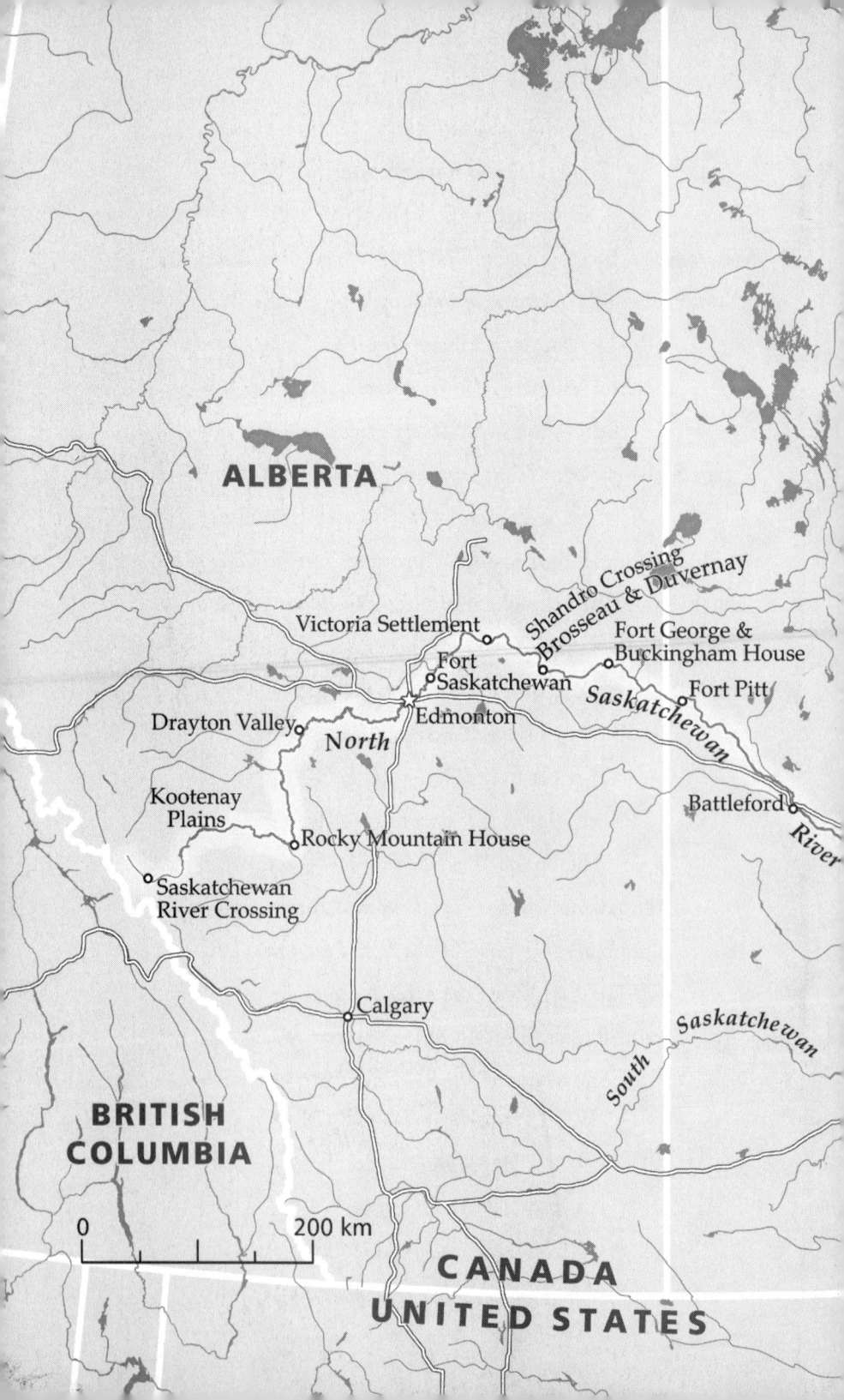

- Shandro Crossing
- Brosseau & Duvernay
- Victoria Settlement
- Fort Saskatchewan
- Fort George & Buckingham House
- Fort Pitt
- Edmonton
- Drayton Valley
- North Saskatchewan River
- Battleford
- Kootenay Plains
- Rocky Mountain House
- Saskatchewan River Crossing
- Calgary
- South Saskatchewan

BRITISH COLUMBIA

0 — 200 km

CANADA
UNITED STATES

SASKATCHEWAN

MANITOBA

Cumberland House

River

The Pas

Saskatchewan

Grand Rapids
The Mouth

Prince
Albert

Nipawin

*Lake
Winnipeg*

The Forks

Fort Carleton

orden Bridge

Saskatoon

Winnipeg

Regina

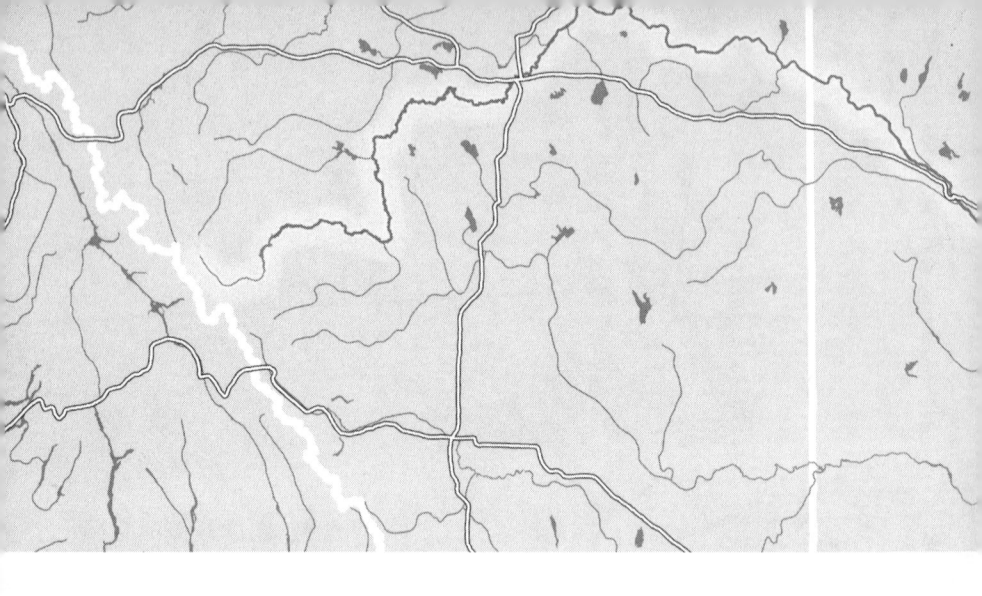

From the glaciers and ice valleys of this great range of mountains innumerable streams descend into the plains. For a time they wander, as if heedless of direction, through groves and glades and green spreading declivities; then, assuming greater fixity of purpose, they gather up many a wandering rill, and start eastward upon a long journey.... This river, which has along it every diversity of hill and vale, meadow-land and forest, treeless plain and fertile hill-side, is called by the wild tribes who dwell along its glorious shores the Kissaskatchewan, or Rapid-flowing River. – William Francis Butler, *The Great Lone Land* (1872)

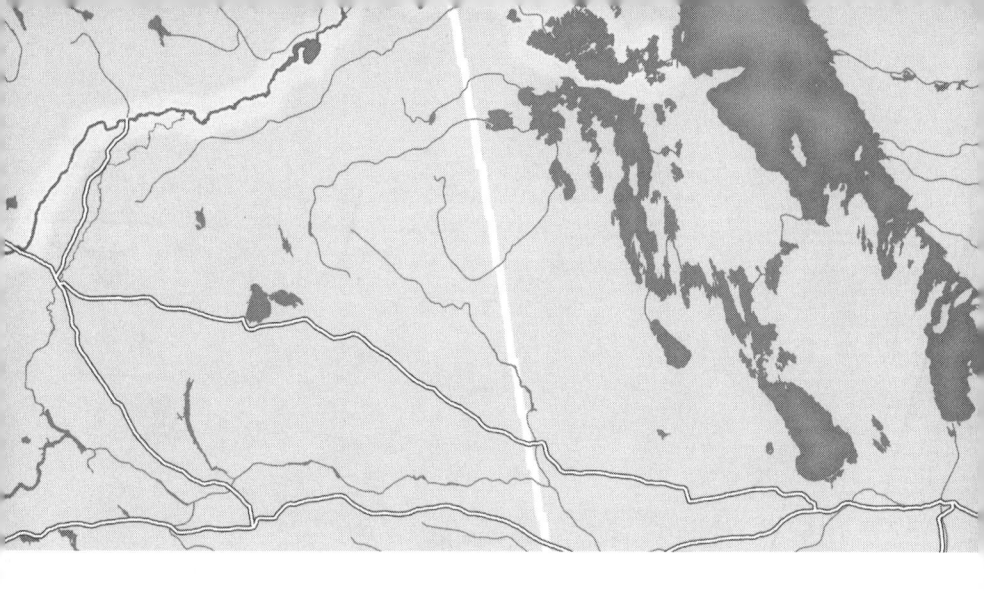

PREFACE
An Essential River

Several years ago, I read the European best-seller *Danube,* in which the author/narrator, Claudio Magris, takes a trip (whether real or imagined) down the Danube through the heart of Europe and into the Black Sea. Along the way, he regales us with stories of writers and philosophers and poets and others, all of them associated one way or another with the great river. It was fun to read, and left me a little envious: together with the German poet Holderlin, for instance, "the greatest poet to sing of the Danube," Magris drags in the voyage of Heracles and mythical travels of Germanic forefathers along the waterway. So much history! So much memory! So much literature!

And then I began to wonder: could we talk about one of the great Canadian rivers this way? The North Saskatchewan River, say, along whose banks I have spent most of my life? The notion seemed ludicrous; after all, just how much history have we made here? And just how old is our poetry? But I soon recognized these

"Here among the stupendous and solitary Wilds covered with eternal Snow..." Trip to Columbia Icefield, crossing the Saskatchewan Glacier, Byron Harmon, *1924*.

questions as beside the point, or rather too "European" in their focus. Much of the very earliest history of the river – the story of Aboriginal interactions with it – remains unwritten, of course, or is at best inferred from European accounts and contexts, but there has been history along this river since the first human communities gathered along it; there's been poetry since the first story described its source, its power, and its gods.

So, my research associate, Duane Burton, and I set out to gather together as wide a variety of stories and tales and anecdotes and reports as we could find that had something to say about the writer's or poet's observations or feelings about the Saskatchewan River, from First Nations legends ("orature") to twenty-first century poetry.

The North Saskatchewan is an essential river. The waterway has been literally life-giving for over a millennium. Pronghorn antelope were once prolific along the south banks of the North

Saskatchewan between Edmonton and The Forks. Trumpeter swans, now endangered, were once harvested in the thousands for their feathers and quills. Grizzly bears were commonly hunted along the river for food and floor covering into the mid-nineteenth century. It supplied drinking water for people and beasts, trickling out of the Saskatchewan Glacier, swelling with its tributary waters from the Brazeau, Nordegg, Ram, Clearwater, Sturgeon, and Vermillion on its way to the Alberta-Saskatchewan border. In Saskatchewan, the waters of the South Saskatchewan and Battle join it in its flow to Lake Winnipeg in Manitoba.

"The nets came up full of fish in all the lakes along it," wrote Emerson Hough, an American writer who came to "Sas-Katch-E-Wan: The Missouri of the North" in 1907. "Its plains were tenanted by the buffalo and antelope. The plover circled about the uplands; the painted wild fowl streamed across; and the wind blew always fresh and keen enough to wash away a strong man's sins." But even as he rhapsodized, steam locomotives and sod-busting were forever altering the terrain; and the people who had once "tenanted" the plains along with the vanished buffalo were sickening on reserves.

In May 2001, the North Saskatchewan River valley in Edmonton yielded 2,920 bags of garbage on its annual clean-up day, an illustration of how most of us – garbage collectors excepted – are heedless of the river as a natural environment. Environmentalists like Adele Mandryk, though, look to Edmonton's river valley in a way that is almost poetic:

> *Can God's grandeur flame out from this unlikely source and shine so close at hand within the river valley system of Edmonton? Chet Raymo, professor of physics and astronomy, in his book* Skeptics and True Believers: The Exhilarating Connection Between Science and Religion, *says: "scientific knowledge enlivens our very experience and tunes us to the deepest mysteries of creation, the hidden rhythms of the world*

that evade our limited senses." Are these deepest mysteries of creation to be found in Edmonton? In our own North Saskatchewan River Valley?

What moved and excited me as I spent two years getting to know "my" river better, was that part of it that flows through its magnificent trench down toward the elegant steel architecture of the High Level Bridge in Edmonton, having turned a bend or two along its sweep past the Kootenay Plains, past Rocky Mountain House and Drayton Valley, along bush and farmland and under the Devon Bridge, then looping through Terwilliger Park before bending again just where I am looking out at it from Victoria Promenade, high on the bank near my home. What impresses me now is to think of how far still this water has to run – past towns and villages and a couple of cities, past First Nations reserves and along railway tracks, past trading forts both reconstructed and abandoned, under bridges and over sand bars, past grain elevators and power plants and bits and pieces of mouldering steamboats and ferries, past cemeteries and memorial cairns, past sacred places and look-out points – before it ends its course in the meandering channels of its mouth, opening into Lake Winnipeg.

And all along its way the North Saskatchewan River has been and is being serenaded by poets, whether they sing the song of the creator Wesakechak, who brought the great waterways of North America into being, or the ballads of the *voyageurs* who laboured at their own Herculean voyages up and down its currents, or the hymns of the Christians as they raised places of worship just offshore, or the battle cries of warriors, the chants of the Sundance, and the requiems for the dead, the dying, the sick, or the melancholic reminiscences of people who abandoned homelands for a sod shack in the middle of a long, long winter, or the laughter of adventurers beating around the bush and careering on rafts, ass over teakettle into rapids…and so on, down to the writers of our own time and places who stop, look, and listen to the river as it slides away beyond our ken.

Who needs the Danube?

The North Saskatchewan River is a big river, streaming through our history and mythologies, our communities and identities, our bedrock and our unwinding time. And we've written the literature to prove it. – *Myrna Kostash*

I felt compelled to write the story of the Kootenay Plains while doing research for this book. I have made every effort to accurately source and represent the material that belongs to the Stoney Nakoda people. – *Duane Burton*

Note: While the most offensive literary references to Aboriginal people have been left out of *Reading the River*, it was impossible to avoid all derogatory references, such as "warring savages," or even romanticized ones such as "full-ridged chest of a tall red-man," or the obsolete, such as "half-breed," as they were deeply rooted and ubiquitous in earlier discourses of Aboriginal and European contact.

Napi [Old Man Creator] kept on travelling north, creating the forests and the big rivers and lakes where the Cree live.... Napi created the Cree and other Indian people along the way and fixed up their country for them. Eventually he left the world and went away toward the west, disappearing in the mountains. Before he started, he said to the people: "I will always take care of you, and some day I will return."

The Piikani [Peigan] mythic account of the Creator walking northwards is a deep time memory of the ice and lakes receding, and the plants, animals and people coming back to these lands we know as the Eastern Slopes of the Rocky Mountains and the Western Plains of the headwaters of the Missouri and Saskatchewan.... – Brian O. K. Reeves, "Sacred Geography: First Nations of the Yellowstone to Yukon"

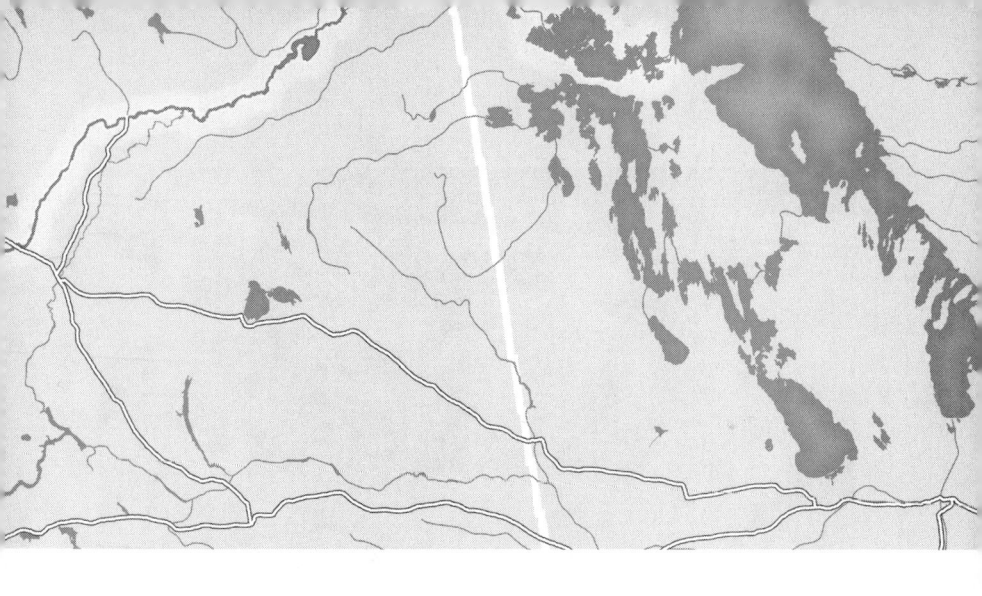

OPENING
A Gift of the Gods

The last great ice sheet of the last Ice Age began its melt 17,000 years ago from the southwest corner of Saskatchewan. About 6,000 years later, the Laurentide ice sheet had retreated northeast past The Forks, where the two branches of the Saskatchewan, North and South, now meet and flow on to Lake Winnipeg. Meanwhile, some 12,500 years ago, back in the Rocky Mountains, a vestige of the Cordilleran ice sheet, the Columbia Icefield, released small streams of meltwater which coalesced into a cascade at the foot of Saskatchewan Glacier, the longest-outlet glacier extending from the icefield. From here the glacial water tumbled on eastwardly, gathering in tributary creeks and what are now the waters of the Howse and Mistaya rivers, just west of the bridge at Saskatchewan Crossing. The future bed of the North Saskatchewan lay still trapped in ice.

"The Forests, the ledges and hills of Rock, the Lakes and Rivers, have all something of the Manito about them." Kootenay Plains and North Saskatchewan River, Alberta, Canada.

> *And* Waka Taga, *who is Life-Maker, then sings into existence these medicine spirits:* Mu *the spirit of Thunder,* Waheambah, *Sun*...Owsni Ti, *the Cold Air Spirit, and the Water Spirits.*

The spiritual roots of those who live at the beginnings of rivers in the Rocky Mountains lie deep, not only in their geography and mythologies but equally in the awareness of the history of generations of humans for whom it was a homeplace. Consider, for example, the migration of peoples after late Pleistocene chinook winds melted the rim of ice in the eastern valleys of the Rockies, or the island-hoppers in the Aleutians; consider the unstoppable movement of caribou and bison and musk-ox herds south into the new pasturelands, humans in hot hunting pursuit, 50 or 60 kilometres in a life span.

The poet Jon Whyte "wrote the west," as in his historical overview, *Indians in the Rockies*.

> *Where the transverse valleys of the Athabasca, the Saskatchewan, the Bow, and the Oldman rivers descend from the mountains to the plains, the glaciers melted first. There the land was lower and warmer. Animals that had retreated south, like the bison, moved north and into the mountains where they found the grasses they'd grown habituated to. They quickly repopulated the mountain valleys upon the ice's melting and the growth of plant cover. The wandering peoples, ever hungry, sought them out.*
>
> *The band of toolmaking hunters entered the Rockies 11,500 years ago. On the south-facing slope of the Bow Valley, at the shore of the glacial lake, they made camp long enough to find flaking rocks to form edged tools for killing and fleshing animals and for butchering the meat. They cured the hides, made clothing and tents, perhaps found moments to relax in the warm summer sun. The ashes of their ancient hearth rested on the soil....*

Through generations of narration, before and even after the invention of a written language, the First Nations reproduced the memory of those primordial events and later historical ones with a concrete vividness akin to the data of professional historians. Those who heard them – at least the ones with narrative genius – in turn passed the stories on in a process of listening and telling that was a kind of "writing," or *orature*. And when the first Europeans arrived in their midst, they told them again, these "sacred geographies" of the lakes, rivers, and streams, of origins and first causes.

"They believe in the self existence of the Keeche Keeche Manito (The Great, Great Spirit)," wrote the explorer David Thompson in his *Narrative of Travels in Western North America,* having wintered on the plains. "They appear to derive their belief from tradition, and believe that the visible world with all its inhabitants must have been made by some powerful being.... The Forests, the ledges and hills of Rock, the Lakes and Rivers have all something of the Manito about them...."

The Saskatchewan is a rather shallow river, varying from a metre to three metres deep, but naturally it flows most copiously in June during the rapid melt of the glaciers and the rains in the foothills. Its watershed, however, is vast, 385,000 square kilometres, and its 2,200 kilometres of drainage, from the lower eastern slopes of the Rocky Mountains to the sea water of Hudson Bay via the waters it feeds into the Nelson River, proved to be part of a superb trade route: Aboriginal grave sites in southern Alberta have yielded up spiral shells from the Pacific Northwest and copper beads traded from the Great Lakes region. Well-developed trails criss-crossed the Rockies and the plains. Obsidian, for arrowheads, from the Yellowstone River area shows up all over western North America, "in such profusion trade must have dispersed it," writes Jon Whyte.

The Saskatchewan was also the route that brought European traders into the continental heartland, looking not for conches and beads but for fur. The beaver top hat, a social necessity in Europe from the mid-1600s to the 1830s, was a felt hat made from the pelt's underlayer of fur wool, and the demand for it at the London fur auctions drove entrepreneurs up the western rivers of Canada. This was ideal beaver country: relatively flat with meandering waterways – lots of opportunity for the beaver to build dams – and well-watered aspen forest.

In ancient times, a race of huge beavers inhabited this world. They were many times the size of beavers in the forest today. These giant beavers lived on the shores and in the islands of a great lake. The giant beavers lived on earth for many, many years until one day the great sacred beaver was attacked by a thunderbird, the most powerful creature in the world. Binay-sih, the thunderbird, carried the sacred beaver high into the air. The talons of the powerful bird were sunk deep into the spine of the dying beaver and the blood oozed out of its body as they flew over the forests. When the red blood of the spirit beaver dropped to the ground, it was absorbed into the rocks and sand causing them to take on a reddish colour.

This sacred beaver was carried to the nest of Binay-sih and eaten by the young thunderbirds. Now the giant beavers around the great lake were without a sacred ruler, and soon they disappeared from the face of the earth, leaving a race of small beavers that had no spiritual leader. These are the beavers our people trap and hunt today. – Sacred Legends

From its headwaters the river flows through Rocky Mountain House, turns north and then once again eastward past remnant fur trade posts from Fort Edmonton to Fort Carlton, winding through swaths of farmland, then enters the land "unfit for tillage," the Canadian Shield, near Cumberland House, sweeps past The Pas, old Pasquia, and discharges its water into Lake Winnipeg. This is a traverse of 1,287 kilometres.

Lonely River

Hugh MacLennan grew fatigued just thinking about the Saskatchewan River. It was, he wrote in *Seven Rivers of Canada*, "the loneliest looking," by which he meant all that pitiless motion of water across the vast, open, barely-peopled plains in the heart of the continent, tireless and relentless and not very dramatic except at its origins in the mountain glacier and in its "final spasm" at Grand Rapids in Manitoba.

> *Often the Saskatchewan passes through bush and parkland, and these were the regions most prized by the fur-traders. But more often it winds through naked plains, and the feeling of loneliness is in proportion to the bareness of the land. The river is always below the surface of the prairie and it seldom floods, for its trenches are extremely deep. For hundreds of miles the trenches of the two branches channel the waters easterly: hundreds of miles of tan, monotonous water with weeds and wildflowers rife along the escarpments when sand-bars protrude from the channels in late summer; hundreds of miles of greenish-white ice against the flat white of the plain in the six-month winter which seems so interminable that the people in the river town hold sweepstakes on the hour and minute of the spring break-up....*
>
> *For along most of the Saskatchewan, whether on the North Branch or the South, the world has been reduced to what W. O. Mitchell called the least common denominator of nature, land and sky. There is also the effect of the weather. It shifts constantly and with it the moods of sky and land, and the river reflects all these moods with total fidelity. Few sights in Canada are more peaceful than the mirroring of the pastel sky-hues on the Saskatchewan on a fine summer day; none more chilling than an eddy of snow in January when the thermometer stands at forty or fifty below and the ice is too hard for a curling stone. The winds here are visible: in summer you see them as a throbbing radiance along a sea of grass, in winter as a drifting lace of ice crystal along a sea of snow....*

Though most of the Saskatchewan flows through the plains its waters rise in one of the most spectacular regions of North America. The North Branch, fathered by the Columbia Icefield, comes out of the glacier on Mount Saskatchewan, and when you stand on the little bridge over the North Fork and look at that lithe, frigid stream, not glacial-green but milky from limestone, so narrow in August that a broad-jumper could clear it, you can have a strange sensation when you think how far this water has to go.

The first contact of Europeans and Natives of the Canadian prairies was made through the agency of the Hudson's Bay Company, the fur-trading consortium of London gentlemen established by Royal charter in 1670 with exclusive trading rights in the whole territory whose rivers drained into Hudson Bay. From the time of the first European explorations westward into the continent, the explorers' movements were concentrated on passage to the headwaters of the North Saskatchewan, for the Indians with whom they traded had spoken of a swiftly flowing river gushing out of the mountains.

It is likely that Henry Kelsey, dispatched from York Factory on Hudson Bay by the Hudson's Bay Company in 1690 to find the Indians in their western camps and persuade them to trade at the Bay, was the first European to move upstream the great Saskatchewan waterway onto the western plains. The first conclusive mention of the French on the river is Pierre de La Vérendrye (son of Pierre Gaultier de Varennes et de La Vérendrye, builder of trading posts in Manitoba), who established Fort Bourbon at Cedar Lake near the mouth of the Saskatchewan in 1741. For the next eighteen years, the French traders worked the lower part of the river. In 1743, François, another son, constructed small Fort Pasquia (or Paskoya) at the confluence of the Carrot, Pasquia, and Saskatchewan rivers, now known as The Pas, Manitoba. It was

Pierre's other brother, Louis-Joseph de La Vérendrye, who first traversed the main river in 1749; he called it La Blanche. On other French maps, the river appears as Poskaiao and Poskoiac and Poskoyac. By 1775, Alexander Henry refers to three names for what we now call the Saskatchewan: River de Bourbon, Pasquayah, and Sascatchiwaine – Cree for "swiftly flowing waters."

When the free traders out of Montreal, who eventually emerged organized in 1783 as the North West Company (NWC), arrived on the rivers of the Northwest the Hudson's Bay Company's monopoly on the trade was broken, and it was forced to move upriver and upcountry to compete for furs directly at posts visited by Native trappers. Their first trading post was near The Pas, upstream from the mouth of the Saskatchewan, in 1773. A year later, they were at Cumberland House. They would keep moving, farther and farther west, until they got to the rapids and built Rocky Mountain House, the posts of the NWC leapfrogging them all the way. In 1821, the two companies merged under the old title and charter of the Hudson's Bay Company.

As to the question of who was the first European to see the Rocky Mountains, the evidence is speculative. We do know that, well before the arrival of these explorers and traders from England

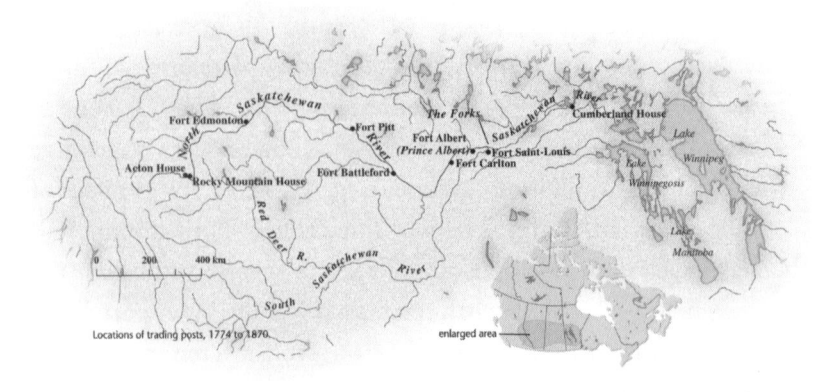

Location of trading posts, 1744 to 1870.

and France, the Cree, *the* great traders in Saskatchewan River country, had been meeting at various camping places along the trade corridor of the river valley and its tributaries between Edmonton and York Factory. There were six important camping places, near which at least four early French forts were later established: *Misipawitik,* "a large rapid" (Grand Rapids), *Opasskweyaw,* "the narrowing between woods" (The Pas), *Nipowiwinihk,* "a standing place" (Nipawin), and *Penahon,* "the waiting place" (Fort-à-la-Corne). As places not only of trade but also of family reunions, marriages, and religious ceremonies, they were a powerful geography.

"Thither come the plumed
and painted sons of the forest"

When William Henry Withrow wrote *Our Own Country* in 1889, he needed a very long subtitle to convey the breadth of his interests: *Canada, scenic and descriptive: being an account of the extent, resources, physical aspect, industries, cities and chief towns of the provinces of Nova Scotia, Prince Edward Island, Newfoundland, New Brunswick, Quebec, Ontario, Manitoba, the North-West Territory* [present-day Saskatchewan and Alberta] *and British Columbia, with sketches of travel and adventure.* In fact, though, it is difficult sometimes to tell whether Withrow was always writing from observation and adventure or from romantic novels in his library. He describes the life of an Indian trapper:

> About the month of August, the Indians of the great North-West procure a supply of pork, flour and ammunition, generally on trust, at the Hudson's Bay posts, and thread their way up the lonely rivers and over many a portage, far into the interior.... They carry a supply of steel traps, which they carefully set and bait, concealing all appearance of design. The hunter

makes the round of his traps, often many miles apart, returning to the camp, as by an unerring instinct, through the pathless wilderness.... In the spring he returns to the trading-posts, shooting the rapids of the swollen streams, frequently with bales of furs worth several hundreds of dollars.... The Indians of the interior are models of honesty. They will not trespass on each other's streams or hunting-grounds, and always punctually repay the debt they have incurred at the trading-posts.... Thither come the plumed and painted sons of the forest to barter their peltries for the knives and guns of Sheffield and Birmingham, the gay fabrics of Manchester and Leeds, and other luxuries of savage life, and to smoke the pipe of peace with their white allies.

Manning the French advance ever westwards from Montreal deep into Indian trading country were the companies' employees, the *voyageurs,* usually Canadian by birth from families in Quebec or from Métis families descended from the first free traders in the West who had set themselves up at strategic locations at river crossings and portages and married Native women. The voyageurs usually spoke several local languages and worked at the posts, where they were expected to live off the land. Trader Alexander Henry's river expedition, for instance, in the summer of 1810, travelled with such Métis voyageurs as Jacques Barbe, Etienne Charboneau, Joseph Dubois, Angus McDonald, Joseph Hamel, among them guides, a clerk, and interpreter. According to journalist-historian Marjorie Campbell's reading of Henry's journals, they also did most of the work: "As his steersman and bowman kept the canoe straight while the rest of the crew tracked laboriously up the river Henry could sit amidships dozing pleasantly or planning his campaign with opposing traders." But as soon as Henry was at the fort, he was all business.

Henry ruled the natives with a strong hand. He had his forts well palisaded. Not more than thirty or forty principal Indians were allowed within the palisades at once, and then only after proper formalities. Young men sent on ahead for tobacco were received first, thus announcing the coming of the older men with whom trading was accomplished. There was a large keg of grog and tobacco for each tribe, the sort of gift calculated to woo those with valuable pelts. Often there was little rum and much Saskatchewan water in the keg, Henry nicely gauging the acquired tastes of the natives....

Buying cheap and selling dear came naturally to Henry. From the natives he secured dried berries, as well as pelts, pounded meat, grease, back fat, buffalo robes, and horses, all very cheap. "A common horse" cost a gallon keg of Blackfoot rum, two fathoms of tobacco, and a few minor items.

"What the horse is to the Arab, the camel to the desert traveller, or the dog to the Esquimaux, the birch-bark canoe is to the Indian," William Withrow quoted a Mr. H. M. Robinson in his own travel book, *Our Own Country* in 1889. And he even quoted, unattributed, a poem to make his point: "All the forest life is in it – all its mystery and magic, all the lightness of the birch-tree, all the toughness of the cedar, all the larch's supple sinews, and it floated on the river like a yellow leaf in autumn, like a yellow water lily."

If it was a "north" canoe, it would be about eight metres in length and a metre-and-a-half wide, made of thin sheets of birch bark sewn with spruce roots, the seams sealed with spruce gum. The voyageur had to supply his own paddles. The canoe could carry eight to ten men, each carrying his personal baggage and food supplies, including biscuit, peas, and pork, tools such as an axe, a towing line, and a kettle, and the trade goods, of course, at least 20 per cent of which were kegs of liquor. When they portaged, the voyageurs packed eighty kilograms each, some heroes of labour reportedly carrying up to seven packs at a time. Besides their wages, the employees were entitled to leggings, shirts, tobacco, knives, and beads. By 1814, they were trading pistols, gloves, and even umbrellas, as well as the usual blankets and beads, for pelts, for the Indian trappers had become "fussier and harder to please," as a recent historian of the fur trade, Elizabeth Macpherson, observed.

But a century later, such workers had become the stuff of legend for the writers of the wild western frontier, such as the American Emerson Hough, a professional journalist who travelled the American west during the transition "from wilderness into a civilized region," to quote a critic, Carole M. Johnson. At some point in the early 1900s, he must have travelled to Canada and to points on the Saskatchewan River, for he published, in 1907, a magazine article that likened the "Sas-katch-e-wan" to the Missouri, for its centrality to the story of the rush of adventurers and traders across the continent to the western sea. Hough writes that the Saskatchewan remained "mysteriously unknown, highway only of the furs."

Perhaps it is fitting that a definitive word on the subject of the fur trade and the contact of Aboriginals with Europeans should come from a descendent of the people who still endure the ravages of its effects upon them. Ralph G. Steinhauer, born on the Morley reserve in 1905 and Alberta's lieutenant-governor from 1974 to 1979, wrote a foreword to Jon Whyte's *Indians in the Rockies* in 1985 because he hoped that a new look at the lives of First Nations people on the eastern slopes of the Rockies and on the plains would awaken the reader to the hardships inflicted on Indian people through the "forced transition from a beloved way of life to one so totally different." The transition was the fur trade – the coming of the white traders, disease, and alcohol, the mass slaughter of the bison, the signing of treaties and the removal of the Indians to the reserves, the forced Christianization, really "a total upheaval" in their lives – and it came up the Saskatchewan River. That is not the only story, but it does remind us that, long before it was the Saskatchewan, this was Kisiskatchewan, and it flowed swiftly, a gift of the gods.

○ Saskatchewan
River Crossing

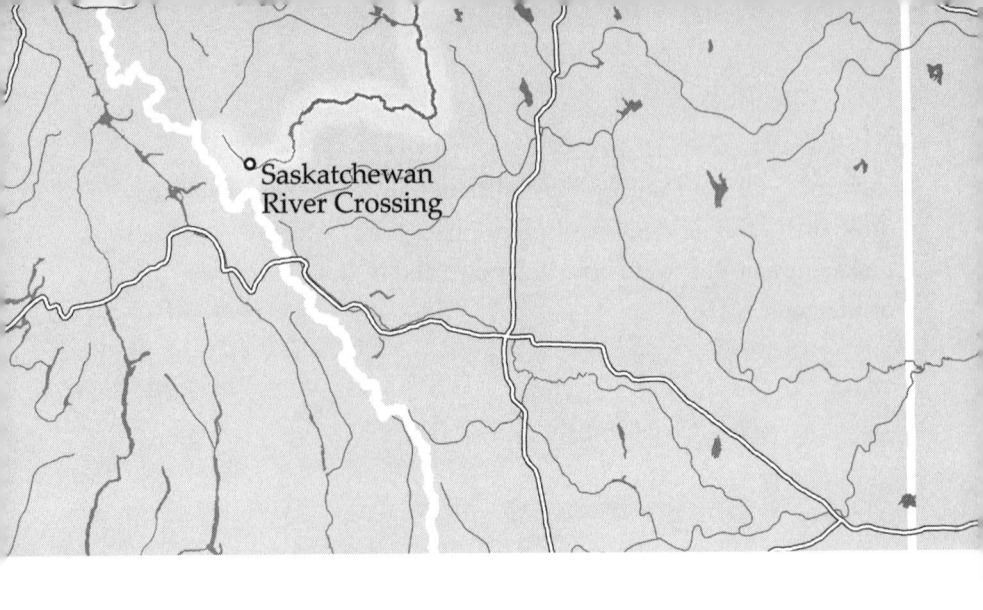

The Mackenzie, the Columbia, and the Saskatchewan spring from the peaks whose teeth-like summits lie grouped from this spot into the compass of a single glance. The clouds that cast their moisture upon this long line of upheaven rocks seek again the ocean which gave them birth in its far-separated divisions of Atlantic, Pacific, and Arctic. The sun sank slowly behind the range and darkness began to fall on the immense plain, but aloft on the topmost edge the pure white of the jagged crest-line glowed for an instant in many-coloured silver, and then the lonely peaks grew dark and dim. – William Francis Butler, *The Great Lone Land*

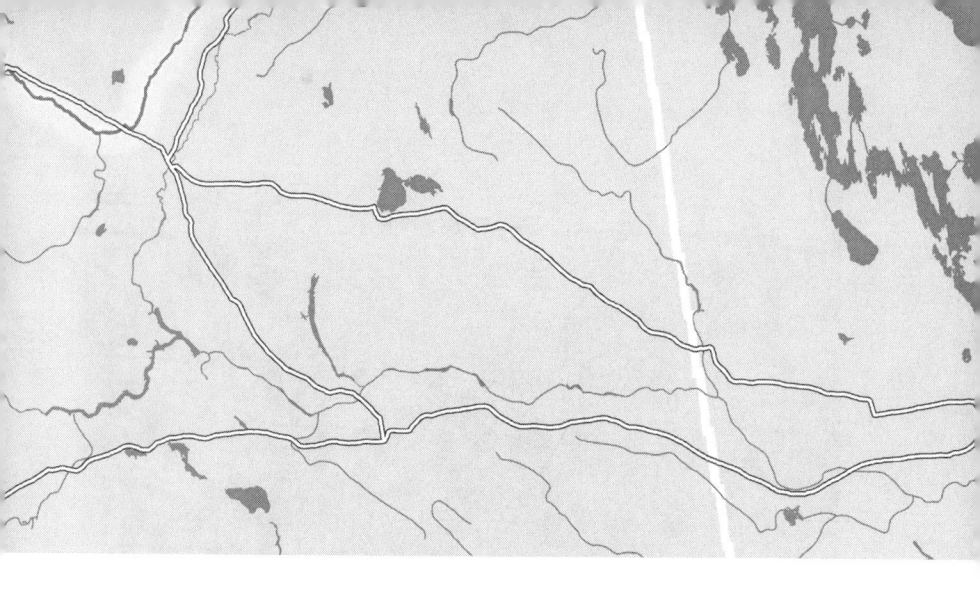

SASKATCHEWAN RIVER CROSSING
The Heart of an Untouched Land

The North Saskatchewan rises at the base of Saskatchewan Glacier in the Columbia Icefield in the Rocky Mountains of Alberta, 1800 metres above sea level between Mount Columbia and Mount Athabasca. You can see all this – the glacier, the meltwaters, milky from limestone, gushing out of the rock face, the roaring whirlpool of the young river churning around its rock bed and then out on the gravel flats by the highway – simply by standing on the shoulder of Highway 93. During the Second World War, a road was built from the newly completed Banff-Jasper highway to the toe of the glacier so that U.S. troops could train on its surface. The glacier has since receded a kilometre but if you hike up Parker Ridge, above the tree line and along alpine meadow, blown about by the winds whipping around the ranges, you can look down, very far down, onto the exquisite blue thread of the a-borning Saskatchewan River. It is making its first descent in the direction of

The river is making its first descent in the direction of the Hudson Bay.

the Hudson Bay through the valley excavated by the glacial stream, its bed a litter of rock and stone, and it is joined in rapid succession by the tributary streams of Alexandra River, Norman Creek, Rampart Creek, Arctomys Creek, Mistaya River, and the bulging Howse River. With these waters, it is about to become the North Saskatchewan River itself, streaming out to the Kootenay Plains.

In the 1800s, pack trains of explorers and fur traders crossed the river here at its meeting point with the Howse and Mistaya Rivers. The Rockies themselves were crossed at Howse Pass by NWC trader and explorer David Thompson and his party (including his wife, Charlotte, and their three children) in June, 1807. They had paddled as far upriver from Rocky Mountain House as they could, then several kilometres up the Howse River until it became impossible to canoe further. They then followed a horse trail along an old fur trade route cut roughly for them the year before by two men out of the House. "Here among the stupendous and solitary Wilds covered with eternal Snow, and Mountain connected to Mountain by immense Glaciers.... I staid fourteen days more, impatiently waiting the melting of Snows on the Height of Land." At snowmelt, they moved on, and on June 22, 1807, Thompson noted in his journal, they reached a rivulet whose current descended westward. They had crossed the Continental Divide. By June 30, 1807, they stood on the shore of the Columbia River.

In 1809 Joseph Howse, a trader for the Hudson's Bay Company, crossed the pass, as did all other traders looking to establish posts west of the Rockies until 1810, when Pikuani [Peigan] hunters blocked it to prevent the trade in rifles to their Kutenai [Kootenay] enemy, threatening "if they again meet with a white man going to supply their Enemies, they would not only plunder and kill him, but they would make dry Meat of his body," as Fred Stenson, who has written a history of Rocky Mountain House, relates.

David Thompson trekked north of Howse Pass and eventually through the Athabasca Pass to the Columbia River system, which became as busy and trafficked as the Howse Pass remained out-of-the-way. But from the 1870s, when the CPR surveyor, Walter Moberly, concluded that Howse Pass was the best route for the railway (he was ignored) right up to the present time, visions have been spun of a highway through the "gentle mountain pass" (to quote the Red Deer Chamber of Commerce in 2003) to connect with the Trans-Canada superhighway north of Golden, British Columbia. The national parks of Jasper and Banff, it seems, represent "one of the greatest inter-provincial trade barriers in the country."

In August 1858, some fifty years after David Thompson and party, the Palliser Expedition, exploring the geology and topography of the Canadian Northwest on behalf of the British government, reached the Rockies. Its leader, John Palliser, then invited its geologist and naturalist, James Hector, to explore whatever seemed to be most interesting for his purposes. Guided by Peter Erasmus and a Stoney Indian whose name he never learned to pronounce and so referred to as "Nimrod," Hector set off intrepidly up the Bow River valley, through Vermillion Pass (now cut through by Highway 93), following the Vermillion River to its confluence with the Kootenay River. The rest of his itinerary makes dizzying reading — Beaverfoot and Kicking Horse rivers, Wapta Falls, Kicking Horse Pass, Mount Hector, and Hector Lake — until finally they gained the North Saskatchewan by coming down the Mistaya River, one of its tributaries in the Rockies.

They reached the Saskatchewan River Crossing area and next tried to locate Thompson's Howse Pass but were so slowed by dense forest and fallen timber up the Howse River that they got no further than Thompson's 1807 winter camp at the foot of Mount David.

There were no trails and little food — they were eating blueberries as they struggled through Kicking Horse Pass — and Hector suffered the indignity of being struck in the chest by his own horse and losing consciousness for a few hours; but they did it in thirty-eight days. Peter Erasmus told the tale.

I found some fresh deer tracks shortly after I left camp, but was too anxious, and startled them before I could get a good shot. Following them I had another running shot, drew blood, but did not knock the buck down. I kept after the wounded deer, and before I realized that I had gone so far, it was dark, and I had lost my directions. It was hopeless to try to find the way in the dark so I built a fire and tried to forget that I was hungry, cold, and worried over the doctor. Nights in the mountains get pretty cold and that one was the longest and most miserable of any time I ever spent on the trail.

Early the next morning I climbed a high place and got my directions from the fog rising from the river. There were no rabbits or bird game of any kind and I decided the deer had not been hurt enough to be worthwhile chasing again. Although I watched for any moving object I could not find any sign of a squirrel. The area was totally barren of any game. Nimrod had gone on the hunt long before I got back empty-handed and tired to the party.... The doctor was still in pain but feeling much better, for which I was thankful.

"The Indians and half-breeds were paid servants and thus not entitled to any praise for their deeds, which were quite frequently at the risk of their own lives." Peter Erasmus, Métis, Alberta, ca. late 1890s.

"Here, at last, lay the mountains"

On a winter journey to observe conditions in Canada's newly acquired western territory, William Francis Butler made the notes that eventually became *The Great Lone Land: A Narrative of Travel and Adventure in the North-West of America*. On December 4, 1870, at sunset on a "calm and beautiful" evening, after several thousands of kilometres of wilderness travel, Butler and his party were now making steady way across the plains toward the foothills. Occasionally, they dipped into a creekbed or coulee and lost sight of the western horizon, but finally they saw clearly, from the summit of a long ridge, the Rocky Mountains that "burst suddenly into view in greater magnificence than at midday." Butler told his companions to go on ahead and make camp, while he rode by himself through some "fire-wasted" bush onto another height bathed in "floods of glory" from the declining sun. "I cannot hope to put into the compass of words the scene which lay rolled beneath...." Yet he did.

> *Here at length lay the barrier to my onward wanderings, here lay the boundary to that 4000 miles of unceasing travel which had carried me by so many varied scenes so far into the lone land; and other thoughts were not wanting. The peaks on which I gazed were no pigmies; they stood the culminating monarchs of the mighty range of the Rocky Mountains. From the estuary of the Mackenzie to the Lake of Mexico no point of the American continent reaches higher to the skies. That eternal crust of snow seeks in summer widely-severed oceans.*

Philadelphia photographer Mary Schäffer was keenly aware that the mountain landscapes she had hiked in 1893 around Lake Louise had already been swept by a tourist tide: "...the tin cans and empty fruit-jars strew our sacred soil, the mark of the axe [grew] more obtrusive, even the trails cleared of the debris so hard to master...."

But she was also fed up with watching male-only hiking groups set off into the high mountain country of still-unnamed lakes and little-known rivers and rumoured peaks (at least to non-Aboriginal adventurers) that she herself longed to investigate around the headwaters of the Saskatchewan River. She was lured by the "squiggles" on the map drawn for her by the Stoney guide Samson Beaver who had once, more than twenty years earlier, been through a mountain pass and to a lake she herself now desperately wanted to see.

Wearing canary-coloured yachting slickers and a pair of heavy boots, with horses and the guide William Warren, whom Schäffer later married, and the cook and packer Sidney Unwin, Mary Schäffer and her Boston friend Mary "Mollie" Adams set off in the summer of 1907 "to delve into the heart of an untouched land, to tread where no human foot had trod before," as she recounted in *Old Indian Trails*, typically oblivious to the history of Aboriginal presence in the area.

In the summer of 1907, Philadelphia photographer Mary Schäffer set off "to delve into the heart of an untouched land." Mrs. Chas. Schäffer [Mary Schäffer] Vaux family, 1902.

Ironically, this was the same year that Emerson Hough had written of the Saskatchewan River country as a "highway only of the furs." From Schäffer we know it was already a tourist destination.

On June 24, 1907, almost exactly a century after Thompson, after four days of trekking through the Bow Valley and growing anxious about the sheer volume of meltwater pouring from the summer snowfields into the Saskatchewan, which they must cross, Schäffer and company arrived at the mouth of the tributary stream, the Mistaya River (also called Bear Creek).

The water was boiling and plunging over the huge boulders and warned us that there was no time to lose. All got over that small stream safely which is not always the case, as the great force of the water is apt to cause a horse to stumble in so rough a river bed. One mile to the west of the entrance of Bear Creek into the Saskatchewan, there is one of the best fords on that river if you are bound for the north. On the Ocean-like beach we took our stand, while "K." [Sid Unwin], mounting the only horse of the bunch which we knew could take care of himself in the great river (Nibs of course), struck into the stream. The little fellow showed not the slightest hesitation as he took to the water but seemed rather proud than otherwise of showing off his ability to his new acquaintances.

Those were anxious moments as we saw "K." cross branch after branch of the great river. He slowly waded in, the water would creep higher and higher about the plucky pony's shoulders till horse and rider almost disappeared from view; they would then back out and try it farther up or down, then emerge to a bar and work over the next channel in the same way. At last after fifteen minutes, we saw him a distant speck in the brilliant setting sun on the north shore. He waved his hand, and we knew that our yet untried horses could be got over without much danger of being washed down-stream.

Yes, we got over without having to swim, but one never wants to take those large rivers which are fed by the great ice fields, other than seriously; the power of the water is that of the avalanche from the mountain-side, and it sweeps along throbbingly, intermittently, cruelly, and relentlessly.

One fine fresh spring day in Manhattan in the mid-1940s, Florence Page Jaques and her painter husband Lee stepped out on to their balcony and sniffed the "delicately cold" north wind. Intoxicated by its "clarity," she pronounced it "Canadian air."

"Why do we put up with these small samples?" Lee asked. "Why don't we go up where they make the stuff?"

And they did, for two months, across the Canadian prairies and up and down the Rockies. They were experienced canoeists of northern Minnesota/western Ontario lake country but they had only been in the Rockies in a train and in a hotel at Lake Louise.

So, another generation, another kind of trekker: Florence and Lee Jaques tramped around the same country as had Mary Schäffer. But the adventure no longer seems one of pioneer mountaineering, as it did at the turn of the twentieth century, but of tourism. There were now "pleasant cabins" available on the trail, and visitors sought sensation in a landscape no longer viewed as remote and therefore dangerous. For Jaques, it is thrilling to stand on the edge of a cliff.

Almost a hundred years after the arduous and near-deadly expedition of Hector, Erasmus, and "Nimrod," a new breed of traveller had arrived in the mountains. Roads had been cut for them and hiking trails cleared, cabins built and firewood chopped; now the pitiless austerity and density of the back country, prised open for them, were exciting. Jaques writes:

> At Mistaya Canyon we walked half a mile to see its black scalloped rock and ice-green water. Bears had clawed the bark of the trees here and the markings were high above my head. They must all be grizzlies here, I said pessimistically. Usually I like to think of the hidden citizens of the country watching us, but here I was too uncabined, unconfined.
>
> And no sooner had we reached the car than a bear did dash across the road, though he was only a chubby cinnamon. It seemed to me that the population of bears in western Canada equaled the human population. It had become quite natural to wonder, whenever I went walking, how near a bear was likely to be.

A new breed of traveller had arrived in the mountains. Cable car on North Saskatchewan River, Alberta, 1915.

  At the Saskatchewan River crossing, a trading post and pleasant cabins made us decide to stay overnight. Perhaps the next day would be less dour. By suppertime we were justified; the clouds had lifted to show great bare crags where mountain goats should have been. The boy who brought us firewood told us he sometimes saw elk down the hill behind the cabins, and after supper Lee suggested exploring the trail.

  Over the slanted earth that towered into snow, a stormy scarlet sky blew into rags and tatters. We walked on and on through the tall grass and brush. It was exciting weather. The atmospheric tensions brought about by storms that were plunging through the dusk made me have the exhilarating feeling that anything might happen.

  But as one storm cloud came lowering heavily down our river valley directly toward us, "I think we'd better go back," I insisted, in spite of Lee's urging that we find the end of the path.

  It is a good thing that we did turn around, for the trail followed the Saskatchewan and its end was a hundred and fifteen miles away at Rocky Mountain House. Our meandering footpath was the road the Indians took to the Calgary stampedes.

I lay awake that night, thinking of the depths of the darkness that lay around us. Mountain valley after mountain valley – what gigantic chalices full to the brim with unbroken blackness! This night was a dense weighted substance, marred by no small man-made glitters or noises anywhere. Except for our few pinpricks of light at this dim river, nothing at all was visible through heavy forest or fearsome labyrinths of stone.

But I was elated rather than cowed by the gloom so solidly massed about our slight shelter. I liked the feeling of implacable hostility surrounding us, the frozen cataclysms poised above us, the unseen storms that prowled about the night. I lay and felt the wind shake at our cabin, and thought with deference of the men who had first confronted these savage places and had not turned back.

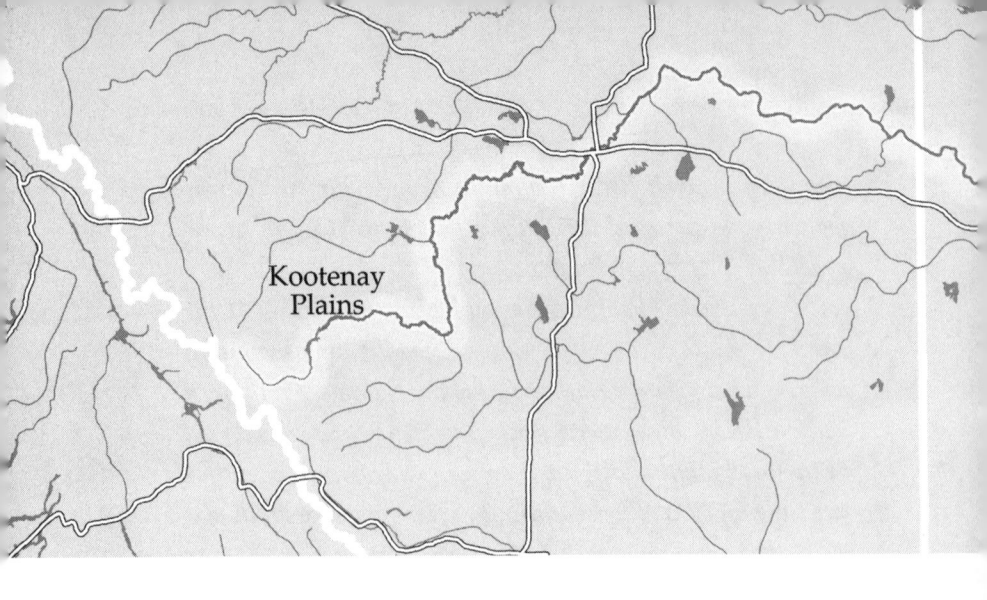

*The land speaks to Nakoda, releasing its medicines,
The rivers show him secrets and dangers
Rock shows his position.* – The Stonies of Alberta

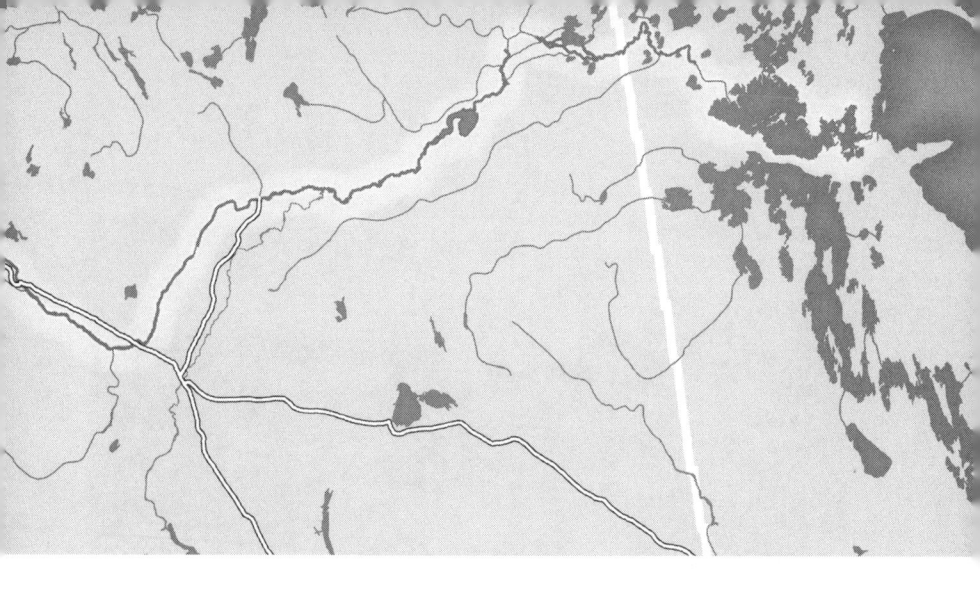

KOOTENAY PLAINS
Meadow of the Winds

Moving swiftly downstream from Saskatchewan Crossing, the river heads east for about 20 kilometres before turning almost due north. It runs in a long lazy "s," then gently shifts to the northeast. Coming out of this curve the river "re-rights" itself and runs straight east to Rocky Mountain House, where it turns due north again. Where the fast rivers that flow into the North Saskatchewan cut into the front ranges along the 's' curve lies a mystical landscape. These are the Kootenay Plains, held protectively alongside the river between the high ridges of the front ranges of the Rocky Mountains and the Bighorn Mountains. Whirlpool Point juts out into the river at the south end of the plains so sharply it is sometimes described as splitting the river in two and actually causing it to reverse directions. David Thompson describes a narrowing to "fifteen yards" with a current so strong it "had to be bucked to its confluence." (Campbell) At the north end looking south and west, Windy Point offers "one of the most breathtakingly beautiful views in Western Canada."

Aboriginal people knew the Kootenay Plains as Ke-don-ne-ha Tin-da, or "Meadow of the Winds." Looking southwest from Windy Point, 1943. A (Mac) McMullen Photo

There are small islands formed by the braiding of the river, and ancient sea bottoms are folded into gently terraced slopes that become plains. June grass, pasture sage, prairie groundsel, and blue flax grow here, with open forests of white spruce, lodgepole and limber pine, aspen, and Douglas fir. On the west-facing plains, there are over sixty bird and fourteen mammal species. The effect of a rain shadow on this leeward side of the Rocky Mountains sweeps the Kootenay Plains with warm, dry, north-south prevailing winds, creating "a benign oasis-like ecosystem that attracts a wide variety of birds and wildlife and supports plant species found nowhere else in the North Saskatchewan watershed." In *The David Thompson Highway: A Hiking Guide*, Jane Ross and Daniel Kyba write that in the early nineteenth century, "travellers crossing these Plains reported a Serengeti-like scene. There were herds of bison, wapiti, mule deer and mountain caribou in the valley...bighorn sheep and mountain goats on or near the slopes. In the woods there were moose."

This place was well known by Aboriginal people, not as the Kootenay Plains but as *Kadonnha Tinda* (ke-don-ne-ha tin-da), or "meadow of the winds." In *Small Moments in Time: The Story of Alberta's Big West Country,* Anne Belliveau writes, "David Thompson's manuscript frequently mentions the Kootenay Plains when he is discussing the Saskatchewan River corridor. At one point his notes refer to the region as "Kootones," which may have been Thompson's attempt to interpret the rapid and flowing Stoney pronunciation of *Ke-don-ne-ha Tin-da,* rather than the generally accepted belief that these plains were named for the Ktunaxa, the original Kootenay First Nation name."

There are many stories about the name of the people who first inhabited these plains. Peter Erasmus wrote: "The Stony Indians were so called because of their preference for the mountainous country where they lived and did most of their hunting." In *A Profile of the Stoney Nakoda Nation,* Peter Lazarus Wesley, grandson of Moosekiller, writes that early European explorers called the people Stoney because they cooked with round stones heated in the fire then placed in water, but the Stoney call themselves *Iyarthe* Na-ko-da, "the people of the mountains." A naming story that has been passed along by various Stoney elders has been written down by Sebastian Chumak in *The Stonies of Alberta:* "Iktomni says: I name you Nakoda, First Stoney Men. You are the fourth. And because Great Star dries you out evenly on this flat boulder, you will be called Stoney."

Stoney origins are sometimes difficult to unravel. Assiniboine is the generic name for Stoney groups and Stoney the name usually used for groups residing in Canada. The Assiniboine come from "the great council fires" of the Sioux. In *Stoney History Notes,* Chief Powderface and Stoney elders explain their history as written down by Peter M. Jonker:

> We are descendants of the Dakota [linguistically] Sioux.... When smallpox epidemics were killing thousands of our people in the mid-1600s, small Bands began to break away and migrate to outlying areas.... One such splinter group moved

With hunting trophies, in winter. L-R: Silas Abraham; Moses Wesley; Samson Beaver. Stoney people, Kootenay Plains, Alberta, 1904.

> west into the vicinity of Chief Mountain (now in Montana, U.S.A.), while another moved first north and then west into the Red Deer and North Saskatchewan River areas. The Band at Chief Mountain filtered northward along the Eastern Slopes and Front Ranges of the Rocky Mountains; its descendants are now the Bearspaw and Chiniki Bands.... The other splinter group became known as the Wesley Band.... The three Bands together form an arc along the Eastern slopes.

The Stoney Indians continue to tell stories about these traditional hunting routes arching along the eastern slopes of the Rocky

Mountains and along the North Saskatchewan River. Both the Kootenai from west of the Rocky Mountains and the Stoney on the east side travelled the North Saskatchewan and Howse rivers through the mountains. An annual Kootenay Plains rendezvous has been documented as the oldest in North America, lasting until about 1870, which is about the same time the buffalo disappeared from these plains. There are 10,000- to 12,000-year-old hunting, fishing, and tool-making campsites here, and ancient trails, parts of which are still visible and in use today.

"We wish to help you hear the whispers of our landscape and feel the movement of our lives entwined in it," Chief Frank Powderface graciously offers in *Stoney History Notes,* to listen to "the stories hidden in this landscape." The Kootenay Plains hold hundreds of thousands of stories, but for the most part, we can access only those few that have been written down by explorers, traders, adventurers, and others who have passed through the plains.

Saskatchewan author and journalist Marjorie Wilkins Campbell tells the story of David Thompson's first trip through the plains in 1806-07, "toiling upriver by horse and canoe" to where Natives said the "Shining Mountains" parted. He travelled "with the greatest secrecy" and "under cover of darkness" in order not to show the North West Company's hand to the Hudson's Bay Company in their competition for furs west of Rocky Mountain House. Thompson, his wife Charlotte, and their three children, "their baby comfortable and cozy on her back," canoed upriver from Rocky Mountain House and camped on the upper end of the Kootenay Plains at Two O'Clock Creek Flats. There, "they came out on a plateau where the air was dry and crisp, the famous grass lands which Thompson called the Kootenay Plains because it was here the Kootenay tribes came to dry their supplies of wood buffalo and mountain sheep. The plain lying to the north of the river is famous for its abundance of game...."

Thompson was on the plains in 1809 and crossed paths with Hudson's Bay Company officer Joseph Howse, who was returning from his successful trip through what Thompson later named Howse Pass. In 1811, as Thompson again travelled through the Kootenay Plains on his way over the Great Divide, he wrote in his journal:

> *In the summer this must be a delightful situation in comparison with the wild and barren mountains which surround the whole. At this time there was not more than two inches of snow, and in many places the snow was entirely eaten up by the buffalo. I observed near the foot of the rocks behind the plain the remains of an old Kootenay camp, where the wood of the tents was still standing.... Moose and deer are also plenty, jumping deer, grizzly bears.... We saw a flock of upward of 100 white partridges [ptarmigan,* Lagopus leucurus*] on this plain. They are very beautiful birds, and very good eating....*

In 1858, Dr. James Hector of the Palliser Expedition travelled in the Kootenay Plains area with Métis guide Peter Erasmus, three Métis voyageurs, and a Native hunter known as Nimrod. Like Hector, Erasmus kept a remarkably detailed journal. Unlike Hector, his voice was not heard until, at the age of eighty-seven, he told his story to an aspiring newspaper reporter, Henry Thompson, who sent the manuscript to the Glenbow Archives in 1976. Erasmus pointed out that "The Indians and half-breeds were paid servants and thus not entitled to any praise for their deeds, which were quite frequently at the risk of their own lives." In describing his experiences with the Stoney Indians, Erasmus said:

> *We were lucky in finding an old Stony Indian who drew a map for us on birch bark that proved to be an invaluable aid*

in our search for a pass.... The Stony Indians were a peaceful people. Their policy was to avoid trouble unlike the Blackfoot, Peigan, or Bloods, their nearest neighbours. They raised good mountain horses that were greatly sought after by the plainsmen. They had great stamina, were sure-footed, and when properly trained were very reliable as buffalo runners. The Stonies were less inclined to migratory habits, and lived in selected parts of the mountain country more or less permanently for the greater portion of their lives. In my experience they were the best trackers of any of the Indian people, and they developed the use of medicines to a degree unsurpassed by any of the other tribes. It was largely through their knowledge of medicine plants that the Crees looked to them as friends and never bothered them when they went after buffalo.

Change came quickly for the Stoney. Methodist missionaries built a "house of God" and a "house of learning" on the Stoneys' seasonal hunting lands on the Bow River, 160 kilometres south of the Kootenay Plains. The settlement that grew up around the church and school was called Morleyville. In 1876, the federal Indian Act was passed, and one year later, the Siksika, Peigan, Blood, Stoney, and Sarcee signed Treaty 7 at Saskatchewan Crossing. Rev. John McDougall had been asked by the government to persuade the Stoneys to make treaty. McDougall successfully used the settlement at Morleyville as an argument for locating the Stoney reserve there. The Stoney received farm equipment, some cattle, and were directed to become self-sustaining farmers on land so poor it grew only stones.

In *These Mountains Are Our Sacred Places,* Chief John Snow tells the story of his people's struggle for the Kootenay Plains. Stoney Elder John Abraham describes his father's claim to the Kootenay Plains at the Treaty 7 negotiations: "He went up in the mountains to what is now known by the name of Kootenay Plains on the Saskatchewan River and there settled.... My father told the commissioner and Rev. John McDougall that he was taking treaty for that land at the head of the Saskatchewan in the Mountains." According to Snow, "...some of my people at the treaty came from the Bighorn-Kootenay Plains, and...they had requested land in their traditional hunting grounds to be set aside as a reserve. An interpreter had to be used and our chief interpreter had been John McDougall. With his interest in settling us on land in the Morleyville area I wonder if he ever interpreted my people's request for land in the Bighorn-Kootenay Plains."

Thirty-three years later, John McDougall wrote that the Kootenay Plains were "the original home country of these people and they have always clung to it.... It was by force of circumstances over which these men had no control that they were given [a] Reserve near Morley." (Snow)

In 1887, the federal government established a 670-square-kilometre Rocky Mountains Park (which would become Banff National Park) to promote the area's hiking and hunting attractions: its "beautiful mountains," "sparkling rivers," "thundering waterfalls," and "true lakes." Tourism would help pay for the new continental railway through the mountains, which in turn would make coal, timber, and other natural resources accessible. Indians were forbidden to hunt or trap within the newly created national park, an outright violation of Treaty 7. Chief John Snow writes: "The buffalo were gone, the crops on the rocky soil failed, the restrictive game regulations, the creation of National Parks, and the influx of Europeans into the area had diminished our hunting territory.... Therefore our people asked, where is the promise that the government made when it stated, 'I will manage your country well'?"

In defiance and desperation, Peter Wesley, a Nakoda Stoney known as Ta-otha or Mooskiller, "one who provides," who grew up hunting in the Kootenay Plains area, moved from the

By 1904, in defiance and desperation, approximately one hundred Stoney Indians had moved back to their traditional hunting grounds. Horses on Kootenay Plains, Alberta, 1908.

Morleyville reserve back to the plains. By 1904, approximately one hundred people had moved back to their traditional hunting grounds with Wesley, among them those who had long resided on the Kootenay Plains: the Beavers, the Abrahams, the Houses, the Hunters, and the Wildmans. After listening to Stoney elders who remembered this time, Snow imagined what might have been Moosekiller's words to the agent when he left the Morley Reserve:

> *My children are hungry, they cry in the night. My young men have empty stomachs and there is no meat in my camp. So I and mine go back to the Kootenay Plains. There we shall have meat and the children shall grow fat and happy. Grass grows there for our horses and no snow lies there in the winter.*

As far as the government was concerned, the Peter Wesley Band were illegal squatters.

The park drew entrepreneurs, mountaineers, guides, packers, tourists, sportsmen and sportswomen. Mary Schäffer was the first female tourist to arrive in Banff in 1907; she travelled by horseback to the plains. Captivated, charmed, even seduced by their beauty and their people, she wrote:

The Kootenai Plains — there is no describing them. To appreciate them one must breathe their breath deep into the lungs, must let the soft winds caress the face, and allow the eye to absorb the blue of the surrounding hills and the gold of the grasses beneath the feet. To us, who had been storm swept, chilled, and baked by turns in the outlying valleys, it was simply heaven.... To see the Plains at their best, one should come over the Pipestone trail in August, and look down on the scene from the rolling hills of the south. Then the golden-brown of the ripened grasses floods the valley with light, for miles the river winds and twists from west to east, an occasional Indian shack comes into view, the faint ringing of a bell denotes that a few tiny specks on the landscape are really horses, and the white dots are tepees of the Indians. Here the air is sweeter, dryer, and softer than anywhere I know, and here the world could easily be forgotten and life pass by in a dream.... Winding in and out among the yellowing poplars, we spied two tepees nestled deep among the trees. I often wonder when passing an Indian camp-ground, be it ancient or modern, if ever for an instant the natural beauty of a location consciously appeals to them. I have seen not one but many of their camps and seldom or never have they failed to be artistic in their setting, and this one was no exception.

After visiting the Silas Abraham and Samson Beaver families, Schäffer and her party left for the North Fork of the Saskatchewan. She carried with her "one of the greatest trophies...a tiny grubby bit of paper on which Samson had with much care traced the lake we had tried so hard to find.... He had been there but once, a child of fourteen, and now, a man of thirty, he drew it from memory — mountains, streams, and passes all included."

At the same time that Schäffer was writing about the Kootenay

Plains and exploring mountain lakes guided by Indian maps, Snow writes,

> ...we had already built houses and planted gardens; we had numerous horses and cattle there. Our fathers and children were buried there. This was our homeland. We were not asking the government to give us somebody else's land; this was land promised to us at the time of treaty and later by the Indian Affairs Branch. We were only asking the government to recognize our right to this land and to register title or patent to it.

Chief Frank Powderface and the Stoney elders remembered Moosekiller's words:

> During his last days Ta-o-tha warned us that we were about to experience a dramatic change in living conditions. The white governors, he predicted, will claim to own most of our lands and leave us on only small Reserves; they will impose laws on us and take away our free will; there will be more and more rules, regulations, and permits; we will have increasingly less choice about how we wish to live, and we will lose our hunting areas.

By 1907, the speculators had arrived: "My dream has come true," German fortune-seeker Martin Nordegg wrote ecstatically in his journal in 1907, recounted in Brian Brennan's *Romancing the Rockies:* "I cannot sleep anymore. I can see nothing but mountains of coal." Nordegg staked the first coal claim on the Bighorn River above its beautiful double falls and downstream to where it flows into the North Saskatchewan River. He went on to build the company town of Nordegg and develop Brazeau Collieries.

In 1912, he planned an adventure trip to Lake Louise for his young daughter Marcelle that took them across the Kootenay Plains. Addressing Marcelle, he wrote:

Ahead of us lay a little prairie where my old friend Philip was sitting on his horse eagerly expecting us.... We forded the Saskatchewan River, a dangerous undertaking even at low water level then. Here too, you showed no fear, although you got quite wet, but the warm sun dried everything quickly. Soon after, we reached the Indian camp and you met all my friends: Hector, Abraham, Silas and his son, their ladies and their children. They gazed at you in wonderment and admiration. You received a bag made of soft elk skin and a necklace that is said to bring good luck and is made of sweet smelling prairie grass.

Both the man and the town of Nordegg prospered, while Snow writes of the many failed attempts to reclaim the Kootenay Plains over several years. Although the Kootenay Plains were officially acknowledged as promised in Treaty 7, all Stoney Nation claims for the plains have been denied.

Eventually, the Stoneys' need for land was acknowledged with the designation of the Special Bighorn Reserve (Kiska Waptan) for the Wesley Stoney Band, but as Snow writes, "Another impasse of misunderstanding had been reached in 1947-48. My people at Bighorn believed that the agreement was a start, however faulty, for negotiations to fulfill the treaty promises, whereas the Indian Affairs Branch thought that it had found a 'final solution'."

In 1969 the government's bulldozers arrived. They came to bring the North Saskatchewan River under control. Snow attempted to describe the carnage:

> *Work crews had moved in with heavy equipment and begun massive destruction of the beautiful North Saskatchewan Valley, near the Bighorn Reserve...knocking over Indian log cabins, destroying Indian graves, and ruining traplines as well as traditional hunting areas.... What I saw was unbelievable – land that the Stoney Indians still claimed – was being bulldozed without consideration for, or consultation with, my people.... The destruction of the land was a terrible thing to watch. Haze filled the air as growing things were burned off to clear the ground. Homes were swept aside by heavy machinery, graves turned over.... Even more far-reaching in the result was the almost complete disappearance of game from the area.... The damage – physical and psychological – that the building of the Bighorn Dam caused my people can never be calculated.*

The hydroelectric dam created the longest man-made reservoir in Alberta at 32 kilometres in length by more than 3 kilometres wide. In a curious and cruel twist the reservoir/artifical lake was named Abraham, after the same Silas Abraham who was visited on the plains by Mary Schäffer, and whose family burial sites now lie under Abraham Lake. The lake's extremely vibrant turquoise colour is caused by "rock flour" (glacial silt), but this spectacular artificial beauty is deceptive: the lake is virtually dead. Its waters are extremely cold, and the valley now acts as a funnel for unpredictable and fierce winds.

Anguish at what is lost is captured by poet Peter Christensen:

On the Kootenay plains
drums beat a lament
against the mountains
it is the last dance

The drums grow thunder
the high cry of song
moves mountains

Among the tents
belled and feathered dancers
jangle move rhythm

Above the camp ground
    politicians attach megaphones
               to their mouths
  flood the valley
  raise themselves over the earth
  their platforms
  scaffold the dead river

Snow's story of his people's struggles continues as ever more stakeholders climb on board:

> *With the growth of the conservation movement, my people might have felt that at last we were getting our message across. Surely this movement would help preserve what little we had left that was natural and beautiful. Perhaps it was not too late! But the conservationist movement and the hopes of its non-Indian supporters were very different from what my people had envisioned. Although legislation was passed to preserve certain areas for conservationist purposes, other government departments continued their mass destruction of the beautiful forests, the open prairies, and the mountainous areas.... The movement itself was to prevent us from going to our ceremonial and sacred places, which all ended up in a park or another restricted area.*

There is a large official provincial plaque on the David Thompson Highway describing the history of the Kootenay Plains. There is no mention of the Stoney.

But those who accept the late Stoney Chief Frank Powderface's invitation "to stop and listen to the stories hidden in this landscape" will know their Sun Dancers have never left the Kootenay Plains. "Many great suns pass. Nakoda does not get old."

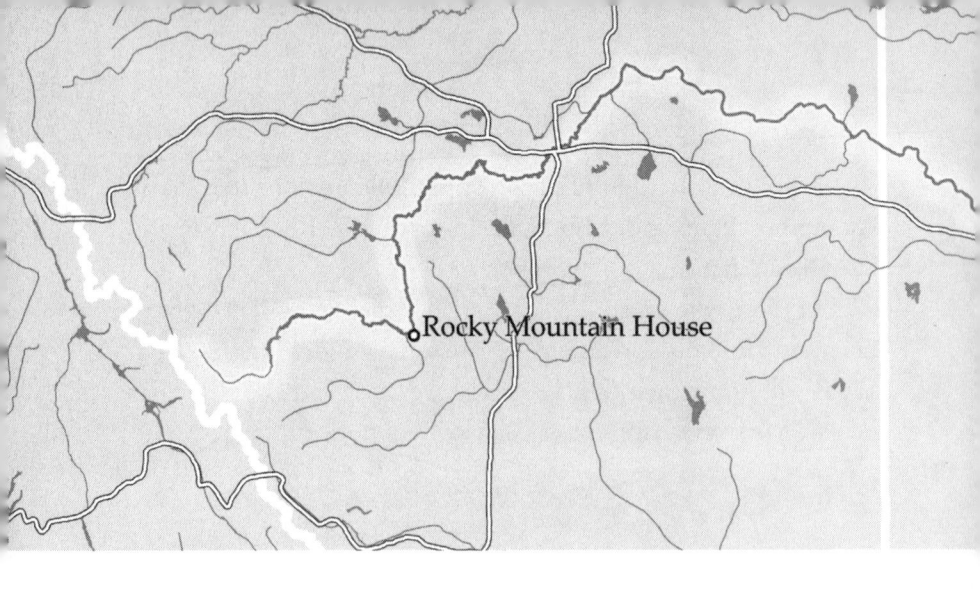

The Hudson's Bay and North West Companies each built fortified fur trade posts here in 1799. The anticipated trade with the Kootenay Indians, who lived west of the mountains, did not develop, but these posts and their successors after the 1821 merger drew in the trade of the Blackfoot, Peigan and Blood Indians, as well as that of the Stoney, Sarcee, Gros Ventre and Cree. The North West Company post was also used as a base for exploration and from it, in 1807, David Thompson crossed the Rockies to the Columbia River. The last fort at Rocky Mountain House was finally abandoned in 1875. – Historic Sites and Monuments Board of Canada plaque

ROCKY MOUNTAIN HOUSE
The Fur Trade

Like German mine-owner Martin Nordegg and his party stumbling through a gap in the bush in 1912, most travellers in the area of Rocky Mountain House after 1875 would have had to piece together – from an eerie ruin of old chimneys on the vacant slope, rotting stubs of timber of a palisade in faint trenches under the tall grass, and a surprising riverside meadow long shorn of its trees – the site of the last fur trading post upstream on the North Saskatchewan River. They are still standing, the chimneys of the stockade's fireplaces, ghost sentinels of the deserted trading post.

In 1799, the North West Company (Nor'Westers) and the Hudson's Bay Company (the Company) established rival fur trading posts, known respectively as Rocky Mountain House and Acton House, virtually next door to each other, on the floodplain of the North Saskatchewan River near its confluence with the Clearwater River. A two-day ride from the Rocky Mountains or a 340-kilometre

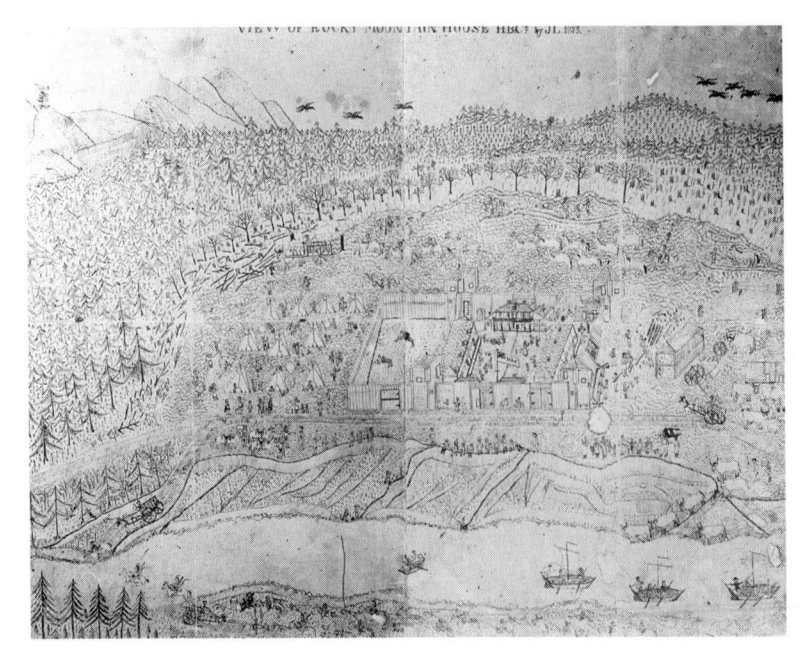

Beaver pelts fuelled the trade. View of Rocky Mountain House, Alberta, 1873, from a sketch attributed to Jean L'Heureux, "View of Hudson's Bay Company Fort and surroundings." National Archives of Canada.

paddle upstream from Fort Edmonton – clear sailing without a portage – they were some 1,200 kilometres from the river's mouth; they were at the end of the line of fur posts on that immense watery artery of the fur empire that was the North Saskatchewan and Saskatchewan rivers. Above them, hazardous waters, rapids, and steep canyon river walls blocked the way upstream.

Further exploration toward the Kootenay Plains and to the Rocky Mountains and over the passes down into the Columbia River system had to be done on foot and horseback, dog-sled and snowshoe. The construction of the Bighorn Dam has radically changed the river's character by regulating its flow and smoothing out the roughest of the rapids upstream from Rocky Mountain House, but at the time it was an agony of labour to judge from the journals of those who tried.

The Trade

For many years Rocky Mountain House was the richest fur-producing area in the Northwest, shipping annually 3,000 to 4,000 beaver pelts as well as great bales of otter, sable, fox, and, later, buffalo hides.

Beaver pelts fuelled the trade: one top hat made of beaver felt in a London haberdashery cost the equivalent of the annual earnings of a fur trader in the bush. The trade year was a cyclical round of spring and fall brigades: flotillas of canoes and then the broad and flat-bottomed York boats bringing in the trade goods, the niceties of life such as tea and flour, as well as the basics – clothes, blankets, knives, awls, hatchets, beads, bells, and, most important, guns, alcohol, and tobacco – and taking away the fur pelts.

To defend its interests, the company built a fort comprising a cluster of buildings of heavy logs surrounded by a stout stockade and defended with cannon. Inside, the trader and his family chopped and hauled wood all winter from the forests holding them hostage, snared rabbits when they ran out of gun shot, ate shrivelled potatoes and turnips, and waited for the furs to come in. Their arrival required a ceremonial parade of Native hunters and trappers to the fort – horses and women staggering under the weight of the fur bundles – long speeches, tots of rum, and shared pipes. Hunters attached to the post scoured the forest for game while woodcutters industriously cut it down to fuel the enormous chimneys and to provide lumber for the boat-builders. Toward spring, buffalo meat had to be made into pemmican for the *voyageurs* and the fur pelts pressed and lashed together in packs.

The North West Company sent Alexander Henry the Younger to the Saskatchewan River in 1808. On his way he met David Thompson at Cumberland House, then wintered at Rocky Mountain House in 1810 – the reality, not the poetry, of roughing it in the bush.

11th. Long before daybreak snow began to fall, with a strong N.W. wind, which detained the Indians; for the storm continued all day. *12th.* Snow ceased, but the wind continued. The river below the rapids was stopped with ice, which caused the water to rise opposite the fort; soon the rapid was also choked with drift ice and all frozen solid.... *13th.* The river appears to be closed for the season, above and below, as far as the rapid directly opposite the house. I am told this remains free from ice the whole winter. I saw a duck in the open space, though wild fowl are scarce here.... This afternoon the ice suddenly moved and the water began to rise fast; the current increased astonishingly, forming eddies along the shore on both sides, where the waves and ice reached the height of three feet, running with great force upon the shore, until the water entirely covered the dry shoals and washed the foot of the high banks. This sudden and violent commotion continued for about twenty minutes, during which the water rose upward of four feet perpendicular, when the current appeared to cease and the channel was blocked with broken ice.... *19th.* A thick vapor from the open space of water below the rapid spread a heavy rime or fog that was not dispersed before ten o'clock. *20th.* B. Desjarlaix hunting; seven men out to raise dog trains: four laying up canoes and cleaning the fort; one making a wood train; one off for meat, one cutting wood, one carting, one making kegs. Our canoes are much split by the frost, and four of our large axes broke to-day, being nearly as brittle as glass. Desjarlaix killed nothing, as the animals about the fort have all been roused by men going for trains, searching for horses, etc. *21st.* About sunset suddenly we had a S.W. gale, and the thermometer rose from 32° to 40° in a few moments. *23rd.* Sawed plank for gates; made trains for journey to Terre Blanche. Two Sarcees arrived from near Wolf river, where buffalo are numerous; they brought a few beavers.

Come spring and icebreak on the river, the boatmen packed the canoes and York boats with three-tonne loads of pelts for the long haul down river to the supply stores of the company on the shore of Hudson Bay.

The most exciting day of the year was the return of the boats, this time loaded with blankets, tools, guns and ammunition, and metal pots, the trade of which began the whole business cycle over again.

Visitors were enthusiastically received, as Fred Stenson records: "It was early morn," John McDougall wrote of a visit with his father, Rev. George McDougall, and Chief Factor William Christie in 1865, "but up went the flag, and the little metropolis was all excitement in consequence of our arrival. The Chief Factor in those days was supreme in his own district.... No wonder the...fort was *en fete* when such ecclesiastical and commercial dignity came suddenly upon it."

In its brief seventy-six year tenure in the fur trade, Rocky Mountain House hosted a remarkable sequence of residents and visitors, pre-eminently the surveyor and cartographer David Thompson, but also numbering chief trader Alexander Henry (1810-11), Rev. Robert T. Rundle, the first Christian missionary to reach the Rocky Mountains (1841), artist Paul Kane (1847-48), James Hector and John Palliser of the Palliser Expedition (1858-59), Father Albert Lacombe, Oblate missionary (1861), and Captain William Francis Butler (1870). In *The Great Lone Land* (which went through five printings in its first year), Butler describes the relief of seeing from mid-distance "the light blue smoke of the Mountain House curled in fair contrast from amidst a mass of dark green pines." Riding up to the river across from the post, he hallooed to the "denizens" within that he had ridden "1180 miles in the last forty-one days," and then plunged with his horse into the water already gelling with rotten ice and into the excited company of the people of the House.

During the dying years of the fur trade on the upper Saskatchewan, some 300 lodges of Blackfoot, 300 of Bloods, 49 of Peigans, 30 of Sarcees, and 109 of Stoneys were trading at Rocky Mountain House, including the Blackfoot messenger Hind Bull and the Blood Indian Medicine Owl, who came to announce the imminent arrival of Rainy Chief of the Bloods, Chief Crowfoot of the Blackfoot, and Chief Morning Plume of the Peigans. According to the *Reminiscences* of Campbell Munroe (as recounted by Hugh Dempsey), who lived at the House at this time, once through the gates the chiefs were treated with tobacco and hats with plumes, and when they departed, they left behind their best horses for the Hudson's Bay Company men.

William Francis Butler described such a scene when, on his winter journey along the fur trade route, he arrived in Rocky Mountain House on December 5, 1870.

The Mountain House is perhaps the most singular specimen of an Indian trading post to be found in the wide territory of the Hudson Bay Company. Every precaution known to the traders has been put in force to prevent the possibility of surprise during "a trade." Bars and bolts and places to fire down at the Indians who are trading abound in every direction; so dreaded is the name borne by the Blackfeet, that it is thus their trading post has been constructed....

When the Blackfeet arrive on a trading visit to the Mountain House they usually come in large numbers, prepared for a brush with either Crees or Stonies. The camp is formed at some distance from the fort, and the braves, having piled their robes, leather, and provisions on the backs of their wives or their horses, approach in long cavalcade. The officer goes out to meet them, and the gates are closed. Many speeches are made, and the chief, to show his "big heart," usually piles on top of a horse a heterogeneous mass of buffalo robes, pem-

mican, and dried meat, and hands horse and all he carries over to the trader. After such a present no man can possibly entertain for a moment a doubt upon the subject of the big-heartedness of the donor.

Business at Rocky Mountain House had been falling off ever since the American fur traders opened their own posts in Missouri River country in the 1830s and drew the Blackfoot south, close to their hunting grounds. In spite of the worsening conditions of the fur trade, Rocky Mountain House eked out an economic existence with the construction of York boats until the winter of 1860-61. On the verge of starving inside the ramshackle walls of the fort, the traders abandoned the post. Finding it empty, Blackfoot raiders burned it to the ground.

A final House was built in 1868; the fur trade era ended, however, when this last fort was closed in 1875, its very foundations eaten away by the river. The Hudson's Bay Company had finally managed to open a post in the middle of Blackfoot country (near present-day Calgary) and no longer needed the services of its men and women on the North Saskatchewan. Whatever was salvageable was simply floated downstream to be reused in luckier enterprises.

In any case, European fashion in gentlemen's hats had changed, and silk, not beaver felt, was the material of choice. Old posts mouldered into the forest floor, and the beaver kept to their immemorial ways, serenely indifferent to the fate of the men and women who had pursued, trapped, killed, and skinned them. Poet Marion Smith imagines their world.

The Indians told me "the beaver had been an ancient race. They were always beaver, not men, and were wise and powerful, but they must not have lived well for the Great Spirit became angry with them and drove them into the water still to be wise, but without power, their only defense their dams, their houses, their burrows...."

You see how he makes his dams.
Our fishing weirs are destroyed by water;
his always stand.
His house is of strong earth and wood
He secures his winter provisions in good time
and makes burrows to escape us.
We could not catch him without much hard work
until the traders brought us
iron traps and axes
and showed us how to use
the female's scent
as an irresistible lure.

Now we are rich,
but when the beaver are gone from here
the traders will move farther west
and we'll be left poorer

The old post's crumbling chimneys were partially restored in the 1930s by townspeople interested in conserving whatever remnants remained to tell a tale, especially once the site had been declared of "national historic significance" in 1926. Archaeological excavations of the site began in 1962. With the opening of the David Thompson Highway, which roughly follows the explorer's own route through the outlying range of the Brazeaus, in 1968, the old economic zone of the fur trade had re-invented itself as a tourist destination.

In 1980 Rocky Mountain House became Alberta's first national historic park.

Sacred Places, and Profane

Given Hugh Dempsey's lifelong interest in the story of white-Aboriginal relations in southern Alberta – he has written several books about the First Nations of the plains – it is natural he would turn his editorial attentions to the journals of the long-suffering Reverend Robert Terrill Rundle, Methodist chaplain for the HBC and among the Aboriginal people of Rocky Mountain House.

On May 8, 1841, Rundle copied into his journal a letter he wrote to John Rowand, factor at Fort Edmonton, complaining of the behaviour of his mixed-blood interpreter, James "Jimmy Jock" Bird, a man clearly torn between his obligations to the fur company and his fierce loyalty to the local Aboriginals among whom he lived. Their first misunderstanding had occurred at Rocky Mountain House when Rundle felt injured by the "impropriety" of long conversations between the Indians and Mr. Bird that went on without translation.

On April 20, a large number of Blackfoot assembled by Mr. Bird sat in a tent in their camp, waiting for the Reverend. Fred Stenson revisits this scene in *The Trade*.

"The missionary sang a hymn and the Indians seemed quite interested in the sound." Reverend Robert T. Rundle, first Protestant missionary in North-West Canada, n.d. From a painting by John Wycliffe Lowes Forster, Methodist missionary, Fort Edmonton, 1840-1848.

> *He rose, dressed and made himself neat before stepping out. He had guessed he would not be alone and that was correct. All around, people sat on the ground in wait.*

At midday, the council tent began to fill, and soon it was crowded to a suffocating degree. The front flap stayed open and more faces crowded there. Children had removed some of the stones to push themselves in under the sides. In the night the wind had changed from a cold north wind to a warm westerly and had gained much strength. A choking dust had risen.

Rundle wiped his streaming eyes. He squinted in search of Jimmy Jock. The crowd was falling silent and that meant it was time. He found his interpreter seated near a far wall, among some older men, talking. Rundle tried but could not get his attention. Before this became embarrassing, he began alone.

The missionary sang a hymn and the Indians seemed quite interested in the sound. Jimmy Jock, with his hymnal open in front of him, went on talking, more or less through the entire song.

Rundle stopped singing. In English he told Jimmy Jock to be quiet or he would not continue. Bird pointed to the hymnal and said he was showing the Indian where the words were that the missionary was singing.

"That is no way to interpret. If, when I am finished, you would interpret the hymn, I would be glad. But not this way."

Jimmy Jock closed his hymnal with a snap.

Concerned that the Indians were becoming too interested in the drama between the interpreter and himself, Rundle read a prayer and, when he finished, said to Jimmy Jock, "You will please come forward and interpret that prayer."

Jimmy Jock said nothing, nor did he move.

Under the veil of English, Rundle spoke more strongly.

"You dishonour the Almighty, Mr. Bird. The gospel I present is a perfect cure for man, whether civilized or savage, and you stand in its way. You are a murderer of souls."

This, the strongest reproof in his arsenal, fell on Jimmy Jock's ears without apparent effect. The missionary felt the first tickling of panic. Trying to control his face, he asked again.

"Just do it this once."

Bird rose from his place and Rundle assumed he meant to comply. He was thanking God in a prayer when he saw that Jimmy Jock was not coming to the front. He pushed through the crowd and out the flap of the tent.

Rundle quickly returned his attention to the people before him. He forced himself to smile. Under the sound of the wind a terrible silence had gathered. The faces studied him but showed nothing. Rundle reopened his hymnal and began to sing, but he had hardly finished one verse when the dust began carving at his throat. It grated so hard his throat closed and the sound of his singing choked off. He tried to speak but even words would not come.

In 1977 Chief John Snow wrote *These Mountains Are Our Sacred Places*, an impassioned and exhaustive account of the long relationship between the Stoney First Nations, their ancestral hunting lands (from the headwaters of the North Saskatchewan to the U.S. border), and European-Canadian interlopers, including the missionaries.

> *Throughout the first three-quarters of the nineteenth century my people, the Stoneys, lived as we always had, little influenced by the whiteman.... We hunted and lived in family groups, coming together in larger bands for special occasions and ceremonial purposes, and for wintering at Morleyville, the Kootenay Plains, or the Highwood River area....*
>
> *By the 1850s, Stoney life had altered in some details. The horse had completely replaced the dog for transportation; firearms had replaced the bow and arrow; trade goods were*

common in our camps. Trading had changed our way of life a little because of the need to trap fur-bearing animals for barter, over and above what was needed for daily use. But trade with the whiteman never became a basis for our economy as it did for some tribes. We continued to support ourselves by our own hunting, trading only when we wanted some useful goods.

It is difficult to assess whether living standards had improved over traditional ones. Steel axes and knives, as well as firearms, reduced the pressure to make our own tools and weapons. Thread and beads were easier for our women to work with than the traditional porcupine quills; woven cloth also entered our lives, although we also continued to use the skins produced by the hunt. Inter-tribal skirmishes declined, especially in the 1860s and 1870s when the stories of encroaching settlement drew the tribes together in a way they had not considered before.

But by and large life continued unchanged. We were still dependent on hunting for our food. The freedom of the woods and the plains and the mountains was still ours and still the most important part of our lives. The land-hungry settlers were still unknown to us. Even the white traders and missionaries, whom most of us saw only occasionally, were still a curiosity.

One of the very first missionaries to visit the Stoneys came in 1840. He was the Reverend Robert Rundle. When he was travelling through this area, he was warmly welcomed and made to feel at home.

Entrepreneurs on the Trail

In 1897, Sam Livingston, an Irish prospector who had already struck out in the gold fields of California, Oregon, and

"...exciting stories about the gold waiting for them in the rubble of the North Saskatchewan riverbed." Prospectors washing gold on the Saskatchewan at South Edmonton, Alberta, September 1897.

Washington, heard next of gold on the Fraser and Thompson rivers in New Caledonia (now British Columbia). While trying his luck near the Rockies, he met James Gibbons, a prospector who had travelled out from Fort Edmonton with exciting stories about the gold waiting for them in the rubble of the North Saskatchewan riverbed. Eventually a party of fourteen prospectors teamed up for the expedition. The story was passed down through a Métis woman, Jane Howse, Sam Livingston's soon-to-be wife, and from her to Lyn Hancock and Marion Dowler.

> *They had to first find the North Saskatchewan River. There was no trail and they had no map. They had to fight their way through thick forests, over high mountains, along rushing rivers. Grandmother Jane said they used the Kicking Horse Pass to get to what we now call Banff. That was 1864 and nobody lived at Banff then. They tried to go across country to*

Rocky Mountain House but they still couldn't find the North Saskatchewan River. Finally the prospectors split into three parties: one gave up and went south to Montana; the second wandered east along the Bow; and the third, consisting of Grandfather Sam and James Gibbons, rode north on horseback.

They followed game trails, Indian trails, creeks and rivers. They drifted about all summer, lost a lot of time and used up all their food. Summer passed into fall and still they hadn't found the North Saskatchewan. By October they had used up all their ammunition and were forced to eat their horses. Eventually they were down to one horse, and they even lost that...to a party of Blackfoot Indians.

Desperate, lost, weak from hunger and shivering from cold, they saw the trail of a travois in the snow and followed it. They had no idea where it led, but they stumbled along it until, more dead than alive, they collapsed at Rocky Mountain House.

Chief Factor Hardisty saved them from starvation. He welcomed them into the fort and gave them all the food he had...rabbit stew...and a bunk to sleep on.... Chief Factor Hardisty let Sam and James rest for a week, then he gave them snowshoes and pointed the way to Fort Edmonton further down the North Saskatchewan River.

The Brazeau Collieries, Alberta's largest mine on the eastern slope of the Rockies, began in 1911. In September 1912, the *Rocky Mountain House Echo* reported breathlessly that German investor Martin Nordegg and his teenaged daughter Marcelle were visiting the area, just west of Rocky Mountain House, looking over the development of the Nordegg Mine and the coal plant in Nordegg town. Nordegg predicted that this country would be a "favourite route for tourists" within a decade; in the meantime, it was rough going.

"They sank into the clay at valley bottom, threshed bravely against the current at every fording of the river, and lost their way in the bush." Alberta Central Railway surveyors crossing creek (possibly Baptiste or Horseguard) near Rocky Mountain House, Alberta, 1910.

In his reminiscences addressed to his daughter, *To the Town That Bears Your Name: A Young Woman's Journey to Nordegg in 1912*, he relives the perils of his party's travelling by pack-train: they sank into the clay at valley bottom, threshed bravely against the current at every fording of the river, and lost their way in the bush with only a faint indentation of old Indian trail to guide them. Of course, they weren't really lost – the country had been criss-crossed by generations of hunters and then by European traders.

Eventually they stumbled into some ruins, through a gap in the trees above the river bank: some pasture gone to weed, crumbling fireplaces, cellar pits. They were standing on the site of the last of the Rocky Mountain House trading posts, abandoned in 1875.

We went down to the Saskatchewan River, climbed a very steep hill to get a view of the construction of the big railroad bridge, then climbed down into a ravine and, for lack of a bridge, crossed a little mountain stream on a tree trunk.

The pack train, consisting of eighteen horses that had been put together with a great effort, arrived at noon after a long wait. In the meantime, two cowboys, the Belgian engineer, our agent Stuart Kidd, our jack-of-all-trades Tom, you and I took the primitive ferry across the Saskatchewan and awaited the transport that moved with less than haste or hurry. The horses were brought in two sections. As soon as the first one had landed, one of the horses tore loose, jumped into the river and began to swim back despite our shouting and screaming. The current was very strong, and we feared the heavily packed animal might be lost. It fought bravely against the current and was first driven downstream. The horse managed to reach the other shore and was, after some heavy lashing and swearing, placed into the second group of horses that now climbed onto the ferry and landed without further incident....

We moved at a snail's pace so that the horses could get used to each other and to their rank in the pack train. After a few kilometres, we reached [the original] Rocky Mountain House, the remnants of the once biggest fort of the Hudson's Bay Company. Only the brick chimneys are still standing. Log cabins and palisades have long since vanished.... It was the most westerly fort, and heavily fortified, and at times it housed up to fifty of those brave traders who were at the same time hunters, explorers and inventors, and who had to endure bloody battles with the various Indian tribes....

We proceeded along the Saskatchewan River towards the West through open deciduous forest, uphill, downhill, accompanied by the crew singing in minor key the song that we would hear so often from now on:

Oh my Darling...

Just before sunset, we reached a clearing where we made camp for the first time....

> *By now, it was dark. There is no dusk in this part of the country. We strolled over to the kitchen fire that burned cheerfully. Bacon and beans had been fried in the pan, and now tea was being prepared. A dirty hand grabbed as much as it could from the tea bag, threw the tea into the boiling kettle and then the mistake happened that I could not correct in five years of trying challenges at Canadian campfires: the tea was now boiled for five minutes. The result was an extract of tannic acid the thought of which makes my hair stand on end to this day. For this reason, I mostly drank cocoa that I prepared myself....*
>
> *I taught you how to undress lying down, because there are no chairs in the tent, how to fold your clothes in a way that they can be reached at once but stay put in their place. Then I wrapped you in your blankets and, accompanied by the roar of the powerful river, you fell asleep in the light tent for the first time.*

With the closure of the coal mines in 1955, Nordegg was abandoned, only to be declared in turn an Alberta Historic Resource in 1993.

"I followed a trail"

American writer Jack Nisbet has "tracked" David Thompson across western North America, consulting Thompson's own field notes as well as early landscape paintings, and coming to rest, as Thompson did in 1800, at a landing spot on the banks of the North Saskatchewan across from Rocky Mountain House.

> *The settlement of Rocky Mountain House sits in open country set back from the river. The main street is laid out wide*

enough for a cattle drive, and the evening traffic suggested that the trading-post culture of the last century had moved only a few miles up to the crossroads. At the bottom of the main drag, I spotted David Thompson Hotel, a two-story concrete-block affair, blue with a bright red false front....

Later that evening I wandered back down to the Saskatchewan. Fresh out of the mountains, the river ran fast and milky under the bridge. I followed a trail that led upstream to a point opposite the cluster of old trade houses and sat down beside a clump of wolf willows to watch it get dark. Along the flat, big cottonwoods rose above the dark green of alder and serviceberry bushes. Pearly wolf willow berries, beads for Blackfeet children, mirrored the ice-green color of the Saskatchewan. A muted laugh rang across the water, followed by the dips and drips of smooth paddle strokes. By the light reflected off the river, I could make out bright orange flags and life jackets suspended over a loose formation of canoes. As they came closer, the laughter increased. Then three dark fiberglass hulls coasted quietly into the big eddy, and the paddlers drew them in, one by one, to scuff up on to the gravel bar for their final stop of the day.

Born in 1770 into an impoverished family in London, England, David Thompson was apprenticed to the Hudson's Bay Company and began his extraordinary journey as fur trader, explorer, surveyor, and writer at Fort Churchill on Hudson Bay in 1784. He was then moved to York Factory and inland to Cumberland House in 1786, where he learned Cree, and in 1787-88 on to the foothills of the Rocky Mountains, where he learned the language of the Peigans.

At Cumberland House, his friendship with HBC astronomer and surveyor Philip Turnor – whose 1790 map was the first to call the river the Saskatchewan – changed his life. He was already a keen student of mathematics and astronomy; from Turnor he learned the science of surveying, and how to determine longitude and latitude exactly for each stopping point, usually the trading post. As he himself wrote in his *Narrative:* "Now I could make of this uncharted land a known quantity and to this end I kept for sixty years records of all observations of each journey made." He could locate and fix a point on the earth by calculations based on the sun and stars, and for this the Indians called him *Koo Koo Sint,* the stargazer.

Perhaps frustrated by the terms of his work with the HBC, Thompson left it in 1797 to work for the rival North West Company. In 1800, together with his Native wife, Charlotte Small, he set up shop in Rocky Mountain House. He combined his work as a trader with that of surveyor at Fort George, Rocky Mountain House, and on the Peace River, to the Missouri and Mississippi rivers, and along the newly established international boundary at the 49th parallel. On expeditions upriver from Rocky Mountain House, looking for a pass through the mountains and a swift route to the Pacific, Thompson and his companions struggled through terrain that travellers after them would revisit, equally dramatically: Captain William Francis Butler, Sam Livingston, and Martin Nordegg. For the Stoney, of course, this challenging country back-of-beyond was home.

Over the seven years of his residency at Rocky Mountain House from 1800, David Thompson explored the region, looking for a pass through the mountains to the Columbia River and the Pacific. Thompson was the first European to survey and map the entire length of the Columbia River (from 1807 to 1812), establishing trading posts and opening up the river routes and mountain crossings that the fur trade depended on.

By the time the Thompson family returned to Montreal in 1812, David Thompson had travelled more than 130,000 kilometres of the Canadian and American west by foot, horse, and canoe – an achievement that dwarfs the celebrated travels of the Americans

Lewis and Clark to the Pacific Northwest – and had assembled all the data that he would draw on for his monumental three-by-two-metre map of the West, covering an area of 3.9 million square kilometres from Lake Superior to the Pacific, which hangs at the Archives of Ontario.

The years of his decline are a melancholy narrative: family estrangements, commercial catastrophes, penury, blindness: he was even denied a clerk's position at the HBC. No publisher came forward to publish his maps (which were nevertheless used as official maps for a hundred years), and he never finished the great *Narrative* of his journeys. His death in 1857, followed three months later by Charlotte's, went unnoticed, and his grave unmarked.

There is no known likeness of him, but David Thompson's "powerful mind" and wordcraft made the deepest impression on Dr. J. J. Bigsby, a fellow member of the boundary commission surveying the forty-ninth parallel, who describes the power of Thompson's storytelling: "He can create a wilderness and people it with warring savages, or climb the Rocky Mountains with you in a snow-storm, so clearly and palpably, that you have only to shut your eyes and you hear the crack of the rifle, or feel the snow-flakes melt on your cheeks as he talks."

In 1916 David Thompson's *Narrative* was finally edited by his champion, the geological explorer J. B. Tyrrell, who had come across his neglected journals, field notes, and yellowing maps. Awed by Thompson's near-forgotten accomplishments, Tyrrell dictated the inscription on the rediscovered grave in Montreal: "the greatest land geographer who ever lived." The fact that Thompson's unfinished *Narrative* was so long unpublished and is again out of print, and his Columbia River *Journals* published only in 1994, has meant that we encounter Thompson as man and writer through the writers who have come after him, sometimes literally in his footsteps.

"Between the years 1883 and 1898, while engaged on the staff of the Geological Survey of Canada," Tyrrell wrote in his preface to the *Narrative*, "it fell to my lot to carry on explorations in canoes, on horseback, or on foot, over many of the routes which had been surveyed and explored by David Thompson a century before, to survey the rivers he had surveyed, to measure the portages on which he had walked, to cross the plains and mountains on the trails which he had travelled, to camp on his old camping grounds, and to take astronomical observations on the same places where he had taken them. Everywhere his work was found to be of the highest order...."

In his own time and for another generation or two, Bliss Carman's prodigious output of lyrical poetry could be found in every library and schoolroom, and poems like "David Thompson," written at Lake Invermere, British Columbia, in 1922, served as a kind of popular history of Canada. David Thompson referred to himself as "a solitary traveller unknown to the world," but here he is a heroic figure.

David Thompson

A Gray Coat boy from London
At fourteen came over sea
To a lonely post on Hudson's Bay
To serve the H.B.C.
A seeker of knowledge, a dreamer of dreams,
And a doer of deeds was he.

Before his feet lay a continent
Untrailed, unmapped, unguessed.
The whisper of the mysterious North,
The lure of the unknown West,
Called to him with a siren's voice
That would not let him rest.

'Twas but a step from the factor's door
And the wilderness was there,
Rivers stretching a thousand miles
Lakes for his thoroughfare,
And forests fresh from the hand of God,
Waiting his will to dare.

Plains that dipped to the edge of the sky
Untracked from rim to rim
The sorcery when the sun was high
Of ranges far and dim,
The summer morns and the winter nights,
They laid their spell on him...

He followed the song the rivers sang
Over their pebbly bars;
By spruce and larch he tallied his march;
The moons were his calendars;
And well he could reckon and read his path
By the faithful shining stars.

From the Churchill to the Assiniboine
And up the Saskatchewan,
Back and forth through all the North
His purpose drove him on,
Making a white man's trail for those
Who should come when he was gone...

With their combined experience as editor and technical writer, biology researcher and field worker, Joyce and Peter McCart travelled David Thompson's routes, closely consulting his meticulous journals to locate themselves on today's highways, logging and mining roads, hiking and biking trails. Thompson's footnotes prove to be an archive all their own.

> *He devoted space to describing the landscapes he rode through, the Indian bands he visited, the animals he encountered (or shot for meat), and the trees that lined his trail. He had a different term for the size of every stream he saw. A "river" meant a river navigable by canoe; a "rivulet" was navigable at high water; a "bold brook" was a sizeable stream or sometimes a swiftly flowing one; a "brook" was a small stream; a "rill" was a trickle that might be intermittent; and a "raveline" was a dry channel....*

Combining travel guide with historical narrative, Joyce and Peter McCart travelled David Thompson's routes in the late 1990s, closely consulted his journals, and interpreted for today's traveller the significance of Thompson's achievements, for example this account of a hair-raising canoe trip near Shunda Creek:

> *For three days, the voyageurs fought the North Saskatchewan. They soon abandoned paddling as useless, and attempted to line the canoe up the river. But towing the canoe from shore proved impossible – the banks were steep and stacked with debris. Getting into the water to tow it was unthinkable – the river was so deep and moving so fast, it would have swept the men away. They tried poling the canoe through the rushing water, but gained only a few miserable yards. They tried hauling themselves along by the trees on the riverbank, but the torrent flooding down defeated them. Finally, the exhausted men couldn't move the canoe another inch, and Thompson ordered them to where they could get ashore, most likely downstream near the mouth of Shunda Creek. After three days of unremitting effort, they'd advanced barely six miles up the river....*
>
> *Thompson and his men were looking at The Gap, a deep, narrow canyon that forces the North Saskatchewan to greater depth and higher velocities as it constricts to squeeze through*

the Brazeau Range. Thompson measured the currents of The Gap – at its slowest, the river was moving at nine miles an hour; at its fastest, twelve to fifteen miles an hour. The voyageurs are often credited with a paddling speed of six miles an hour, a rate that might have meaning on a mill pond. On the North Saskatchewan that June, paddling at six miles an hour meant they would have been moving backward, and as it was, the river brought them to a standstill. But once Thompson abandoned all hope of reaching the mountains and ordered the men to turn around, the river gave them a bonus. From The Gap to Rocky Mountain House, they shot down the North Saskatchewan at over ten miles an hour, paddling "no more than was barely necessary." Travel Alberta's Reach Reports estimate the time for this run at two to three days; the voyageurs made it in five hours and fifty minutes.

The Lure of the Downstream

Darrin Hagen is said to be the only human ever to be voted both Sexiest Man and Sexiest Woman in Edmonton (for several years running). He began his extraordinary career by running away from Rocky Mountain House. Adventurers heading upstream battled currents to get there; in *The Edmonton Queen (not a riverboat story)*, Hagen contemplated the lure of the downstream.

> *The Greyhound bus leaves Rocky Mountain House twice a day: 7:00 am and suppertime. Not being a morning person, my ticket was for the latter. That way I could say good-bye to Mom, pack my clothes and my accordion, and go watch the North Saskatchewan for a while.*
>
> *When you stand on a bridge, an illusion occurs. Watching the water slide silently past you in July, the first thing that*

occurs to you is how clean the water is. A brilliant aquamarine blue that I've never seen anywhere else. The water flowing underneath makes it feel like the whole bridge is moving backward. Suddenly I'm Barbra Streisand on the boat in "Funny Girl" holding that impossible long note.

In Rocky Mountain House you don't tell people you listen to Barbra Streisand.

I took my journal, some school papers, and the love letter from an older man in Edmonton that almost got me thrown out of the house.

An older man. He was 33 then. I'm 33 now. I'm hardly an older man.

I stood on the bridge, ripped them to pieces, and watched them spin and flutter down to the water, where they gradually disappeared into the brilliant clear blue.

I wondered how long it would take to float to Edmonton. If only I had a boat. I knew where I would end up....

The Greyhound stops at Alhambra, Leslieville, Benalto, Eckville, Sylvan Lake and Red Deer....

I could have gotten there faster on the river. I could have floated *into town*....

At Red Deer, Calgary and Edmonton are exactly the same distance away. Why north? Would things be different if I had turned South?

Probably not. Besides, the river runs north.

And it's my river.

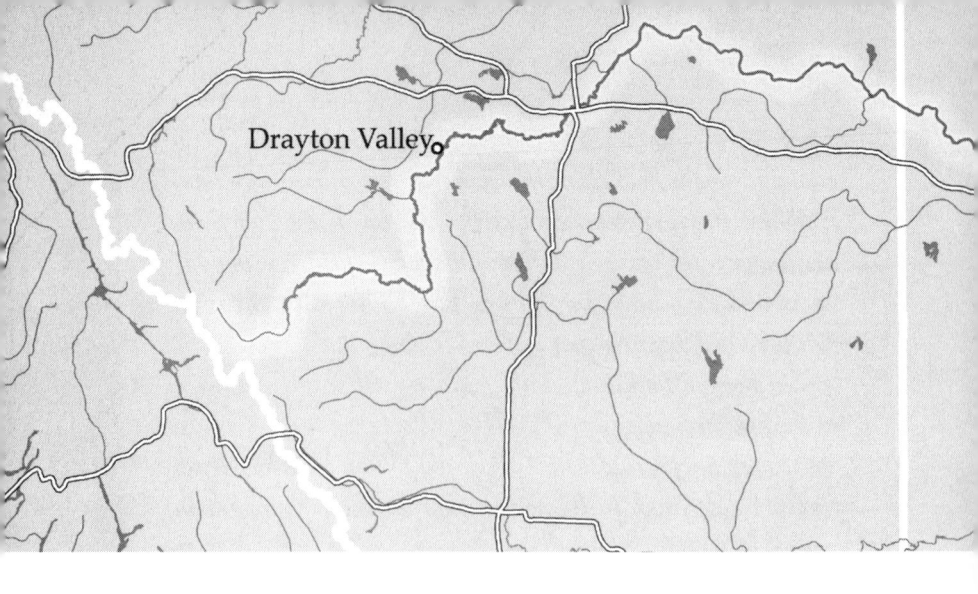

So, the channel was narrow, because of this island. And all of a sudden we shot down in a sharp bend and there was a great big white birch tree that was too near the water's edge and the flood or something had washed the ground away from it. And the big tree fell out into the water. The roots were still on land, but this tree was in the water. And we went right under the darned thing! – Keith Merkley, "Old Raft Story"

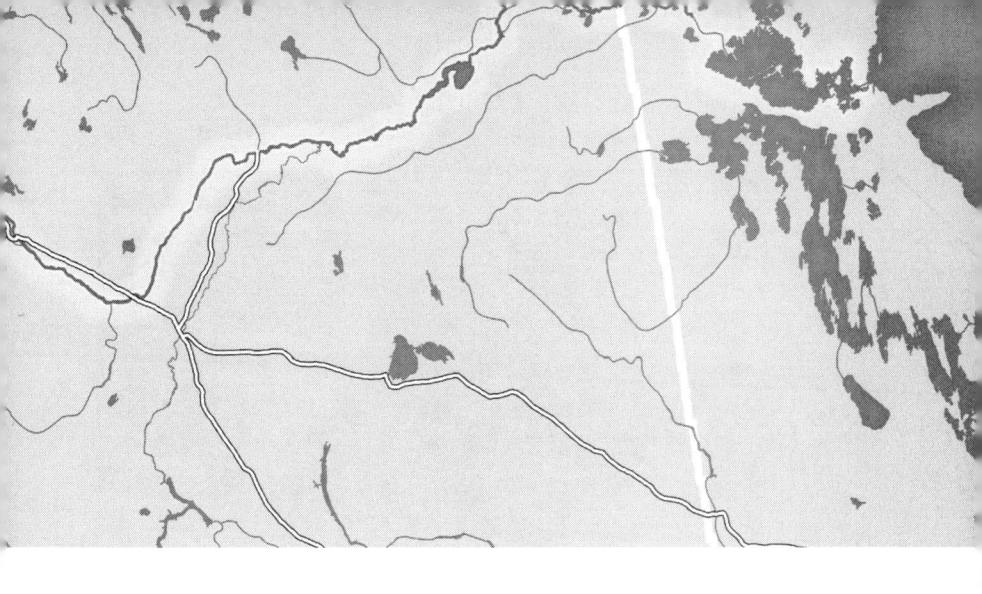

DRAYTON VALLEY
The Great Secret of the River

In 1953, Drayton Valley, a settlement that sits on a high plateau between the North Saskatchewan and Pembina rivers, was also found to be sitting on top of Canada's largest oilfield, the Pembina. Families of settlers had been making a modest living as lumbermen and trappers and farmers there since 1907-08. Since there were no roads in the district, settlers walked to Edmonton or floated their fur bales down river by raft. They returned on foot or took the train to Rocky Mountain House, built another raft, and used the North Saskatchewan as their "highway" back to Drayton Valley.

It was the river which brought the first European to explore the general area of the Drayton Valley – David Thompson, working for the North West Company and travelling with Alexander Henry in 1810 – but land wasn't broken for another hundred years, when a bit of a lumbering industry was set up, and cut trees and logs were simply floated down river to the sawmills in Edmonton.

Surveyors brave the river on the smallest of rafts. Crossing the North Saskatchewan River near Edmonton.

On the eve of the oil strike, the forests had all been harvested, the lumber mills were shutting down and closing the work camps, leaving a small town of approximately fifty residents "with little history and even less future," to cite the town's website. A decade later, the town was issuing half a million dollars' worth of building permits, and the bar was open twenty-four hours a day.

Edmontonians proved to be tourists of their own river. Keith Merkley and a party of friends – eleven young men and women – left Edmonton by train in the summer of 1907, descended at Innisfail, and hitched a wagon-ride with a farmer all the way to the Clearwater River about 80 kilometres from its junction with the North Saskatchewan below Rocky Mountain House. There they lashed logs together into two rafts, loaded up stove, food, bedding, dishes, and tools, and pushed off...into shoals, sand bars, and islands, and uprooted trees hanging over the riverbank.

In 1956, another set of raftsmen, Don Hepburn and Ted Kemp, Edmonton school teachers, surprised their friends, colleagues, and students by roping together a wooden raft on five oil drums and setting it in the North Saskatchewan River right under the David Thompson

Bridge at Rocky Mountain House. They planned an idyllic float downstream to Edmonton, but instead endured a "nightmarish" two-day battle with "vicious currents, shoals and swirling white-water rapids," as the *Edmonton Journal* reported it. They gave up at Drayton Valley, and hitch-hiked the rest of the way back to Edmonton.

In his account of the aborted adventure in *Rod and Gun* magazine, Kemp admits that neither he nor his friend had the least fear of the river; in fact, their plan for the excursion was to read books and mark papers, while getting a suntan. They even prepared bacon and eggs on their Coleman stove, the first day, "and then we entered the wilderness." They could not keep their craft from rushing over to the far shore whenever they turned a bend, nor from getting caught in shallow gravel shoals, and they did not see the tree bent over the water that then whipped off their tent.

> *Moreover, the constant pounding of the waves and the rocks against the barrels had caused them to loosen the floor boards, which were now popping up at such an alarming rate that we began to consider the possibility of proceeding down the river, each of us with his own individual barrel. To avoid this, we moved rapidly about the raft with our hammer, striking out viciously at uplifted nail-heads.*
>
> *And so we passed our time for most of that first day. I was unable to find the time to mark a single philosophy paper. In fact, I did not even remove the papers from the waterproof bag inside the waterproof box where, out of concern for their safety, and upon the insistence of my professor, I had stowed them. Don, on his part, did not have time to regret forgetting his book....*
>
> *The next morning our feet were swollen hugely. I could not get my shoes on, and Don could barely force his feet into his. We broke our camp, I carried the equipment to the edge of the gravel shoal, and then Don carried it to the raft, where I loaded it.*

Almost Relaxed

We placed our equipment carefully in the centre of the raft. Boxes were on the outside, and soft equipment pushed down between the boxes. Then we nailed tent posts to the deck around the boxes to secure them.

The second day was not quite as bad as the first, and, in addition we had learned better how to adapt ourselves to the river. By watching the river far ahead we were able to see where the water divided to pass through different channels. Thus by applying at the right time the minimum control of which we were capable we were sometimes able to determine which channel we would take. When there was no alternative, and this often happened, we learned to accept the fact fatalistically.

There were now stretches where for as much as half an hour we were able to almost relax. Don unshipped his mouth organ, and although it sounded pitifully weak against the rushing sounds of the river, it seemed to humanize the unpopulated wilderness through which we passed. I took out the binoculars and scanned the river banks. We noticed, for the first time at leisure, the rugged beauty of the countryside, the steep rock banks with their vari-colored strata exposed by the river, the dense growth of evergreens, here and there patched by the light green of poplars and grassy spaces. We saw where the lightning had struck many times along the same stretch of shore, leaving trees shattered and lying like broken toothpicks in a box. Three times we saw deer watching us as we passed close to the shore. We felt much better....

Shortly after this we entered the Pembina oilfield, where on either side of the river the pumps worked silently as we passed. We saw drilling rigs, and held brief shouted conversations with the men who worked them. We began to feel quite heroic.

Nevertheless, we hoped to get as far as the Drayton Valley ferry by nightfall. We planned to come ashore there, if possible, and either leave the river, or at least phone our wives. In our innocence, we thought they'd be worrying....

Fortunately, the ferry was at the shore of the river where we wanted to stop. On it were four men, watching us with interest, not to say amazement, as we bounced along toward them. We struck a gravel bank just this side of the ferry landing and with the help of those four were able to beach the raft.

So ends our saga. We decided to go no further. We left the raft and hitch-hiked to Edmonton, stocking foot, with our equipment. The Golden Hind was dismantled by the neighbouring farmers who had use for the barrels which floated it.

Oil and Water

In his poem, "The Oil," George Bowering is driving along "white man's tracks" up and down prairie highways ("but our things are straight lines"), on the surface of the deep and oozing dark, "I mean oil." The Peigan don't live here anymore.

Perhaps the poet is riding on top the Pembina oil field on which lucky Drayton Valley itself sits, amid a frenzy of Cadillacs.

The Oil

Sleepy old mind, I'm driving a car
across the prairie shivering under snow sky.
Old sky: I suddenly see with one rise of road
old buffalo fields,
                    there is nothing
but buffalo turds on the grass
         from which we keep
              the home fires burning.

Alberta
>floats on a pool of natural gas
>the Peigans knew nothing of
>in their fright
>in their flight
>>to the mountains.
>>>>We owe them that.

This straight line of highway
>& ghost wheat elevators
>everything there is straight lines
>>except the Indian fields,
>>>>they roll
we say, rolling hills,
>>but our things are
straight lines,
>>oil derricks, elevators, train tracks
the tracks of the white man
>>>the colour of
no white man, but
>>dark as the earth
in its darkness,
>>deep down oozing things:
I mean oil.

>>Alberta's unnatural heritage
concocted of Catholic adoption agencies
>& fundamentalist
crooked coffee-stained neckties
at the expense of Indian boys,
now Catholics with horses removed
from under them,
>>the Peigans crosst the Rockies

to British Columbia
    where oil is more scarce
& people.
 In the high trees they rise now,
with campfire smoke,
    the smell of needles burning.

Buffalo shit smoke
    burning in Alberta
by the road, highway 2 North.

Now a
 Cadillac, I see a
    nother Cadillac, & there
is the black straight road, &
    a Cadillac,
      two Cadillacs
on the road, racing, North,
    the mountains to the left
blurred by a passing
    Cadillac.

On April 24, 2003, kayaker Robert Pruden was already out on the North Saskatchewan River, for his fifth paddle of the season. After each paddle he would post an account on the Internet, including closely observed detail of the particular part of the river he had launched into.

Yakking the River

Today the river is flowing a bit high. The water at the Devon put-in is usually kinda fast and disturbed but with the higher levels everything was smoothed flat. The day was a very com-

fortable 15° C with sunny skies and light winds. The trees were well into their spring growth routine, greening well and scenting the warm air with the sweetness of their saps and resins.

I would remind you that the name of the (ka)yak VJ Guardian Spirit (VJGS) has significance for me. VJ is short for Victoria Jason, the first Canadian woman to paddle the Northwest Passage solo. Guardian Spirit is a name that my sweet 9-year-old daughter offered up via a poem. After wrecking my yak last year she figured I needed an angelic reference whenever I paddle.

I enjoyed watching the riverbank pass by as I floated along while I attempted to fire up my GPS to check my location and altitude. I was floating uncontrolled while the VJGS slowly spun sideways to the current. The GPS showed my speed at 7.3 km/h, altitude at 633 meters. As it would turn out the present speed would turn out to be my average speed for today's trip.

It seemed to me that I spent a lot of time looking at eroded riverbanks tunneled by beaver. We had record snow falls last winter and it showed on the banks. All along the river the high muddy banks had suffered slides that sent huge sections of mud cascading into the water. I saw whole trees appearing to grow out of the water after they had miraculously slid down the slopes to come to rest in an upright position. Huge islands of gray mud had moved into the main current creating eddies into which the detritus of the spring floods collected. I saw the rings of time in the exposed sedimentary layers of previously hidden underground history. Although I see these eroded banks every time I paddle I never get tired of studying the geology and wildlife I see.

I saw a deer grazing on a very steep hill, the usual mallards, possible grebes and luckily enough, a cormorant that was hanging out with the Canada geese. The Canada geese effectively rule the river: they were everywhere. There were loads of *sandpipers scooting like sandpipers and flying like F 16's just over top of the water. I love watching those little birds fly with their impossible turns. I dubbed them my favorite river bird today. I had many encounters with beaver, from confused babies to wily adults. One really really big beaver was digging a new tunnel into the riverbank and espied me first. It literally sprinted down the bank and hit the water with such a splash that I almost needed to do a self-rescue. Another beaver, one I have encountered before in the city, trailed me for the longest time before I finally stopped paddling so it could catch up to me, pass me then allow me to trail it.*

I decided to catch up to the little guy and paddled beside it for a short time. The beaver eyed me and paddled harder to avoid me but did not do his slam-dunk-and-whump routine. I figured a near-beaver experience like this wouldn't happen again so I pulled out my digital camera and took a couple of pictures of my new paddling partner. He soon veered to the shore so I left the little guy as I adjusted my path to get set for my put-out at the Magpie Canoe Launch located at my favorite city park, Emily Murphy.

Mark Morris gets out of his kayak at Drayton Valley and rests, in order to watch the river, look at it, and think about it. Morris is an experienced kayaker and outdoorsman who came to western Canada from Europe after years of travel and moving about and found himself mesmerized by the landscapes of Alberta and its rivers. Whenever he is anywhere near the Saskatchewan River, he tries to get to it, to cross it, to move along it.

I think the great secret of the river is what it would be like if it wasn't there. It's one of those things that everyone takes for granted, not because they are indifferent to it, but because its

Going to town involved shopping for groceries, getting parts, buying feed, and stopping at the library; best of all, it meant crossing the river. Ferry crossing North Saskatchewan River, Alberta, 1908.

effects are subtle and work on us like the undertow rather than the surface of its waters. So we would only really understand its undulating influence if it suddenly disappeared, and the land was flat, and ready for those Wal-marts and Zellers. I think that's part of the secret of the great North American rivers, that one is driving along flat prairies, and suddenly there is a great hidden living slash dropping into that flatness. It's so sudden, I always find it exciting, that unexpected corridor of cottonwoods whose tops were not high enough to float over the lips of the valley, the road changing altitude as if one was in an aeroplane starting its descent approach, and then the bridge, and the bridges across the big rivers are some of the best fusions of human thought and nature, all the more so for being at cross-purposes, as the river goes at one right angle and the road at the other. And then the take-off up the other side, and over the other lip, and the river is as if it wasn't there, not even in the rear-view mirror.

Do you know that road that crosses the Saskatchewan by Drayton Valley? The road drops down and curves, and there are always road workers there trying to patch up the battle between river rising and asphalt, but on the right there is a little picnic place, where one can sit and gaze at the river, and look across to the flat expanse beyond the bridge, a widening of the valley, where there are usually geese sitting placidly, and one realizes that in the river valley and all around it as far as one can see humankind simply hasn't known how to encroach.

And I think that wilderness is there in Edmonton or Devon, as you look at the way the river has entrenched the valley, and you see sheer sides of layer upon layer of thousands of years of sediment exposed, because it is often too steep for the vegetation to take hold, and you know that stuck in there in those mud rock banks are almost certainly arrowheads, and below, in the lower layers, the fossilized bones of bison, from before even arrowheads had ever been made. And of course it's real wilderness along the marvellous road from Rocky Mountain House into the mountains, and there is that tremendous rushing waterfall whose name I forget vaulting over a high fault-line of one of the river-heads, and that always reminds me that the river there is really young and exuberant and heedless, but nonetheless has grandfathers – or is it the gods? – of the mountains watching over its birth.

The Saskatchewan continues to drain the Rocky Mountains in to the Atlantic Ocean. But its flow is no longer wanton, no longer wasted. Or it won't be when the engineers have completed their work, backed by the co-operation of four governments. Perhaps the most exciting feature of the entire story of the "river that flows swiftly" is the resemblance of the men who are developing it today to those who explored and mapped it. The fur trader-explorers were men with an eye for every detail in every bend in the river, seeking men who found answers to their questions. So are the engineer-developers. Both groups have managed to combine the utmost in vision with the utmost in practical achievement. That, it would seem, is the Saskatchewan way. – Marjorie Wilkins Campbell, *The Saskatchewan*

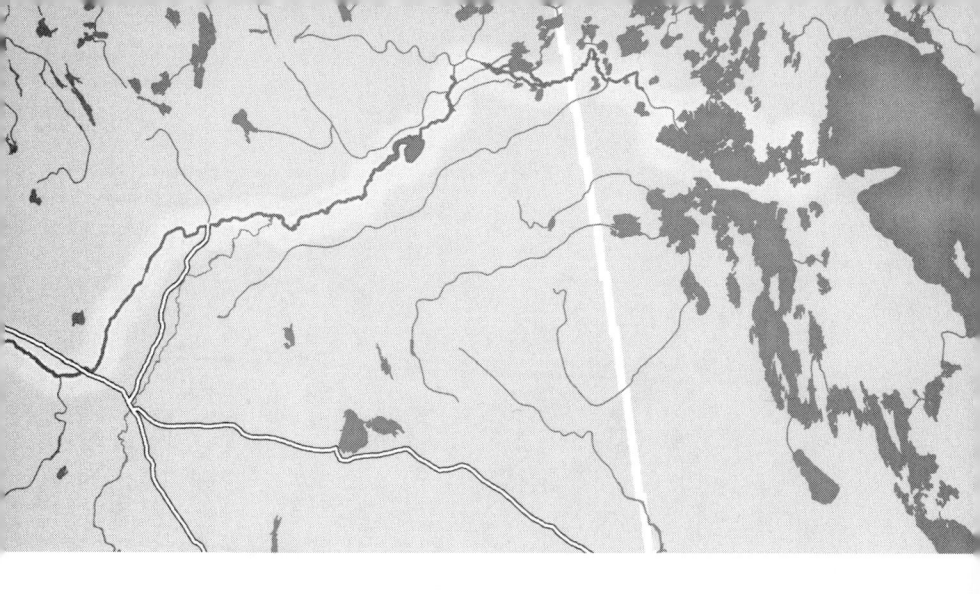

EDMONTON
The Watery Highway

The valley of the Saskatchewan River is 10,000 years old, but much, much older are the black coal seams from the age of dinosaurs 70 million years ago, and the sand and gravel deposits on the city's western edge. These latter are remnants of ancient sediment beds deposited by a broad pre-glacial river where mammoths, muskoxen, horses, and camels grazed 25,000 years ago, and where predators and prey have mingled their bones. Three thousand years later this river disappeared beneath the glaciers of the Late Wisconsinan age, and when these eventually melted and receded, disappearing in a torrent of meltwater, the glacial waters from the Saskatchewan Glacier in the Rocky Mountains began their work as a river, pushing across the plains through silt all the way down to Cretaceous bedrock that formed the valley bottom for the Saskatchewan River.

Twelve thousand years ago, during the last of the glaciations, Lake Edmonton formed at the foot of the receding continental ice

"What I like best about the river, though, are its twists and curves and oxbows, so you are never certain what is ahead." Aerial view, Edmonton, Alberta, ca. 1920s, showing river through the city, from 100th Street east to Highland district.

sheet and lingered long enough to deposit silty clay, or gumbo, as springtime gardeners in Edmonton call it, while the river dropped layers of sand which remain today as the topographical relief of low hills – favoured camping spots.

"Although summers may have been as warm as they are today, [glacial] Lake Edmonton was not a place you'd choose for a beach holiday," write Barbara Huck and Doug Whiteway. The lake was walled in on three sides by sheets of ice and dotted by icebergs, "an inhospitable, often savage place."

> *When the lake disappeared, it did so in a flash of geological time. As the ice dam began to thin at its southern edge, water found a low point under it on the height of land between the North Saskatchewan and Battle River basins and began to flow south. The force of the flow ate at the ice above and the*

ground below, rapidly enlarging this sub-glacial drain until, in a torrent of water and ice and rocks and soil, the lake poured out of its icy basin and into the Battle River, carving a deep channel as it went....

Moving south and east, the deluge carved an enormous trench across the province, forever commemorating the passing of the flood. Today a small stream follows this course, which we know as the Battle River Valley. Aboriginal Albertans had a more accurate name for it: sípíy wayutinaw, *"the river that flows in a great valley."*

With the disappearance of glacial Lake Edmonton and the retreat of the Laurentide ice sheet, the glacial North Saskatchewan River began to establish the course we know today, eroding through the alluvial silt, glacial till and preglacial river gravel of the Empress Formation. Within a thousand years it had reached the Cretaceous bedrock. Bison bones found on the highest river bench, 55 meters (180 feet) above the present channel bed, have been dated to 11,000 years BP (before present).

For the next 3,000 years, the river continued to carve the valley walls at a rapid rate, creating a series of lower benches leading to the modern flood plain. Here, alluvial soil from floods in the last century overlies sediments containing bone and wood as much as 8,000 years old, proof that the river has done little downcutting in the past eight millennia.

In Edmonton's southwest corner, the North Saskatchewan makes a great meander around Terwillegar Park residential district; just to the southeast the land rises to a knoll called Rabbit Hill, a relic of the ice age – sand and sediment deposited by meltwater – and one of the highest points in the Edmonton area. From here hunters watched for the movement of bison and deer to the drinking spots at the bend of the river below.

The pinkish streak in the riverbank strata dates back 6,800 years to the explosion of Mount Mazama (now Crater Lake, Oregon), which covered most of central and southern Alberta with ash. Perhaps 5,000 years ago, early Alberta toolmakers camped regularly in present-day Rundle Park, manufacturing stone tools from quartzite, a river rock harder than steel. Archaeologists have identified fourteen prehistoric sites in gravel pits in the Hermitage Park area.

Gail Helgason's novel, *Swimming Into Darkness,* opens with a lyrical description of the power of the North Saskatchewan river as it moves through Edmonton. The narrator, an Icelandic-Canadian woman who is researching the life and poetry of an Icelandic settler, Markus Olafsson, stands in today's Terwillegar Park, the site of his homestead, and thinks about the deep attraction of the moving water below.

> *Like Markus Olafsson, I'm drawn to this river, with its water chilled by glaciers on the Continental Divide, water that slices deep clefts into the soft clay banks, so that those who build houses beside it, as Markus did, never really know, season in, season out, whether this will be the year they will be defeated by the blasting forces of wind and rain and water and snow. I prefer this river because it is always in motion, always hurrying, no matter how calm the surface appears. In winter, under thick ice, gravity pushes the current onward. In summer, even the shallows are tentative, never quite at rest.*
>
> *Unlike that prairie lake of my childhood, fed by deep and hidden springs, the source of the North Saskatchewan is easily traced to the glaciers and mountain valleys Markus immortalized. Its beginnings hold no mystery. I find this calming.*
>
> *What I like best about the river, though, are its twists and curves and oxbows, so you are never certain what is ahead. The need for watchfulness can never be forgotten.*

No bridges crossed the river then, and even frozen in winter it had the feel of a thing aflow. View of Fort Edmonton in winter, looking west from the flats. York boat and Red River carts in foreground. December, 1871. C. Horetzky.

> A prairie lake can be too translucent, too full of the sky, too dreamy, too much like a mirror. It can pretend to tell you everything and tell you nothing. It can lull you to sleep when you most need to be alert. A river like this one, heavy, silt-ridden, intricately braided with unseen currents, makes no such false promises.

Pre-contact Indians of the Saskatchewan River country hunted and traded in an economy of great natural abundance, following the bison herds, drying the meat and fish, preparing clothing and shelter from the skins, and moving along the "highways" of the rivers to the next fork or ford, for example, to present-day Rossdale Flats, in impressive assemblies of hundreds of tipis. Life was good, and in a sense the white traders needed them more than the Indians needed the Europeans. As historian Phillip Coutu points out, the Indians' basic needs were met from the buffalo hunt; "the trade in beaver pelts [with the Europeans] merely provided for unaccustomed luxury items such as Brazil tobacco, decorative beads, Jamaican rum and European firearms. Blankets, cotton clothing, metal cooking pots, knives and axes also greatly enhanced their living standards but could easily be obtained through trade with neighbouring tribes" in trading networks that spanned the continent. Writer James G. MacGregor, popular historian of the fur trade, remarks that as soon as the Hudson's Bay Company established its first post on Hudson Bay in the early 1670s, "word travelled up the river from one Indian camp to another, until it spread to the mountains.... At first, it was too far for them to make the trip down to the Bay, but they began sending furs down in small amounts by the intervening tribes." By 1700, the hunters and trappers were making the trip themselves, taking all summer to canoe to the Bay to trade.

In the summer of 1795, a young clerk employed by the NWC at Fort George, Duncan McGillivray, wrote in his diary of the company's plan to build a new post upriver at a place known as The Forks (of the Sturgeon and North Saskatchewan rivers, near present-day Fort Saskatchewan): "This is described to be a rich and plentiful country abounding with all kinds of animals, especially Beavers and Otters, which are said to be so numerous that the Women and Children kill them with sticks and hatchets," cites historian of Fort Saskatchewan Peter Ream. Fort Augustus – *Old* Fort Augustus, named for the Prince of Wales, Augustus Frederick – was duly constructed, and, like clockwork, competitor William Tomison of the Hudson's Bay Company immediately built a neighbouring post – "within a musket shot" – and named it Edmonton House, after the birthplace in Middlesex, England, of the deputy governor of the HBC, Sir James Winter Lake.

As the Historic Sites and Monuments cairn for Fort Augustus/Fort Edmonton summarizes, rather stentoriously: "Rivals in trade, allies in danger, these companies carried the flag and commerce of Britain, by way of the great rivers from the shores of the Atlantic Ocean and Hudson Bay, to the Pacific and Arctic Oceans."

In 1797, the beaver trade at Edmonton House had reached 12,500 skins. By 1802, however, this had dropped to 1,756. Moreover, after seven years of prairie winters, men had to tramp farther and farther for firewood in the area. Rather than haul wood to the fort, the traders pulled up stakes in 1801 and moved 44 kilometres upstream to where the Rossdale power plant in Edmonton is now located. These were the *New* Fort Augustus and Edmonton House. The river was fordable (near where the High Level Bridge stands), bordering the buffalo plains to the south; by short portage to Fort Assiniboine, traders had a route to the Athabasca and Pembina rivers to the north and west, while the Saskatchewan remained the main waterway east to Red River and Hudson Bay.

In 1810, both posts were once again moved, back downstream to the mouth of White Earth Creek, a tributary of the North Saskatchewan near modern Pakan; but in the winter of 1812-13, they were both definitively removed to present-site Edmonton. A directive had been issued by exasperated governors of the HBC in London: "Stop moving Fort Edmonton about, or adopt a new name for each location." The fort had become the most westerly point that fur brigades from the east could reach before winter freeze-up, and a provisioning post and agricultural centre that produced potatoes, pemmican, and barley, and raised horses.

And a decade later, with the fusion of the two companies, the amalgamated enterprise became known finally as Edmonton House, and a fixed point on the map. By 1826, Edmonton House had become one of the most important stopping and trading points on the river and was developing as a mercantile centre; it was described by trader William Tomison of Buckingham House as "the neatest, most commodious and yet the most compact" and as "the best adapted for defence of any Inland Establishment."

In 1830, after a flood, the fort was moved to higher ground just below the site of the present Legislature. The new house took two years to build, but when it was done – Rowand's Folly, some called it, after its chief trader, John Rowand, the "brawling, roaring, fur-trade king of the Prairies" – it was the finest fur trade post on the North Saskatchewan, the biggest house between Winnipeg and the Rocky Mountains. James Carnegie, the earl of Southesk, surely one of the Northwest's first tourists, visited in 1860, and was much impressed by the "important" size and character of the buildings, as well as by the "almost precipitous descent to the river, which at this part seemed to carry a great body of water."

Rowand's decades at the post (1823-1853) witnessed the decline of the buffalo herd, the first cattle drives from the south, the mutual destruction inflicted by inter-Indian wars, liquor, starvation, disease, and the arrival of the missionaries. "The worst thing for the trade is these ministers and priests," Rowand famously complained. "The Natives will never work half so well now – they like praying and singing."

The Watery Highway

In the early years of the fur trade between Indians and Europeans, most of the goods were hauled by canoe, but eventually the traders switched to the flat-bottomed York boats in which eighteen men could haul as much as forty men in canoes. But the labour was punishing. Father Albert Lacombe, who arrived at Fort Edmonton in 1852 as a passenger in one of the boats, wrote of the "burning sun or beating rain" in which they toiled from early morning until darkness fell. "Without having seen it one can form no idea of the hardships, the cruel fatigue of these boatmen," he told his biographer, Katherine Hughes. Even the sick still stumbled along as best they could, strapped into tracking-harness to haul the heavy boat and its cargo when the waters became impassable.

The steersmen, bowmen, and boatmen who left Edmonton House in the spring had more than 2,000 kilometres of lakes, rivers, and rapids to travel before they reached York Factory on Hudson Bay. They were mostly Orkney Islanders or Métis, and the working pace they set was brutal. They would paddle six to ten oar strokes a minute for fifty minutes, then rest for ten minutes, and keep this rhythm for ten to twelve more hours a day. (Perhaps the couple of drams of trade rum doled out each day helped.) When they couldn't negotiate a set of rapids, they were forced to "track" or pull the boat upstream. Most of them didn't last long on the river: they suffered from hernias, tendon problems, and broken bones. Those colourful sashes they wrapped dashingly around their midriffs? They gave the men vital support while they lifted 40 kilogram bales; the biggest cause of death among voyageurs was strangulated hernia.

But the journey of the brigades back inland in the spring was truly celebratory as they neared their destination at the fort. The new shipment of trading goods signalled the opening of the trading season. The fort's guns gave a salute, the boatmen raced in, singing the old French and Algonquin canoe songs, *En roulant ma boule* and *Moniang nind onjiba*, while all along the river banks above the flats people cheered the arrival of the boatmen, who were decked out in their finery for just this occasion, and for the dancing. "It is at Edmonton House where the ancient tribal drums of the Prairie people would meet the fiddle of the Métis and the traditional Indian dances would encounter the raucous Red River jig. At the fur trade rendezvous, Blackfeet, Cree, English, French, Iroquois, Michif, Ojibwa and Sioux languages would all be spoken intermittently," writes Phillip Coutu.

The river was not the only means of transportation for the trade. Red river carts, ramshackle and squeaky affairs, graceless and shaky on rough ground but "a marvel of mechanism" to their experienced Métis carters, they were easy to pull through bogs, light enough at river fords, and tough in bush. They freighted furs and skins, pemmican and general merchandise on trails from Fort Garry in southern Manitoba via Fort Ellice to the Saskatchewan River at Fort Carlton, and from there to Fort Edmonton. According to James G. MacGregor, William Francis Butler, Dr. Walter Cheadle, Captain John Palliser, Father Albert Lacombe, and Rev. George McDougall all came to Edmonton over the Carlton Trail.

In January 1875, "Parson" John McDougall, son of Methodist missionary George McDougall, on return from Fort Edmonton to his mission in Morleyville, had the company of Colonel W. D. Jarvis of the NWMP for about 100 kilometres of his journey. Jarvis had been in command of a contingent of policemen who had made the gruelling trip across the prairie to Fort Edmonton to set up a police post in the Northwest. McDougall heard all about it. "It was a keen, cold winter's night, and we were in the open camp under the lee of some willows, and the Colonel gave us a graphic account of the trip from the Red River to Edmonton." McDougall was unimpressed by the story; in fact, he was infuriated.

> *After he [the Colonel] had cursed the Canadian and British governments and the whole North-West country, the rivers especially, and wound up expecting us to applaud such wonderful heroism, and I said to him, "Colonel, nine or ten miles north of Edmonton there dwells, when at home, a French half-breed who, when the spring comes, will load his carts with his winter's trade and catch of furs and pemmican, and, with his wife and children, will take the trail you came by, crossing all the streams you crossed. In due time he will reach Fort Garry; then he will sell his furs and robes, and purchase his fresh supply of goods and articles of trade, load these on to his carts, turn his face westward, recross all the streams, now at their*

highest, reach his home north of Edmonton, put up several stacks of hay, fix up his winter quarters, mend his carts and harness, and having carefully stored his goods, he and his family, with the same horses and carts, will cross the Saskatchewan and travel out from two to three hundred miles on to the plains, make a big turn through the country, run buffalo, stand on guard day and night, make many bales of meat, make many bags of pemmican, and finally, being now well loaded, return over the long journey to their home north of Edmonton. And still, it is not yet winter; and thus this native has travelled about three times the distance you and your party did Colonel; and they had no government behind them, and what they have done is a common occurrence in this Western country."

It is needless to say that the Colonel saw the point, and we heard no more about the greatness of the feat of crossing the plain on an old trail in a summer's time.

"The centredom of the great Saskatchewan country"

In the 1850s, Fort Edmonton had a permanent population of about 150, among them builders of the York boats for the brigades that would take the furs down to Hudson Bay. These boats, adapted for the shallow western rivers, rarely lasted more than three trips. The residents planted a potato crop, ground some tolerable flour, and ate, in total, two buffalo a day. Food was always a problem. James Hector, the geologist on the Palliser Expedition, observed at Fort Edmonton in May 1859 that not only did the boatmen have to provision themselves but also deliver food to other brigades as they journeyed downstream, "while in the fort are to be left the women and children with perhaps only two or three men, and if the buffalo are distant they will certainly suffer a summer of great privation."

The itinerant American Jesuit priest Pierre-Jean De Smet wrote of HBC Chief Factor John Rowand that he was a "typical trader, a miniature emperor who possessed the impetuosity of the Irish in an exaggerated degree." Rowand's temper was legendary, and was to play a part in his downfall, in a meeting of the HBC Council for Saskatchewan District that same year, 1848. But it wasn't just a question of one man's irascibility; whole environments were changing on the western plains. After 1850, journals and letters from the trading posts mention running out of trade goods and, because fewer Indian hunters were bringing in meat, they also mention hunger and even starvation. Novelist Fred Stenson narrates the situation from the point of view of the "miniature emperor," John Rowand, known as One Pound One.

> *Whole herds of buffalo had been consumed by fire in the fall of '46. They lay down in their thousands to die. The wheel of such a disaster keeps turning. At Council, his Chief Factors told One Pound One that snow had fallen to such a depth during the winter of his furlough that the weakest buffalo could not dig down to the grass. The stronger ones, digging, found nothing but char. They starved and died again. More rotting carcasses, more wolves. When the wolves run out of buffalo carrion, they come for the horses....*
>
> *As for the charge that One Pound One was too critical of the men...well, the poor darlings. It was not that many years ago (before the damn priests started poaching) that you had men here who could row from dark to dark, who tracked and portaged at a run, who were either never sick or had the good grace to die quickly.*
>
> *Just looking around the boat on which he sat as he returned upriver to his district, One Pound One had evidence aplenty of the decline in the labouring and paddling class. After watching the poor weak things try to row for half the*

summer, his intention was to sit down the moment he got to Edmonton and complain again! At length!

Fort Edmonton, 1849-50

The winter was again ushered in by fires. This time they were to the east, around Pitt and down to Carlton. The Indians starved like dogs and the trade was so bad it went backwards. At Carlton, they were eating their own oxen. What can you say of a trading business that cannot feed itself?

In 1887, frost destroyed most of the crops in the fledgling settlements around Edmonton. A year later, reports of starvation came in from the reserves near Lac La Biche, and in the Edmonton region reserves reported more deaths than births, from hunger and an epidemic of measles. On February 23, 1888, Chiefs Alexander, Alexis, and Michel sent a telegram to Prime Minister Sir John A. Macdonald, alerting him to the situation among their people, that they had begun to kill the reserves' cattle in order to have something to eat. The *Edmonton Bulletin* published their statement two days later, and it is reproduced in Elizabeth Macpherson's narrative of the fur trade around Edmonton, *The Sun Traveller*.

Alexander: "We have come here to make a complaint that the government has not used us as they agreed. If they continue to use us during the rest of the winter up to the present time perhaps a few will see the spring but those who do will be too weak to do anything to help themselves.... If the government will do anything for us we beg they will do so right away. We cannot stand the hunger any longer. If we do not get help at once we will have to kill the cattle the government has placed with us for our use, and we do not wish to do that as we know that would be our own loss. The government knows that other

> winters we were able to help ourselves killing fur which we could trade for food. With that and what the government then gave us we could live well enough. The government promised that in years of failure such as this they would help us more, but instead of doing so in this year of scarcity they have lessened the usual supply of food by more than one half."

Rev. John McDougall, very much a working man himself in the Northwest, confirmed in 1868 that Fort Edmonton "is a prominent place; has been on the map of Britain's empire for scores of years.... Edmonton as she really is, stands for the centredom of the great Saskatchewan country." But it was not yet a place of much importance to anyone outside the Trade. "Are there any hotels? None. Are there any churches? One, a Roman Catholic. How many stores? One, the Hudson's Bay Company," McDougall is quoted by a historian of the Methodist missions, James Nix. Even in 1873, Edmontonians were still almost 2,000 kilometres from the nearest post office and 2,640 from the last railway station. It took seventy-three days of overland travel to reach Edmonton from Winnipeg. No wonder, McDougall exclaimed, so many travellers found the Great Northwest "interminable."

When the HBC sold its governing right to the area to the Dominion of Canada in 1870, huge tracts of the Northwest were offered for purchase, and settlement soon began outside the fort walls. By 1875, the prospects for commerce seemed at least as attractive as the current proceeds from the fur trade: John Walter quit the Company to establish a ferry as well as a boat-building business on the south bank of the river. On a return visit to Fort Edmonton in 1882, Father Albert Lacombe, who had first set eyes on the place in 1852, now regarded it in disbelief. Gone the stockades and bastions of a proper fort; in their place ran a low plank fence. On the hills rising from the riverbanks, small clearings had been cut and log shacks set down. The trail winding eastward could even be viewed as a kind of village street.

Cutting ice on North Saskatchewan River, Edmonton, Alberta, 1908-09. Pillars for high level bridge visible to right. Buildings of old Fort Edmonton, centre, rear, with Legislative Building under construction, left centre.

Now the settlement had a schoolhouse, a telegraph wire, and a printing press. The buffalo were gone, and the Cree hunters and families were cooped up on reserves, and there was hunger on the land. "Where," Father Lacombe lamented, "has my wilderness gone?"

The fort was dismantled in 1915, the Board of Trade having determined that no buildings from the city's past were worth preserving – the city was "too young" to have an interesting history – and though the people of Edmonton were told the materials were all being marked for future reassembly elsewhere, it has never happened. The structure at Fort Edmonton Park is a replica.

Edmonton's Most Historic Intersection

The water is moving downstream to what historian Tony Cashman has called Edmonton's most historic intersection, at what are now called The Flats in Rossdale. For up to 8,000 years before the arrival of Europeans, Aboriginal people chose what is now called Rossdale as a highly desirable place to set up camp beside the North Saskatchewan River. "'It's flat, it's on the flood plain, it's wide open, it's on the sunny side of the river and it's on the river itself...,' senior city planner Duncan Fraser told the *Edmonton Journal*. 'There were many, many people coming and going. This was a meeting area.'"

In 1845, Archibald McDonald, a chief factor in the HBC, was wintering in Fort Edmonton when three of his children were struck down with scarlet fever. They were buried in a common grave, and McDonald returned to Montreal.

The burial ground – holding the remains of an estimated two hundred Indian, Métis, and European people – had been established by the fur traders outside the walls of the main trading posts, and was in use from about 1800 until 1871. In 1902, the Edmonton Electrical Lighting and Power Co. built a power plant on or near the site of the forts, now known as Rossdale Flats.

A 1977 study for the province called the Rossdale site a rare and significant historical find of national interest, but it wasn't until 2002 that the bones of three children were found during digging at the cemetery site. The power company, Epcor, announced it was cancelling the proposed expansion of its power plant on the Rossdale Road, which swings off the Walterdale Bridge and over some of the graves. In 2004, reporter David Howell wrote an update.

> *"For me, I have a hard time walking over this," says [Duane] Goodstriker, head of the Blackfoot Nations First Thunder Society.... Every day, some 10,000 cars, trucks and buses coming north across the Walterdale Bridge exit onto the section of Rossdale Road that runs directly over the historic graveyard and aboriginal burial ground.... For five years, Phillip Coutu, Good Striker and others have fought for the road to be closed*

> *and a permanent memorial built to honour the Cree, Blackfoot, Metis, Sarcee, Dene, European and other Canadians buried there. They have erected homemade crosses and spears to mark the spot.... At no time was consideration given to leaving the road open and relocating any of the bodies. "Right at the outset, the aboriginal elders we talked to said the souls that are down there are at rest, and the worst possible thing that we could do would be to disturb the rest of the souls," says David Schneider [city official in charge of the memorial]....*
>
> *An archaeological report for Epcor concluded that the enclosed area of the old cemetery contained at least 91 and perhaps as many as 129 graves.... Between 1908 and 1981, the remains of 24 people – ranging from skulls to complete skeletons – were unearthed during pipeline installations, other underground utility projects and road construction. More human bones were discovered in 2001."*

In John Lent's poem from his 1990 collection, *The Face in the Garden,* a man with the apparently normal job of operating a "cat" on an ancient hillside near the river digs up more than anyone bargained for.

In the Rear-View Mirror of the Finning Cat

> *Under the skin, is a huge rubbish heap of crumbled congealed magma and dead bodies, pressed into stone over countless millions of years.* – Edward Hyams, *The Changing Face Of Britain*

> the first bones it unearthed were fresh;
> heaved pets the rattling carriages of birds
> traces of human foetus recent death

you can ignore this close archaeology he thinks
and the weighted cat carves farther into this hill
the underpinning of the old site of Strathcona
his burrowing part of an effort to relieve
a traffic problem: dissecting Edmonton's valley
walls into efficient corridors knifing deeply
into its exfoliate past

but as the week wore on and he increasingly inward
the low fall sun the vacuum of the headphones
buried him inside the cab the only point of contact
that squared cast-iron jaw extending beneath him
churning up more and more bones farther in

as if it were his jaw

and his eyes bore into the hill in front of him
saw the skeletal death emerge before it was hoisted
Clinging tendrilled history over his head
sifting down like reasonable patterns into trucks
drawing up behind him to receive this freighted past
saw part of then the full force of the Old Vision:

primeval Sponge: ironic inverted Babel
we dance our straining jig upon our feet kissed
by its growing decayed suction smacking
our leaps forever deeper downward into some thing:

a world of after-images

of the Worm

laughing dancers sway hoist faces upward

into sun half men half meal
only the torsos twisting in the delight of eyes
while the old jaw works away draws
the tableau down into the calcium ritual:
a last dream of sponges final ironies alive
by empty spaces once the shouting dancers themselves
now a quiet vacuum of this breathing undulating thing
fed by negatives in its own dry way alive

it was shortly after this assignment that he'd go
to the Strathcona Bar too often sit there
comfortable in the patronising indifference of
his future: lilting in the students' laughter

it was their bar their dance now

tap his anemic foot on the sponge of the broadloom
slapping spilt beer to the persistent clumsy jaw of the juke
box

his head an unearthed hill

The Modern River

In 1873, the families of George McDougall and of his son John McDougall crossed the North Saskatchewan to Fort Edmonton. "To make a crossing of a big river in 1873 in the North-West meant something," John wrote later. "By dint of much wading and splashing and shouting, and often many disappointments, you urged your stock to take the current." Still to get across were the carts and wagons which had to be taken apart and loaded onto skiffs, which were pulled and tracked upstream to the other bank, an operation repeated all day. The pioneer of today, McDougall asserts in 1910, with the advent of government bridges and licensed wire-rope ferries, "is a misnomer. There is no pioneering today."

In a sense, we can mark the beginning of the "industrial" city in the West in 1882, with the operation of the first cable ferry to cross the North Saskatchewan, for now begins the history of the river as an obstacle – an acknowledgement that the river was not so much useful as the highway of trade as an obstacle to its development. The ferry was owned and operated by John Walter, who had arrived in Edmonton in 1870. To reach his destination from his native Hebrides, he travelled the classic route: by steamer for Hudson Bay, then by York boat and dog train to Edmonton. But, by the 1880s, people needed to get *across* the river as much as they went up and down it. The Oblate missionary Rev. Father J. A. Ouellette, for instance, writing to his Order in 1910 about his work in the Bonnyville area, explained that to travel there, "no mean task," involved the CPR to Strathcona and then across the North Saskatchewan to Edmonton by ferry, which was "a large pontoon held by pulleys that travelled a steel cable stretched from shore to shore. When the pontoon was manoeuvred to the proper angle to the cable, the force of the river's current drove it forward."

The High Level Bridge opened in 1913, that bravura of steel girders that nails together the yawning jaws of the river banks just upstream from Fort Edmonton – which still stood there, in 1913, when the first train rumbled across – and Walter finally dragged the ferry out of the water after its last run.

The Industrial River

Peter Erasmus's exciting dog sled race on New Year's Day, 1856, on the frozen North Saskatchewan at Fort Edmonton belongs to the era of the pre-industrial river. No bridges crossed it then, and even frozen in winter it had the feel of a thing aflow, as teams of dogs and their drivers careered through snowdrifts and flew over overflow ice, 5 kilometres up and down the channel between the banks. But, some thirty years later, we can mark the beginning of the "industrial" river, with the operation in 1882 of the first cable ferry to cross the North Saskatchewan.

To the chagrin of the residents of Edmonton on the north bank, the Calgary and Edmonton Railway, a CPR subsidiary, stopped practically on the edge of the steep banks south of the river in 1891, and a rival town, named after CPR founder Lord Strathcona, sprang up around the railway terminus. "The crossing of the Railway into Edmonton in those days was an absolutely impossible proposition," William Griesbach recalled in his memoirs. "At this point the Saskatchewan River winds through the valley from one-hundred-and-fifty to two hundred feet below the general surface of the surrounding country.... Passengers, arriving by rail, had to drive from South Edmonton [Strathcona] to Edmonton, crossing the river on two ferries, one operating immediately below the present Legislative Buildings and the other operating at two points at different times, one immediately below the present Macdonald Hotel or at a point about half a mile below."

The end of May 1901 found Bernard McEvoy on a cross-Canada trip, dispatching "descriptive letters" of his tour to the Toronto *Mail and Empire*. "My object was, and is," he wrote in a preface to these collected dispatches, *From the Great Lakes to the Wide West*, "to enable stay-at-home people to see with my eyes and hear with my ears some of the sights and sounds of the western half of our great Dominion." He writes with remarkable good humour of his crossing from the railway terminus in Strathcona to Edmonton on the other side of the river behind a team of horses.

> *Seven or eight of us mounted one of the rigs of the district to which these honest horses were harnessed, and we soon had*

cause to be thankful that our driver was an experienced and able whip. Edmonton was on the other side of the gorge of the Saskatchewan. This we had to descend by a steep incline, to cross the river by a suspension bridge, and to climb the two-hundred-foot ascent on the other side. Moreover, the road was of the "dirt" description and there had been frequent rains. It was not getting through one Slough of Despond – there were scores of them. Rapid change of level on the part of the occupants of the vehicle was inseparable from this sort of road. At one time you were apologizing to your neighbour for sitting on the top of him, and at another three or four were sitting on you without apologizing. I never knew before how far a rig will topple without going over. On either side were the solemn woods, seen dimly in the faintly-breaking dawn. At last we came to the descent, and our driver clapped on the brake, and we prayed that nothing might snap. Then a long bridge across the rapid river, and after that the tremendous climb, during which the horses had to stop three times and breathe, and only the good little brake kept us from going over the river bank backwards. Edmonton, electric-lighted, with its two thousand inhabitants (in their beds) was at the top, and we found a surprisingly good hotel and went to bed by daylight.

Father Albert Lacombe, who had first arrived at Fort Edmonton in 1852, expressed his forebodings in 1894 about a railway, this "road coming on...cutting its way through the prairies.... Like a vision I could see it driving my poor Indians before it...." Nevertheless, a year later, Father Lacombe was in Ottawa, accompanying the mayor of Edmonton to lobby the federal government for a bridge across the Saskatchewan in Edmonton. The bridge, the Low Level, was soon built, writes his biographer, who calls it a "monument to Father Lacombe's diplomacy."

The Low Level Bridge was a sight to behold, for it accommodated pedestrians, horses, automobiles, and streetcars as well as the Edmonton, Yukon and Pacific Railway. Construction of low level bridge, Edmonton, Alberta, early 1901. Boorne and May, Edmonton, Alberta.

And so it was that, on April 4, 1900, old-timer and hotelier Donald Ross, swinging a massive sledgehammer, drove home the last rivet on the Low Level Bridge, and it was finally possible for Edmontonians and Strathconians to cross the river on a permanent structure. It was a sight to behold, for it accommodated pedestrians, horses, automobiles, and streetcars as well as the Edmonton, Yukon and Pacific Railway. The EY&P chugged down Mill Creek ravine and across the bridge, dropping off its first load of Klondike-bound miners in 1902. The present-day Mill Creek trail follows the old track bed and trestle bridges of the EY&P.

"Never was there an event so long expected, so long and earnestly worked for, and so impatiently awaited, which took place with less ostentation than the arrival of the first train in Edmonton." Mayor William Short declared a civic holiday.

In 1905, when the Canadian Northern Railway came on to Edmonton from Battleford, it supplanted the old fur trade route by continuing on into the mountains at Jasper. "It was not long before the stillness of a summer's evening at any point on the Saskatchewan was broken by the far-off whistle of an approaching train," writes James G. MacGregor in his history of the Saskatchewan River, and "no sound was ever more welcome to mortal ears than was the sound of a locomotive whistle to a settler." The transcontinental railways were the new "Saskatchewan."

An Ideal Camping Spot

Able to hurtle themselves across the river with no trouble, Edmontonians turned their attention to the scene below, the stupendous work of nature that was their river valley, also known as the Hudson's Bay Flats.

In 1912, the City of Edmonton purchased 155 acres of river valley bottom from the HBC, truly a heritage site, for the floodplains of the Rossdale Flats, with their southern exposure, sandy soils, fish, and proximity to freshwater creeks, made an ideal camping spot, long before the establishment of trading posts here. Phillip Coutu writes that the "North Saskatchewan River valley was blessed with a pleasant variety of berries, edible mushrooms, medicinal herbs, and plant life that attracted deer, rabbits and small game.... In the winter months the great buffalo herds sought refuge in the shelter of the river valley providing a readily accessible and stable food supply."

The $310,000 sale was made with the stipulation that the land always remain parkland, a condition that was out of step with much entrepreneurial thinking of the time. Edmonton's river valley had become an industrial zone, accommodating dozens of coal mines, brick yards, lumber operations, and even a couple of gold mining operations and boat builders. But the purchase had also been recommended by Minneapolis architects Morrell & Nichols and landscape architect Frederick G. Todd, who supported the establishment of a river valley park system. It was a prescient recommendation. The river valley is now one of Edmonton's glories, winding 48 kilometres and offering the largest and most continuous area of urban parkland in North America, encompassing 1,825 acres, twenty-two parks, and 160 kilometres of trails along the river. The system is twenty-one times bigger than New York's Central Park.

In 1914, a group of prominent Edmonton women lobbied city council to change the name of the original Hudson's Bay Flats to Victoria Park. The park was a popular success, as picnic grounds and for horse stables, a rifle range, and a cricket pitch. During the winter months, the slopes served as a series of sleigh, toboggan, and ski runs.

The river valley is now one of Edmonton's glories, winding 48 kilometres and offering the largest and most continuous area of urban parkland in North America. Golf course, Edmonton, Alberta, with High Level Bridge in background, 1921. McDermid Studio, Edmonton, Alberta.

But the playground that was the river valley frequently flooded: in 1830 (which had forced the removal of Fort Edmonton to higher ground), again in 1899, and most spectacularly in 1915. Heavy rains in June caused the North Saskatchewan to rise a terrifying 13.2 metres and overflow its banks, inundating thirty-five city blocks. Eventually, dams would be built upstream to help control the volume of water carried down river, but in 1915 people could only watch helplessly as the rushing water swept chicken coops, barns, and shacks from the countryside and slammed them into the Low Level Bridge, which threatened to collapse under the pressure. The

"Probably the whole city of Edmonton was on McDougall Hill waiting for the bridge to go out." Ross Flats flood from McDougall Avenue [100th Street], Edmonton, Alberta, 1915. McDermid Studio, Edmonton, Alberta.

Canadian Northern Railway parked two trains loaded with coal and sand on the bridge, hoping to stabilize the structure. "Probably the whole city of Edmonton was on McDougall Hill waiting for the bridge to go out," Stanley Noel Smith, who was sixteen at the time, recalled later, to a newspaper reporter. A tent town for evacuees was set up on the grounds of the new legislative building.

Will the bridge hold? Low level bridge with train, Edmonton, Alberta, 1915. McDermid Studio, Edmonton, Alberta.

By the time the water peaked, 2,400 people were homeless, 60 buildings had been swept away, and 700 houses were submerged. The water supply was contaminated and the power plant knocked out. The only reported death was that of an infant who slipped from the arms of its mother, who was walking precariously along a floating sidewalk and dropped her baby into the rushing water.

A Working River

A photo taken in Edmonton about 1938 shows a shantytown built on Grierson dump on the river bank. Living in holes cut into the river bank and in crude shacks assembled out of scraps from the dump, as many as sixty-five men earned a scant but independent living by chipping coal out of abandoned mines and selling salvage.

The situation of the vagrants was extreme – these were the years of the Great Depression – but not unusual. Early immigrants to the Edmonton area also "made do" with the river banks while earning money for their families on the homesteads.

In the spring of 1901, Peter Svarich took off for Edmonton from his farm near Royal Park to hunt for a job; "I felt it was a waste for someone of my youth and talent to remain on the farm in the bush," he confessed in his memoirs. As his subsequent career would show, he was prodigiously talented, but in 1901 he worked at whatever was available, whether cranking the press that printed Frank Oliver's *The Bulletin* or unloading shingles at a lumberyard (and subcontracting a job to another immigrant who delivered logs). He agreed to build a house for the family with whom he lodged, for forty dollars, but first "I had to cut trees for lumber and float them on a raft down to the bridge. This took me a week, and I almost drowned in the river." This was the river still capable of running in swift currents up- and downstream; in its last act as a force to be reckoned with, still powerful enough to bear men away to a grave in Hudson Bay.

When the railway workers' union called a strike for better pay in May 1901, Svarich discovered a company of fellow Ukrainian immigrants milling about Edmonton without work, "dirty, ragged, and sunburnt like Gypsies, and helpless," and immediately organized them into a work gang. City officials needed about four acres of riverbank cleared of bush to make way for an exhibition site.

> *The men were eager to work, and in a few days, we fulfilled the terms of our contract, received our pay, paid our debts, and still had enough cash left to live on for a few days.*
>
> *In the city, there were several abandoned shacks, and we occupied them as our quarters for the night. A couple of them were [later] moved to the site of the present-day Macdonald Hotel, to serve as a market place on the riverbank. Here we made our headquarters and storehouse for flour and other provisions....*
>
> *On the slope at the foot of the bank, we improvised kitchen ranges and heaters. We collected tin cans from bacon and conserves and used these as utensils for cooking, frying, and drinking. We baked flat cakes and biscuits, and cooked* pyrohy *and noodles which we greased with lard and greaves [rendered pork fat chopped very fine]. We enjoyed our meals which we usually topped off with tea without milk, and, at times, without sugar. If we managed to earn more than we needed for our provisions, we would divide sacks of flour in two and send a half bag to the wives and children of each of the unemployed, out in the country.*

Not to be outdone by the Edmonton, Yukon and Pacific Railway, which finally crossed over to the north side of the river in 1902, the Canadian Pacific Railway built its own connection to the north side. Its siting is linked with Aboriginal oral history, which knows the river ford directly west of today's High Level Bridge as a junction with the "Old North Trail," the prehistoric migratory pathway that ran along the eastern slope of the Rocky Mountain range.

Construction began on the High Level Bridge in 1910, with construction crews working night and day, 50 metres above river level, for three years. Four massive reinforced concrete piers, each 38 metres tall, were set in the river bed, and almost 1.4 million rivets were hammered into the girders that hold the 8,000 tonne bridge together.

Construction of the High Level Bridge, the second to span the river within the city limits, was completed in 1912.

Four workers lost their lives, one falling to his death. The handsome black shaft of iron and steel that serves up one of the most spectacular views of the valley is their memorial. So is Wade Bell's imagined reconstruction of the thoughts of a fellow worker of that awful death.

> *And outside, beyond the stand of poplar trees, the bridge, ugly and cold in the sun, half-built and ugly....*
>
> *It is a small house we live in, and we have one room of it only. It is a poor house, unlike others behind it that were built by men who have been here a decade or more and are becoming wealthy as the city grows.*
>
> *This house, and our room in it, have what many rich men's houses do not have, and that is a view that other men think desirable. It is a view of the bridge, of the skeleton bridge thrust from the riverbank, partly made, already immense and*

to my mind ugly, already looking cold and ancient as if the winds of the North Saskatchewan had layered it with a century's grime and the northern clouds bathed it in sour rain. It is easy to imagine the bridge abandoned rather than new, to see it rotten and decaying above the spring colours of the valley....

It is the bridge. It is the ugliness of the bridge that I am seeing today and it is the fear of it that has erupted in my mind this day. It is because of Campbell that I will leave. It was only a few hours ago that we were let off work although it seems like it has been days. We were let off in the middle of the afternoon because of Campbell. Because of him and because of this afternoon I will leave. His life was not worth the bridge, nor is mine. I realize that now. It is the bridge and it is Campbell's dying. It is the bridge and Campbell's death that make me go. I know that now. I am afraid to die.

The bridge could give me work for many months. After it is built I could find an easy job here in this city and this room could be my home and the woman my woman, and we could sit in the evenings and watch the heavy engines cross the bridge and watch the river flow beneath it. We could live here and die in our time. I could do this but I will not. I will leave. It is not the whisky I have had this afternoon that has made me afraid, but it is the whisky that shows me my fear in this vision of another man falling. Campbell fell this afternoon and Campbell falls now, over and over his body is falling, falling and falling without end or so it seems but it does end although I did not then and do not now see his body land as it landed among trees. But I see him falling. I do not have to close my eyes to see him. I see him begin to fall.

Gertrude Balmer Watt, a lively journalist writing from a middle-class woman's point of view on a rapidly changing Edmonton of new immigrants, lived in an old red brick house at the privileged corner of 116 Street and 100 Avenue, overlooking her beloved North Saskatchewan River. From her perch there in 1908, she looked down the banks of the river and along the flats, where lay an "unknown country" to her.

Here it is that the coal camps pitch their tents, the men who haul the sand and gravel erect their homes, and here I found myself one day not long since, a flitter-by in a carriage, barely touching, barely getting a look at this new phase of life in this wonderful little city of ours – but keenly, vitally interested in what I saw....

The first thing that attracted my attention was the little group of stores in close proximity to Norwood School. Quaint country-like places of trade where there were any number of farmers' wagons hitched in front, and inside you could purchase anything from a violin to a roast of beef.

And then we were out among their homes, in the midst of another Edmonton, where life apparently throbs with quite as rapid a heart-beat as in the fashionable west end homes in the centre of the Capital, and where, I am free to confess, I saw far more to interest me....

Leaving the tents and houses in the rear and cutting down the slope to the river, we came upon such a lively panorama as would astonish anyone acquainted with winter conditions on the Saskatchewan. Teams everywhere – horses' heads touching the carts in front, apparently an unending stream of them, but with a small break, they were there again. Loads of coal and loads of gravel...for all the world like a long circus procession.

And where there weren't carts there were men; men with picks chopping gravel, thawed by the aid of little fires built on the ice, others loading the waiting teams – a scene of never ending activity.

I intend to learn what life means to the man who lives just over the hill...here you come close to something real...you begin to realize that there are other things to life than back-biting your dearest friends. It comes to you that existence is after all a solemn thing.

By 1926, when H. Dumas wrote his lyric about the river, bridges spanned the waterway, railways connected the city to the rest of the continent overland and bush pilots pushed at a new frontier north of the parkland farms. Edmontonians would look back on the not-so-distant past from a reverie of the pastoral, right there on the river bank under the shadows of bank buildings and department stores

Sur les Rives de la Saskatchewan

J'ai longtemps cherché dans mes voyages
Dans mes courses sans trèves,
La joie que j'éprouve sur cette plage;
Objet de mes rêves.

Refrain: Sur le bord de la Rivière
Près de la ville
Je construirai ma chaumière
Vivant tranquille,
Je chanterai pour toujours
D'une voix fière,
Le doux souvenir de mes amours.

Where the Saskatchewan Flows

I longed for a place where I could dream
Of my childhood days
Now I've found the spot thus it would seem
Where gleam joy-lit rays.

Chorus: Where the Saskatchewan flows
Down by the city
Where the brown-eyed Susan grows
In simple beauty
I will come and dream once more
Of sweet days of yore
Where the Saskatchewan flows away.

Adventurers and Tourists

As the new age of mass transportation drew to the Saskatchewan not only settlers and merchants, it also became the hub of a pioneering tourism. Jaded, perhaps, by the sophistication of old urban centres and drawn by the romance of the frontier at the end-of-steel, travellers arrived in Edmonton as early as 1905. By 1907 the Yankee tourists had started to come to Edmonton, and they found the river not frightening but a sporting challenge to be overcome, promising a kind of Kiplingesque manly, even homoerotic, adventure for the bored cosmopolitan. The American Emerson Hough, for instance, in *Sas-katch-e-wan: The Missouri of the North* (1907), revels in the very name of the river, "spoken as though it came from the full ridged chest of a tall red-man, thin in the flank, hard in the leg – spoken as though with the exhalation of lungs full of rugged northern air." Compared to his fellow Americans "wheezing with fat," this Saskatchewan still has wilderness in its legs, "youth still in its eye.... Wherefore, let us...get us to Saskatchewan."

Unlike the adventurers of the fur trade era, these men and women travelled in an age of amenities, even though, in their own heated imaginations, the train station in Edmonton "is your station for the North Pole," in the words of John Foster Fraser.

Fraser actually knew better. He was a professional journalist and inveterate traveller (including a bicycle trip around the world starting in 1896), and by the time he arrived in Strathcona in 1904 the place was already lit by electricity and boasted six grain elevators storing 250,000 bushels of wheat, he recalled in *Canada As It Is*. Across the river, Edmonton was already an old town, "as towns count in Canada," and the jumping-off place for the "great north hunting country," now that the fur trade east and west was a dwindling economy. Fraser is much taken with the idea of the hunters trailing to the wilds, "even to the Arctic circle," loners in the bush, beyond the blandishments of the city.

Some five years after Fraser, on a sunny August afternoon, the travel writer Agnes Laut shoved off in a canoe built for twenty from a river bank near Edmonton into the silty North Saskatchewan together with a female companion and a "thoroughly competent" paddler, and headed downstream. She was conscious of the fact that her adventure no longer belonged to that era on the river when "any one man knows Saskatchewan River from end to end," but now depended on finding guides and paddlers who knew the river in sections.

"The banks are high, high as the Hudson [river] ramparts.... Trees and hills are intensest green, and the birds are singing, for the season is late," she wrote of her first impressions of the Saskatchewan. She notes the "vistas" of heavy-headed wheat in fields on the north bank, hears the hoot of trains "pouring settlers at the rate of a quarter of a million a year across this last of the world's frontiers," and is charmed by the exotic sight of the "Galician" (Ukrainian) women washing linen down at the shore (one wonders what they made of her, perched in a canoe in her long skirt and big hat), but this evidence of a tamed geography does not get in the way of her rapture of the wild.

> *Beyond the Galician Settlement for a hundred miles you are traversing a wilderness primitive as the day when white man's boat first penetrated these lonely wilds. Hawks shriek from*

topmost bough of black poplars ashore. Whole colonies of black eagles nod and bobble and scream from the long sand-bars. Wolf tracks dot the soft shore mud; and sometimes, what looks like a group of dogs, comes down the bank watching you till you land, when they lope off, and you see they are coyotes. Again and again, as we drew in for nooning or supper to the lee side of some willow-grown island, black-tail deer leaped out of the brush almost over our heads and at one bound were in the midst of a tangled thicket that opened magic way for their flight. Early one morning, a little fawn came trotting down to the shore of a long island and ran abreast of us, unconscious of danger for half an hour; and one night when we drew in to a lonely bank for camp, we found the mud heavily tracked by large footprints like cattle; but there were no cattle within a hundred miles; and from the dew claw, it was apparent the tracks were of moose.

Popular historian of the river Marjorie Campbell has pithily summarized the age of steamboat navigation on the Saskatchewan: "*SS Marquis* beached at Prince Albert, 1886. *SS Northwest*, wrecked by high water at Edmonton, 1903. *Northcote*, run ashore at Cumberland...on a meadow opposite the Pas River." She does not mention *The City of Edmonton*, stuck in the mud in 1917 and unmoveable, but she makes her point: sternwheelers all, they came a cropper on the shoals, sand bars, and muddy bottom of the river which the much smaller and lighter York boats had been able to negotiate by simple expedient of being hauled along from the banks.

In the fall the water level was barely high enough to float the steamboats; in the spring the ice piled up, fogs lay along the valley, and sudden floods could carry boats away right off the beach, which proved the fate of the *Great Northwest* in the flood of 1899, which lifted it from its dock on the beach of Rossdale and swept it away to its disintegration far downstream.

Edmontonians loved being tourists on their own river. Press Association on picnic, Edmonton, Alberta, 1912. McDermid Studio, Edmonton, Alberta.

But the citizens of Edmonton did enjoy a few seasons of pleasure cruises along the river or to picnic spots on its islands, when boatman Walter Leslie, an Orkneyman who arrived in Edmonton in 1910, navigated the *City of Edmonton* on weekend excursions. Edmontonians loved being tourists on their own river, as local historian, Tony Cashman, relates.

> *The* City of Edmonton, *132 feet long and paired with smaller* Scona, *was in her second season when Walter Leslie arrived, carrying ten years' experience on salt water – most under sail – fishing and freighting around his native isles and on the world's oceans. Adjusting to a river was a challenge: "That was a bad river to navigate, the Saskatchewan."*
>
> *The murky surface, always in motion, hid shifting sandbars and unmoving rocks. Low water was a complication. High water was usually a boon, except when smokestacks were laid flat to squeeze under the Low Level Bridge in order to reach the passenger landing. And there were the sudden night fogs. As the boat approached the landing with a load of picnickers from Big Island, the bridge piers would suddenly vanish.*

Through the workweek, the boat was a freighter, its big stern wheel churning the thick river down to Shandro Landing, up to John Walter's log booms at Poplar Creek, and beyond to the Rocky Rapids near Drayton Valley. On holidays and weekends, she was transformed to an excursion boat, taking holiday crowds of four hundred up to Big Island or down to Fort Saskatchewan. At a daily operating cost of thirty-five dollars, excursions were good business – so good that the staterooms on the lower deck were ripped out and a maple dance floor laid down. A floor scuffed by sacks of grain coming up from Shandro Landing would be polished smooth again by flying feet....

Walter Leslie said you had to understand the eddies, make them work for you. Old Captain Grant never could. A grand gentleman, master of many oceans, he didn't understand the effect of eddies – or the current either. One day they found him in the wheelhouse steering away for all he was worth – and the boat firmly aground on a hidden sandbar. With the current breaking white over the bow and carrying flotsam past on both sides, Old Captain Grant had to be convinced he wasn't taking the City of Edmonton *upstream as ordered....*

In the end, it was low water that got her – in the fall of 1917 while she lay at the dock. Through the fatal night the river fell without warning and dropped her on the muddy bottom. Mud grabbed her hull along the entire length and defeated all efforts to free her.

The Mark Twain superstructure was recycled. Railing made good fences. The maple dance floor, blessed by memories of holiday cruises to Big Island, was put down in the farm home of John Walter's son at Sandy Lake. But the river never released the hull. It's still there off Kinsmen Park.

"That was a bad river to navigate, the Saskatchewan." Walter Leslie knew.

"...you had to understand the eddies, make them work for you". View of Marvin Nelson on the shore, North Saskatchewan River, who swam from the High to Low Level Bridge, Edmonton, 1931. McDermid Studio, Edmonton.

The City on the Hill

Give the city its three names
Alice Major

A city needs three names – the public one, the priestly,
and a secret, sacred name
for the god we do not realize protects us

The winter day is hushed
like a child holding a snowflake on a mitten.
Behind us, city towers send white vapour
to join low clouds. The river path is empty,
the dark is coming down.

A coyote cries, silver yodel.
Everything stops – even the prowling dusk,
even our breath – to listen.

Edmonton. A public name, polite gesture
to mother country, mother company.

The palisaded fort in wilderness
named for a suburb of London, birthplace
of an aide-de-camp in the enterprise
that piled fur and profit at the feet of the gentlemen
    adventurers of Hudson's Bay.

Rough buffalo, stiff-haired beaver,
wolf and milky ermine. All the dead creatures
in whose luxuriant pelts the traders' fingers wandered
to grasp, assess.

And sometimes simply to caress.
Fur can seem as though it's still alive,
a silent offering of spirit warmth,

Beside us, the river is a parallel
white path, almost untrodden. A few tracks cross
its snowy fur. Not the mechanical slide
of skis or flopping human footprints,
but the dotted autograph of paws,
hooves, the light, living feet of birds.

For a time, this outpost had another name –
Fort Sanspareil. An unusual flight of fancy
for round John Rowand, that 'most pushing, bustling
man in the service,' chief factor
who turned profits like a card trick, whose bones
    were boiled bare
and shipped home in a rum barrel
for burial in Montreal.

Sanspareil. A name from the *coureurs de bois*,
from the tongue of the missionary priests
who strung their rosary across the prairies
and into the dark pine woods.

Into the aching dusk
Coyote cries again.

*We hear but do not recognize
our secret name.*

By the 1920s, Edmonton was a city in earnest. It had its first radio station, CJCA, its first neon sign, and its first concert by the Edmonton Symphony, a university (including a francophone college), the first licensed municipal airport in Canada and, in the wake of the international stock market collapse in 1929, a local branch of the Ku Klux Klan.

By the 1940s, journalist Marjorie Wilkins Campbell tells us, the North Saskatchewan had spawned a brand new sport "that demands the utmost in skill, knowledge, and tact," namely, canoeing downstream on the look-out for old fur traders' sites at all the likely places – confluences of streams and the river, promontories, protected river bottom. "Trees, growing out of silt-covered ruins, indicate age. Hearthstones and chimneys, cellars and old *glacières* are important finds." The river became a treasure hunt for amateurs.

Marjorie Campbell, who traced the history of the river from its Ice Age origins to its modern course through agricultural and industrial land, was not at all nostalgic about the old river. She believed that it was time that "scientifically acquired facts" replace traditional "feeling" in the discussion of the future of the waterway. She had in mind, for example, the fact that the annual flow of the Saskatchewan River is some 18-million acre-feet by the time it gets to the Saskatchewan-Manitoba border, having drained off 150,000 square miles across the prairie steppes, "enough wasted water to irrigate hundreds of thousands of acres of dry land." Campbell was impatient that this uselessly free-flowing water should be tapped for its potential – it takes up to 30,000 gallons of water to grow a bushel of wheat, she pointed out – and she could foresee, in 1950, the needs of the oil, potash, and pulp and paper industries in Alberta. Extrapolating from the derring-do of the fur trade past, she could even imagine their ultimate triumph.

On February 13, 1947, Leduc Oil Well Number One blew in, spurting water, drilling mud, and oil over a crowd of five hundred government officials, businessmen, and newspaper reporters, propelling Edmonton into the global petroleum industry.

The River as Feeling

"How can they?" I once heard an American woman say as she stared at the wind flattening the prairie grass beyond the Edmonton airport. "How can they want to live in a country like this?"

On winter days when forty-mile-an-hour gales tear across the prairie snows, this writer from gentle Nova Scotia has often had the same thought. There is no use in pretending that the Saskatchewan River country is a kind one to its people even now; half a century ago it was as cruel as the Pole. This is one of the sternest terrains I know inhabited by people living normal civilized lives. But the very fact that it is inhabited by civilized people has an historical significance most of us forget in these comfortable times.... I remember the feeling of fear it gave me as a boy when my mother told me of a relative who had gone to Saskatchewan from Nova Scotia, and how she had watched her son walking alone across the prairie to school until he because a tiny dot on the horizon.

In Hugh MacLennan's confession of his primordial fear of the prairie winter, we read the transition of the literature of the Saskatchewan River from reportorial and narrative voices to the language of feeling and sensibility, for example, MacLennan's view of the Saskatchewan River country as a kind of challenge to the moral fibre of a writer overcome by dread. A river flows through it. After MacLennan, we may say, the river "means" whatever the writer or poet or poet-philosopher brings to it from his or her own imagination. Essayist Ian MacLaren, who understands "cultural memory" as essential to a shared sense of space, urges us to abandon the fast lane of our modern lives and to slip into the river's slow lane on a passage of meditative recall.

> *Many students I teach at the University of Alberta know nothing more about the river than the name – the North Saskatchewan – flowing just outside the building where we convene; not where it rises, where it debouches on salt water, which are its tributaries, and what other settlements lie on its banks....*
>
> *Place makes little claim on their knowledge or their interests. The World Wide Web proffers blandishments of operating*

"...already immense and to my mind ugly, already looking cold and ancient..." High Level Bridge, Edmonton, Alberta, 1914. McDermid Studio, Edmonton.

in the fast lane. Similar technological creations prompt one to classify as perfectly useless anything that lacks speed....

The two key components of a sense of place, nature and history, do not move with speed. Meanwhile, the aspens in the river valleys of the parkland apparently still tremble. They cheer the soul of those misfits who urge a canoe into the water and claim the river valley for a day. Here is the slow lane, in which reflection can keep the acquisition of information at bay. Take in the valley on the valley's terms, at the valley's speed....

From a scene now dominated by the busy-ness of Low, High Level and Light Rapid Transit (time-emphatic) bridges, a legislative dome and the sounds of commerce, step back and imagine just the sounds that come to life: Cree and French, perhaps a few English voices, perhaps Blackfoot. The snort of buffalo. The susurrus of silt-laden waterway, coursing across the prairie and down to Hudson Bay. Screeching falcons. Neighing horses. Trembling aspens. Nothing supersedes the river and its valley; nature and, therefore, place dominate all human activity in an invigorating balance....

This is our city!

For poet Eli Mandel – whose collections bear very suggestive titles like *Stony Plain, Out of Place, Life Sentence, Dreaming Backwards* – the river does not so much flow in a crevice of earth as through fissures in time.

FROM THE NORTH SASKATCHEWAN RIVER

when on the high bluff discovering
the river cuts below
       send messages
we have spoken to those on the boats

I am obsessed by the berries they eat
all night odour of Saskatoon
and an unidentifiable odour
something baking
        the sun
never reaches the lower bank

I cannot read the tree markings

today the sky is torn by wind:
a field after a long battle
strewn with corpses of cloud

give blessings to my children
speak for us to those who sent us here
say we did all that could be done
we have not learned
what lies north of the river
or past those hills that look like beasts

In "Edmonton October Poem," written in 1970, Douglas Barbour contrasted the grey dullness of the city's "executive thought" and the nostalgic melancholy of "buffaloes without thunder growing old," with the still-bright colours of the natural wonder of the river "swaying" in its valley. In a 2005 poem, the urban landscape has now become part of a shockingly globalized urbanism bewildering animal and human alike. But the river, even if only in glimpses, saves us.

Saskatchewan Drive

Every morning along the Drive
above the bluffs along the river

I pedal beside or into the low slanting sun
for it is autumn here now & the light has laid it slantwise
upon the evergreens the yellowing leaves of aspen &
maples elm & oak that make up the woods
to my left shading down over the edge of the hill
towards the flowing mirror below
occasional individual to my right upon lawns
well tended by those hired by those high enough in
the economy of the city to afford these homes once human
sized for a family felt as such now being disassembled as
the architect of the hour deploys his conventional forces to
bring down that passé habitation & replace it with the singular monstrous building he has erected along all such
drives in Phoenix Chicago Reading Glebe Edmonton
Calgary everywhere the same already built & sold as many
times as the market rose & fell or half-completed
on earth upturned where last week that home stood but I
pedal into wind past the noise of construction money
makes viable although the building overwhelms the site as
down the street do others
trees sometimes gone the birds
whirling to land where they used to
their little brains askew like the landscape or
no longer offering shade &
protection but standing diminished now
against the backdrop of building no
longer fitting in but asserting something I can hear all too
clearly but for the lack of clear articulation sun
in my eyes now I pedal past look out across green grass
bush & woods to the blue sky this morning
the quick glimpse of pearl river below
beyond

Places Far from Ellesmere: A Geografictione – a fiction of geography – Aritha van Herk's fourth work, approaches the blurred boundaries of fiction and nonfiction in postmodern writing with four essay-like fictions about the narrator in rural Edberg, Edmonton, Calgary, and Ellesmere Island in Nunavut. Part memoir, part literary criticism, sometimes a travel journal, the narrative is a re-reading of earlier experience and identity in places that shaped her, as a student in Edmonton in the 1970s, for example. Now she reconstructs the city and its river as pages of a text.

Edmonton, long division

The North Saskatchewan cutting the town in half: north/south; business/pleasure; government/learning. The few bridges incidental to separation and the high brows of the river banking their own domain. Here is the city that will divide you from the country, that will wean you from Edberg, its wide streets and narrow alleys leading toward seduction. This is the quandary you face, your problem in long division: north/south....

If you can only get to Edmonton in one piece, you now the Indian coming with your skin, your fresh eyes up from the Battle River country, through the Gwynne Outwash Channel, looking for a trade, something of use in the long winter ahead....

Long division: attainable in this outwash city overlooking its own autumns. Your landlady accuses that you work too hard, you read too much: she knocks on your door at all hours seeking to distract you (she teaches you to despise distraction), while you only want to return to words, the neat enlistments of notes, the swollen pages of portentous papers. Edmonton is a reading, an act of text, an open book.

Alice Major's *Contemplatio* takes its framework from the ancient ceremonies used to found a colony of Rome. In this sequence of poems, the poet fills the role formerly filled by an augur (hence our word "inauguration"). It seems to Major that artists "found" their cities by making them significant, defining their distinguishing features, and celebrating what is particular and what is universal about their history and landscape.

Envision the Outline

To found a city, call upon a seer.
The augur who will call its pattern from the sky
and place it on the earth. Who contemplates
the found site and finds – in hovering stars,
a trail of clouds, a skein of birds
flung downwind like a lariat –
the sacred polygon, the templum, the shape
it is meant to be.

From this viewpoint, looking south
the valley sinks its verdant basin
of aspen and evergreen.

A glimpse of river gazes back at sunset,
accepting its colours, as the cursive stroke
of a character takes the shade of ink.

Brass letters rim a nearby fountain –
"From this ragged handful of tents and cabins,
 a city will arise." Thus the brash
commercial visionaries of 1880
surveyed the future.

Already, in a short century, a succession of cities:
Handsome turn-of-century stone
squared off at corners. The small dry houses of the thirties.
Much torn down to throw up glass towers.

That ragged encampment
is now a formless scrawl over farmland.

Water laps the brass letters, smudges
their shiny confidence to bronze. I keep an augur's eye out
    for birds
and the cuneiform of cloud. The new moon in a rift
is a fine arc drawn precisely
by a silver compass.

To find a city's outer shape,
first locate its centre – the axes that cross,
cardo *and* decumanus. *Ancient, orthogonal grid.*

The river is the city's hinge, its east-west line.
Crossing it from south to north
geese make their high way overhead,
a silent, migrant beat
from the heart.

Fort Saskatchewan

Plans provided for a stockade of hewn pickets to be fitted closely together, sunk five feet in the ground and rising to a height of ten feet, with a bastion of squared timber 16 feet high in the north-west corner.... The principal buildings were built of squared pine covered with handmade shingles. There were: a stable with large hayloft, a cook house, a guardroom and several shops, all of which were one storey high, built of logs and roofed with mud. – Peter T. Ream, *The Fort on the Saskatchewan*

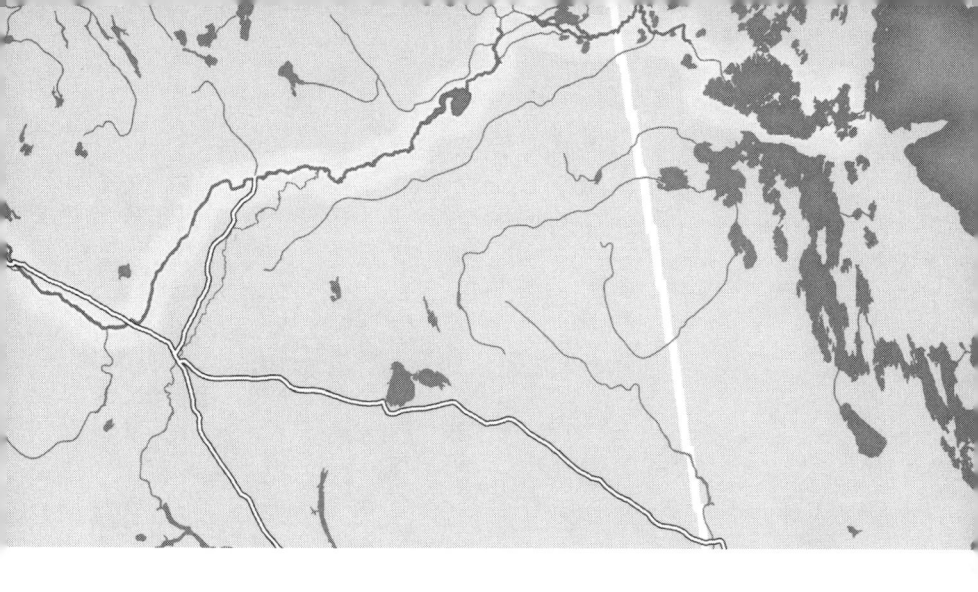

FORT SASKATCHEWAN
Mountain Trout and Roasted Beaver

The modern city of Fort Saskatchewan, boasting Szechuan restaurants, health-and-wellness centres, Chamber of Commerce Home and Trade Show, and the plant of Dow Chemical Canada Inc., is saturated by the history of the comings-and-goings of Aboriginals and fur traders using the river as the main east-west transportation artery well before the arrival of the Canadian Northern Railway in 1905. The river flats around the mouth of the tributary waterway, *mi-koo-oo-pow* or red willow, had long been an ideal site for building canoes.

The Lamoureux brothers, François and Joseph, arrived in 1872 from the Montreal area, farming and lumbering on the river's north bank, having given up on the idea there was gold in the valley. In 1875 they established the first military fort in northern Alberta, initially called the Sturgeon Creek Post. In 1886, after the tragic drama of the 1885 Rebellion, the fort became headquarters for "G" Division, whose members were responsible for policing the vast

Aboriginals and fur traders used the river as the main east-west transportation artery well before the arrival of the Canadian Northern Railway. Laying steel over North Saskatchewan river, 1905, Fort Saskatchewan, Alberta. Bell (photographer).

territory from Innisfail (near present-day Red Deer) in the south to Fort Simpson and Peace River in the north as homesteaders moved in. By 1905, 170 teams were reported carting freight through to Edmonton in one morning alone. The census of 1907 reported 585 residents. By 1911, forty-nine businesses and an opera house had opened in Fort Saskatchewan.

"Within a musket shot"

Anthony Henday was the first European to canoe past on his way back to York Factory on Hudson Bay in 1755, laden with furs purchased upcountry. But it was another forty years before competing fur trading posts – the North West Company's Fort Augustus and the HBC's Edmonton House (in one of its several incarnations) – were established close by each other at Birch Hills. It began with Angus Shaw of the NWC, who built Fort Augustus in the spring of 1795, leapfrogging past the HBC posts downstream. By October 1795, however, the Bay men had established Edmonton House "within a musket shot" of the Nor'Westers – it took them until the following April to build a proper palisade – and the race for the furs was on again. All this moving back and forth, up and downstream with the same names attached to the posts leads to much confusion when reading the journals of the day. That meticulous editor of the journals of David Thompson and Alexander Henry, Elliott Coues, writes a footnote to Henry that the "old Fort Augustus," north of which he is passing through, was just one of several posts maintained on the Saskatchewan which "successively or simultaneously shared the name or epithet, "Fort des Prairies." In 1821 the two companies merged. (A cairn placed in 1926 on the east side of the road going north from the hamlet of Lamoureux tells the tale.)

As an enthusiastic explorer of western historic sites, Arthur Silver Morton successfully located the remains of Fort à la Corne at the forks, the Francois-Finlay Fort at Nipawin, and Peter Pond's post west of Prince Albert. In his 1937 sketches, *Under Western Skies*, which he subtitled a "series of pen-pictures" of the Canadian West in the time of the early fur trade, he describes the visit of fur trader Anthony Henday along the North Saskatchewan River in 1755.

In 1754 Anthony Henday, a servant of the Hudson's Bay Company, came in from York Factory with Indians who had been down to the Bay to trade. He visited the French post at The Pas, came up the Carrot River where the party abandoned its canoes to drift at the rate of five or six miles a day, hunting and feasting, drumming and dancing, all the way across the Prairies to within sight of the Rockies. After trapping north of the head-water of the Red Deer River, Alberta,

> Henday moved north-eastward to the North Saskatchewan somewhere below Edmonton and passed down on the ice to a spot where the materials for making the birch-bark canoes, with which to return to the Bay, were to hand. This was somewhere in the neighbourhood of Fort Saskatchewan Settlement, Alberta. The entry in his Journal for April 23, 1755 runs: Displayed my Flag in Honour of St. George; the leaders [chiefs] did the same after acquainting them and explaining the reason. In the Evening we had a grand feast with Dancing, Drumming, Talking [Speeches], etc." I like this picture of a lone Englishman, some 1300 miles from his nearest compatriot, determined on celebrating the day of the English patron saint, explaining it all to a council of Indian chiefs, who join with him in breaking the Union Jack upon the breezes of the Saskatchewan of 1755.

In 1874, the North-West Mounted Police "A" troop, under the command of Inspector W. D. Jarvis, straggled along the final 110 kilometres of the hideous HBC trail close by the south bank of the river. Sergeant-Major Sam Steele, who would later play an important role in the 1885 North-West Rebellion, described how "the trail was worse than any we had encountered. It was knee-deep in black mud, sloughs crossed it every few hundred yards, and the wagons had to be unloaded and dragged through them by hand."

Sam Steele was the very essence of a man's man in the Victorian age of imperial expansion, serving as a volunteer in 1870 on the expedition to Red River to quell the political insurgency around Métis leader Louis Riel; sent north along the Carlton Trail in 1874, driving sick livestock and exhausted police recruits to Fort Edmonton, raiding whiskey traders along the Saskatchewan, and building a barracks in 1875 at Fort Saskatchewan.

"The reader of Colonel Steele's book," wrote J. G. Colmer, C.M.G. in introducing *Forty Years in Canada: Reminiscences of the*

Great North-West, "will be impressed with the simplicity and vigour of the man." A recent biographer refers to his "skills as a scout and tracker, and his experience fighting a crafty adversary in thick bush," merely echoing what London newspapers had said of the man in his own time: "Fighting Sam," "the world's greatest scout."

In the winter of 1874-75, mail orders came in to the commanding officer at Fort Edmonton from the NWMP commissioner to build a barracks on a site on the south bank of the North Saskatchewan, "anywhere" between Edmonton and Sturgeon River some 33 kilometres east. According to Steele, Inspector Jarvis chose the low banks upriver from the old site of Fort Augustus and right across the river from the settlement of Lamoureux.

> *In April, 1875, we set to work to build our new quarters. The men's building was 90 feet by 22 feet, whilst the officers' quarters were of a size suitable for two or three. To these were added a guard-room and stables.*
>
> *We made our own shingles, raised the walls, put on the roof, a new experience to many; but a few of us had been bred in the rural districts in the east, where every boy in those days was supposed to have an axe in his hands within a few weeks of his birth, and where, in the early days of our boyhood, retired army and navy officers might have been seen on the roofs of their log barns, shingling them or handspiking at the log heaps to make homes for their sons. So there were we teaching ex-graduates and Irish land agents' sons to place shingles.*
>
> *Our food at this time consisted of pemmican and mountain trout. The smallest trout weighed 5 1/2 lbs., and many were over 12 lbs. These fish have a flavour quite equal to salmon, but one does not so soon tire of them. As an addition to our larder large quantities of wild duck eggs were obtained from the shores of the lakes in the Beaver Hills, to the south of*

our post, and an old Indian moose-hunter, who lived in the hills, brought us quantities of game in exchange for flour and tea. The favourite was beaver, which when roasted is delicious food.

In July the Company's steamer Northcote *arrived on her maiden trip, the first steamer to navigate the Saskatchewan. She brought great quantities of mail for our division, the first mail of any consequence since we left our camp at Dufferin more than a year before.*

In 1883, eight years after the erection of Fort Saskatchewan police post, the family of NWMP Inspector Arthur Henry Griesbach, the Northwest's first "mountie," arrived to take up residence. The son, William, only five years old at the time, nevertheless had vivid memories of the wagon train that transported them from Calgary to Edmonton to Fort Saskatchewan. "The road was a mere cart track," he recalled in his memoir, *I Remember,* "and frequently the whole party had to stop and build or repair a bridge." Life in the barracks was a matter of some improvisation. Little William's mother contrived white "linen" summer suits out of discarded flour sacks. With this he wore a straw hat, "good enough as far as it went." He went about barefoot, as weather permitted.

The Griesbach family remained at Fort Saskatchewan throughout the events of 1885, which were caused in part, Griesbach speculated in *I Remember,* by the "curious" disappearance of the buffalo on which the Indians had so completely relied for food, clothing, and shelter, "and which, moreover, provided them with a profitable trade by which the French half-breeds had largely lived. Many of these French half-breeds had retired before the tide of advancing white men and had located themselves on the banks of the Saskatchewan from Prince Albert to the West."

The first sign of trouble in the region came early in 1885 when runners, or agitators, as Griesbach called them, arrived from the

Prince Albert region and circulated among the Indians and Métis, hoping for support for the insurgency organized under the leadership of their spokesman, Louis Riel, at Batoche. The murderous skirmish between the "rebels" and the police and volunteers in March at Duck Lake, from which Supt. Lief Crozier ordered a strategic retreat, encouraged the Métis and stunned the mounties. The Métis runners spread the news far and wide. At Edmonton, Griesbach's father organized a home guard and put volunteers to work bolstering the defences. At Fort Saskatchewan, his command consisted of twenty mounted police.

At the very moment of the outbreak of the Rebellion the Mounted Police were changing over from the short Snider carbine to the .45-75 Winchester rifle, which was a nine cartridge magazine repeater and considered to be the very latest thing in a repeating rifle. There were, I think, from three to five of these rifles in the possession of the Mounted Police at Fort Saskatchewan. The log stockade at this point had been planted in 1875. It consisted of logs fifteen feet in length and ten to fifteen inches in diameter and ten feet in height above the ground. By 1884 these logs had rotted in the ground and were being blown over by the wind, leaving gaps in the stockade. In 1884, using prison labour and Mounted Police labour, my father began to take down the old stockade, saw off the rotten portion of the logs and replanting the remainder four feet in the ground, it gave a new stockade from five and one-half to six feet high and that was the stockade standing at the outbreak of the Rebellion in March, 1885. It was obvious that it was not high enough. My father met that by going into the reserve supply of fire wood which was piled up outside the Fort waiting sawing up as fire wood. This fire wood was dry trees about twelve to twenty feet long and from four to six inches in diameter. He dug a trench inside the stockade and planted the butt end of this fire wood in the trench, leaving the remainder of the wood projecting at an angle over the top of the stockade. This must have given the Fort from the air the appearance of an unfinished basket....

"Out there on a river in the middle of nowhere"

With the collapse of Métis and Indian resistance to the colonization of the Northwest, the way was opened for the federal government to sponsor mass immigration of farmers to homestead the newly-surveyed territory. From the Galician provinces of Austria-Hungary, for example, came waves of Ukrainian-speaking settlers, known popularly as "men in sheepskin coats."

Harvest scene on the river near Fort Saskatchewan, Alberta, 1927. McDermid Studio, Edmonton.

Harry Piniuta published his book, *Land of Pain, Land of Promise: First Person Accounts by Ukrainian Pioneers 1891-1914*, during the heyday of official multiculturalism in Canada. Stories such as those of Maria Yureichuk, which Piniuta found "as told to" Dokia Humenna in her book, *Vichni Vohni Alberty* (Eternal Flames of Alberta), became the core narrative of cultural minorities in Canada who, though Canadian-born, felt entitled to claim the immigrant story as essential to the larger Canadian tale.

Maria Yureichuk's story was published as "How We Traveled on a Raft from Edmonton to Our Homestead," an interesting parallel text to the canoe trips of tourists, of whom more and more arrived on the river to amuse themselves. Yureichuk's group of families arrived in Edmonton in 1899. Their countrymen awaited them down river in the settlement of Victoria, and so Maria's enterprising husband lashed together some spindly logs for a raft, loaded it with their worldly goods, and poled them into the river, headed downstream.

> *Everyone had a good laugh, and we heard someone say, "Galician go homestead." The kind man who had helped us did not want to accept any pay for carting the chest; he only waved to us and said, "Bye-bye."*
>
> *It was already afternoon when we launched our raft and shoved off from the shore. The water in the river was very shallow, and the raft drifted sluggishly. Toward evening of the next day we docked at Fort Saskatchewan, twenty-five miles east of Edmonton. We met some German people who could speak Russian, and we learned from them that Victoria was still a long distance away and that it would take us a whole week to reach it. We had just enough food to last us a couple of days, so my husband dashed to the store at the Fort and bought some potatoes, pork fat, and bread. On the raft, we had a pan in which we built a fire and baked potatoes.*

We smeared them with the pork fat, and that was our meal.

To shelter us from rain and storm, and to provide a place for the children to sleep at night, my husband built a hut on the raft. As the raft floated at night, one of us would nap while the other kept watch lest we founder on the shoals or smash up against the riverbank.

On the third night, heavy snow began to fall. We wrapped ourselves in blankets and huddled in the hut. We failed to notice that our raft had run aground on a sandy shoal and come to a dead stop. To free it, we had to get down into the water with our bare feet, but no matter how hard we pushed the raft and struggled with it, in no way could we dislodge it from the sandbar. Morning found us there, crouched at the entrance of our shelter. And the snow came down like an avalanche, as though it were trying to bury us alive. To pitch a tent was out of the question, for the snow that had fallen during the night was over twenty inches deep. The firewood that my husband had picked up in Edmonton got soaked and would not burn. We were so cold our teeth chattered, and we were afraid that by morning it would be the end of us. I wept bitterly over my fate and cursed my husband and his Canada.

It was already late morning when some Indians who lived near the river noticed a strange object sitting on top of the sandbank and came down to investigate. They took us into their home (an old shack), made some tea, gave us some dry biscuits to eat, and we gradually thawed out....

I will not forget that incident as long as I live. Just picture what it was like to be out there on a river in the middle of nowhere, surrounded by water, wading in mud, heavy snow beating down on you without letup. You don't know where you are or how far from your destination, and no people around to help you push the raft back into the water. It *was a blessing from God that the Indians caught sight of our raft, for without their help we would have perished there.*

It owes its origin to the missionary efforts of the late Rev George McDougall, whose lively interest in the good of our Indians led him to induce quite a large band to settle [in 1862] and begin the cultivation of the soil. – Saskatchewan Herald, 10 Feb. 1879

VICTORIA SETTLEMENT
The Great Valley

The site of a traditional Aboriginal encampment (dated to 6,000 years ago), a river crossing, and convergence of trails, Victoria Settlement was located on the Alberta segment of the Carlton Trail – initially a path created by nomadic Aboriginal tribes – which, proceeding west, branched at Fort Pitt (at today's Alberta/Saskatchewan border) as the North Route or Victoria Trail. It tracked through parkland forests, skirting the lake on whose north shore the settlement of Frog Lake would be built, and moved out across the glacial meltwater coulees of the Moose Hills and Dog Rump Creeks, past Saddle Lake and the Snake Hills, finally to descend at the Victoria Mission on the North Saskatchewan River. By the time of the McDougalls' mission in the 1860s, the trail could accommodate carts and wagons as well as pack horses. In 1872, Sandford Fleming, engineer-in-chief of the CPR, was able to travel in relative comfort by buckboard while he surveyed the trail as a possible route for the railway.

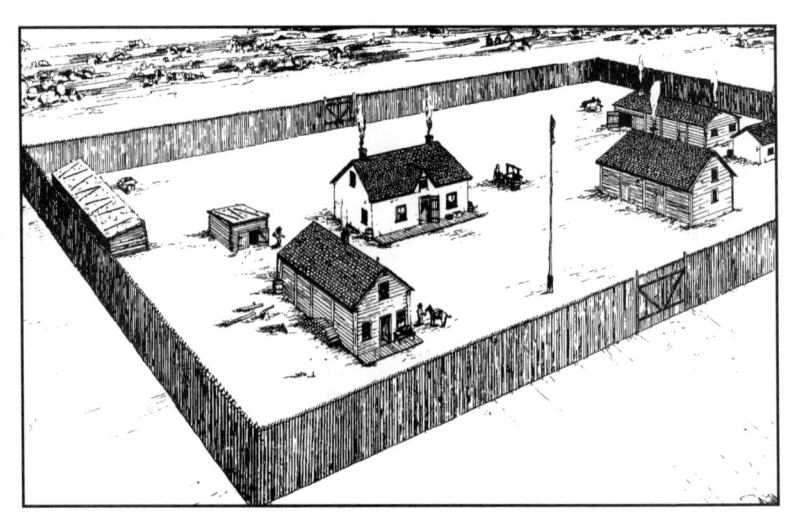

Artist's conception of Fort Victoria.

In 1860, the Canada Conference of the Wesleyan Methodist Church appointed Rev. George McDougall as chairman of its Northwest missionary district; in 1863, the Reverend, his wife Elizabeth, and six children took up residence in a one-room log cabin, hoping not only for the evangelization of souls but also the "civilizing" influence of agriculture. Eventually there would be a new house and stables, gardens and a church, the log cabin converted to a schoolhouse, all surrounded by a palisade down by the river.

The system of river lots was introduced by the first Métis immigrants to the area, who arrived in 1865 and settled east of the Hudson's Bay Company's Fort Victoria and the Methodist Mission. When Sandford Fleming's trans-Canada expedition visited the settlement in 1872, Reverend George Grant's account noted that "the log houses of the English and Scotch half-breeds, intermingled with the tents of the Crees, extend in a line from this west end along the bank of the river, each man having frontage on the river, and his grain planted in a little hollow that runs behind the houses."

The HBC's post, Fort Victoria, was established to take commercial advantage of the Woods and Plains Cree hunters and free traders gathering at the mission. It opened in the fall of 1864 to trade mainly in buffalo robes, buffalo tongues, and dried meat, but within a decade the supply of fur-bearing animals had dwindled drastically, hunger set in among the Aboriginals, and the post was closed in 1883, reopened briefly in 1887, and closed permanently in 1898. But it had done its job: "If the Company prospered during these years," historian Leslie Hurt reminds us, "it should also be noted that this was by and large at the expense of its native customers. While admitting that the quality of the goods supplied to the Indians was not lacking, the remuneration afforded them for their furs was usually out of all proportion to the market value of the skins in England."

Encouraged by the McDougalls, mixed-blood farmers and buffalo hunters moved to Victoria Mission from Manitoba; by 1871-72 as many as 250 people would show up for church services and 70 children attended school. The settlement now stretched 20 kilometres along the river bank.

An Indian agency in 1880 dispensed flour, beef, and soup for the destitute Indians of the area (this moved to Saddle Lake in 1882).

By signing Treaty 6 in 1876, the chiefs and their people had agreed to settle on reserves and become farmers in return for relief, medical care, and protection when needed, schools and farm implements and seeds. They could see what was coming: in a petition by Cree and mixed-bloods at Victoria Settlement, reproduced by Historic Sites writer Peter Melnycky, they described how "some are afraid that when the white man comes our hunting grounds will be destroyed and our lands taken for nothing, and we and our children left to perish.... They see the gold workers along our rivers, and some settlers making gardens in our lands.... The buffalo tracks are growing over with grass...."

In 1887, when a post office was established at Victoria Settlement, officials requested a new name for the community to avoid confusion with Victoria, British Columbia. Pakan was chosen in honour of Cree Chief James Seenum Pakannuk, or Pakan, a Christian convert, whose band fished and farmed on their reserve north at Whitefish Lake.

Attracted by the very fertile soil, the abundance of open prairie land along with building timber in the bush, an influx of mainly eastern European homesteaders gave the area a new lease on life. The mixed-blood families gradually moved north and all but disappeared from the area, but the Methodist mission saw new opportunities among the Ukrainians and in 1901 appointed Rev. Dr. Charles Lawford as missionary and medical doctor at Pakan. The Ukrainians built for themselves the wooden St. Elias Russo Greek Orthodox church north of Pakan and consecrated it in 1906.

A busy little town grew up to service the new inhabitants, with general stores, mills, a blacksmith, farm equipment dealerships, until it all collapsed with the arrival of the Canadian Northern Railway line and the establishment on it of the soon-to-be-important town of Smoky Lake in 1918. Even the hospital was moved there. In 1920, only fifty souls lived in Victoria/Pakan, alongside one hundred graves.

Approaching the centenary of the McDougalls' mission in the west, Rev. Ernest Nix undertook a labour he believed western Canadians had been needing for a long time: a factual account, stripped of folklore, about the "astonishing story" of these zealous missionaries "with a burning passion for souls." It was a story that had first appeared in print in the letters Reverend George McDougall sent to the Methodist Missionary Notices, and then in the "Boys' Own" tales of wild west derring-do by Rev. John McDougall, in his own memoirs.

A Beautiful Spot

Converted by a Methodist lay preacher in Ontario, George McDougall determined to become a missionary himself. In due course he was assigned mission work in the Methodist district that extended from Oxford House (in Manitoba) to the Rocky Mountains. On an exploratory trip up the Saskatchewan in 1862, George McDougall visited Rev. Thomas Woolsey's struggling mission post in Smoking (now Smoky) Lake and persuaded him to move to the site on the "great river" at a point called Victoria, long favoured by Aboriginal hunters and fur traders as a meeting and crossing point between parkland and prairie. It soon attracted about 150 mixed-blood settlers (of Cree, Scottish, or Orkney descent) who arrived by ox-cart caravan from the Red River communities in Manitoba, in spite of the fact that the nearest doctor was back in Fort Garry and mail was delivered only once a year. "It is a beautiful spot," George McDougall told his interpreter, Peter Erasmus, "and the very place we need. It will give happiness to our people just to live here."

In *Blankets and Beads: A History of the Saskatchewan River*, James G. MacGregor writes a sympathetic account of the Protestant missions in the Saskatchewan country, from Prince Albert to Rocky Mountain House. MacGregor took a look at the Victoria site almost a hundred years after the McDougalls' arrival:

> Today at Victoria there lives only an old retired Hudson's Bay trader in the original post building. But of the mission no sign is visible to the casual traveller. West of the road about three hundred yards, however, are the stone cellars of the mission buildings, and in front of the site of these old buildings are the graves of John McDougall's two sisters and his wife – victims of the smallpox epidemic of 1870-71. Below the hill, the scene of so much fortitude and devotion to a cause, flows the dark Saskatchewan.

As for his own contribution, *Mission Among the Buffalo: The Labours of the Reverends George M. and John C. McDougall in the Canadian Northwest 1860-1876,* James Ernest Nix believed that the McDougalls' story was a "portion of the continuing narrative of the Acts of the Apostles; and it is here offered." As Nix writes of the mission's first months, life was a succession of "pioneer" tasks: hay-making, construction of log buildings, timbering and lumbering for the small church, and the beginnings of farming.

> *Early in the summer McDougall made a serious beginning at agriculture at the new mission. Seed grain had been brought during the winter from Lac La Biche, White Fish Lake and Edmonton. A few garden seeds carefully stored by Mrs. McDougall were measured out to the Indians by the thimbleful. So far there was only one plough and an assortment of hoes to do the agriculture and gardening in the settlement. By this time the church and schoolhouse were up, the mission house had been finished and a stockade built around it, and the carpenter Larson was hard at work making furniture. One or two fields had been fenced and planted, and the garden patches began to give the place the aspect of an established settlement.*

Although the McDougalls shared with the local Aboriginal community in the scarcity and back-breaking labour of life in the bush or on the plain – fishing, trapping, hunting, breaking trail – and witnessed the depletion of the buffalo herds in this waning era of the fur trade, they were optimistic about the region's agricultural possibilities. Anticipating white settlement in the wake of the treaties and reserves, John McDougall himself had visions of industrial prosperity based squarely on private property.

Writing in the late 1890s, though, John McDougall indulges a kind of nostalgia for the open land, spreading so magnificently from the trench of the North Saskatchewan, that he knew so intimately from his youth, before railways and farms and war.

> Soon after this I started with my family and two Indian boys for Victoria. Reaching that point, I took with me the two boys and started with three carts and some loose horses to meet father. Mother had not heard from him since I was last at Victoria, but we thought he must now be on the north side of the Saskatchewan, between Carlton and Fort Pitt. Our horses were in good flesh, and this was hardened on them as we drove early and late down through the northern slopes of the great Saskatchewan valley, the lovely country which had so enamoured my more youthful senses when first in 1862 I rode through its rich pastures and over its richer soils. Six years of wider range and larger view had been mine since then, but now as I ride over the many leagues my previous judgment is but strengthened. As we pass Saddle and Egg lakes and cross the Dog Rump, and Moose and Frog creeks, and wind between and over the Two Hills, and all the time behold fresh and picturesque landscapes, and note the wealth of nature's store, self-evident on every hand, my patriotism is enthused and my faith invigorated. And to one born on the frontier, and already having witnessed great changes, it is easy to imagine this easily reclaimed part of our great heritage dotted with prosperous homes. All day long (and somehow those autumn days were unsurpassable in the combination of their glorious make-up) as I rode on in advance of my boys and carts, I was locating homes, and selecting sites for village corners, and erecting schoolhouses and lifting church spires, and engineering railway routes, and hoping I might live to see some of this come to pass, for come it would.

Caravans to the River

Jane Mary Howse was the daughter of Henry Howse, HBC employee at Victoria, part of the mixed-blood family abandoned by Joseph Howse of the HBC. They moved south just before the smallpox outbreak of 1870.

Lyn Hancock and Marion Dowler describe how Jane (by then "Grandmother" Jane) travelled six weeks with her family in 1864, the 1,450 kilometres from Red River to Fort Ellice – the first major stop on the Carlton Trail – and then on to Victoria across the two biggest obstacles of their route: the South Saskatchewan and the North Saskatchewan rivers. They devised yet another version of the Saskatchewan River ferry, and carried on, following the riverbank.

> "We made a raft of buffalo hides," she explained. "First we soaked them, then we laid them on the ground and sewed them together with sinew. Next we stretched them between the logs over wooden crosspieces. When the skins were dry, we rubbed buffalo tallow into the seams to make them watertight and left the whole raft to dry again for a day.
>
> "Then came the hard part. Father attached heavy ropes to each end of the raft, swam across the river and tied one of the ropes to a tree. We then ran our carts, one at a time, onto the raft. Back came the empty raft and over went another cart. It took us two days to get everything and everyone across, but that was less time and trouble than taking our carts apart like we did on buffalo hunts."

As Grandmother Jane and her family continued west through the Northwest Territories along the north bank of the North Saskatchewan River, they passed several more places which are now famous – Battleford, Frenchman Butte, Fort Pitt, Frog Lake. These were places the Cree chiefs, Big Bear, Wandering Spirit and Poundmaker, fought with the Métis for *their own land and freedom against the North West Mounted Police and Canadian troops. Father had several books in his library that told of many daring raids and exciting battles.*

But all that happened twenty-one years after Grandmother Jane travelled the Carlton Trail.

"When we went it was quiet," she said. "Father and mother knew many Métis people who had already moved west, so we visited with them in their homes on the banks of the Saskatchewan rivers. They gave us fresh vegetables from their gardens. We stopped at Fort Pitt too, to get pemmican from the Hudson's Bay Company. Fort Pitt was a very large trading post then."

After travelling for a few more days along the banks of the North Saskatchewan River, they reached their destination – Fort Victoria.

Jane Livingston admitted to her grandchildren that in 1864 Victoria mission wasn't much to look at – a church that doubled as a school for a while, a few log shanties, some skin tipis strung along the steep riverbank, and the beginnings of a new fort – but it grew quickly. "So many Indian and Métis people were attracted to it," she recalled, "that the settlement stretched for six miles along the riverbank" in that arrangement of long and narrow river lots facing the river that can still be discerned.

Her own life changed dramatically the day freighter and buffalo-hide trader Sam Livingston stumbled out of the riverbank bush with his buddy James Gibbons, having snowshoed down the frozen river from Fort Edmonton.

The winter had been bad in Fort Victoria and we had eaten very little fresh meat. Suddenly we heard strange voices coming from the direction of the river. As they got louder, we realized that men were climbing up the steep banks towards us. They were shouting as if in trouble on the slippery chunks of ice.

Nellie and I used the trees and bushes for cover and ran closer. We didn't want to be seen because a few days earlier a Blackfoot raiding party passed by our settlement and we had all been frightened. We hoped this wasn't to be another one. We got to the poplars on the bank, then knelt to peer through the bushes.

We saw snowshoes first, digging like pickaxes into the ice, then two pairs of long flailing arms, two bobbing heads, and finally, two men hauling themselves over the bank.

"They won't hurt us," I whispered to Nellie.

"They look like walking skeletons," she whispered back. One man was older, taller than the other, but I remember most the long golden hair dangling to his waist. His wide-brimmed hat was little protection against the cold winter wind, his buckskin jacket was frayed, his moccasins shredded. The other man was much younger but he looked tired and ill.

Nellie and I stole from bush to bush along the river to follow the two strangers into the settlement. As soon as they appeared, the dogs barked wildly and children stopped playing to run and hide behind their mothers' skirts. Reverend McDougall hurried out of the Mission House to see what was happening. We strained our ears to hear. The taller of the two strangers introduced himself as Sam Livingston, and his companion, James Gibbons. They called themselves prospectors.

Sam Livingston and Jane Howse were married by Rev. George McDougall in the Methodist church and settled down in a log shanty, but by 1873 they realized they could not make a living from the trade on a dwindling supply of furs and hides in the country around the Saskatchewan. They pulled up stakes and moved south to John McDougall's Methodist mission at present-day Morleyville. This entailed crossing the river one last time.

> The caravan of twenty-nine carts, thirty-five people and numerous horses and cows left Fort Edmonton very early in the morning. It had rained overnight and everyone was anxious to cross the North Saskatchewan River before it rose too high. It was already late October and drifting ice would make things worse.
>
> "This was the first time the children had to ride a cart across a river," said Grandmother Jane. "As soon as they saw the rising waters, they started to cry. Grandfather Sam put Jane on the saddle in front of him and took her across on his horses. Then he came back for Nellie. George rode with me in the cart and Grandfather guided us across. Once they were up the slippery banks on the other side, I think they enjoyed the adventure. At least, crossing by horse and cart was better than swimming and towing your canoe in your teeth, like the Indians used to do. It took two days before we made the crossing. The only bad thing that happened was our potatoes froze."

Reveille on the River

In October 1874, with the quashing of the Red River insurgency among the Métis in 1870 already under his belt, Sergeant-Major Samuel Benfield Steele, descended from a long line of British officers and gentlemen, found himself slogging along the Victoria Trail, that first land highway in Alberta used by explorers, traders, freighters, missionaries, mounties, and, eventually, settlers. They were tramping to Edmonton as part of the company of North-West Mounted Police sent westwards from

Ontario to do something about the terrors of the western region: murderous whiskey traders and wolvers from Montana, greedy gold seekers, various outlaws, and desperate Indians trying to keep them all at bay.

Steele kept notes: August 21, 1874: "Stewed prairie chickens and ducks usually formed part of the evening meal." September 6, 1874: "The pemmican was cooked in two ways in the west; one a stew of pemmican, water, flour and, if they could be secured, wild onions or preserved potatoes. This was called 'rubaboo;' the other was called by the plains hunters a 'rechaud.' It was cooked in a frying pan with onions and potatoes or alone. Some persons ate pemmican raw, but I must say I never had a taste for it that way." October 6, 1874: "Axes and spades were in constant demand to repair the numerous bad spots on the trail, long stretches of which were under water, often for hundreds of yards. There is a saying that Canadians are born with an axe in their hands."

In 1885 Sam Steele was back, with a scouting force, in pursuit of Cree Chief Big Bear and the warriors who had sacked the Frog Lake settlement (144 kilometres east of Victoria) in April in the early days of the North-West Rebellion. Rumours that the Saddle Lake Cree were planning a raid on Victoria caused a general panic and people fled from their homes.

A journalist from Quebec and an untried sergeant volunteering in the 65th Mount Royal Rifles under General Strange, Charles-Roger Daoust wrote in the foreword to his memoir of this campaign: "For four long months a whole nation had its gaze fixed on the vast territories of the North-West. During this time, hundreds of young French-Canadians braved all kinds of misery, fatigue and even death, to re-establish peace and suppress revolt."

In May 1885, the regiment set out for Victoria Settlement.

Reveille next day was at 4:30, for a start at 6:10 in the morning. The weather was very fine and quite warm. Crossing of the Wasetna [Waskatenau] Creek. The soldiers followed the guides who made their way by paths, more or less passable, to the banks of the Saskatchewan River. Our route took us a way along the shore. The view of the Saskatchewan and the countryside spreading out in twists and turns all along its course was really very pretty.... At 4:00 we arrived at Victoria and made camp.... The weather was fine the next day.... Several officers visited Fort Victoria, which presented an image of utter desolation; there wasn't a single occupant....

Two days later,...we broke camp and set off for Fort Victoria.... That evening, a courier brought the news to camp of the defeat of the Metis, the capture of Louis Riel and Dumont's escape....

That final day of our journey by water was very pleasant, and the novelty of this new mode of transport entertained the soldiers hugely. The Saskatchewan River is not so wide; its banks are high and beautifully wooded. There are several openings of the land which afford ravishing views for the traveller. The water isn't very deep and has a muddy appearance.... What could be simpler than this system of navigation aboard boats on the Saskatchewan? You only have to follow the current which is very strong; from time to time a smart stroke of the oar is all it takes to change the boat's direction and steer clear of a sand bank.

After the meal, several of the men climbed up the river slope and, seated around a bonfire, sang together the cheerful refrains of local songs. The weather was calm and, high up in the sky, the moon and stars smiled at the carefreeness of the singers, and seemed to repeat in their sublime sphere the emotional chords that chimed in all these Canadian hearts.

A government ferry was set up. Horse-drawn buggies driving on to the ferry to go over North Saskatchewan River, Alberta, 1914.

The Ferryman

On the recommendation of Superintendent A. H. Griesbach at Fort Saskatchewan, who argued that the trails on the south side of the North Saskatchewan River were much superior for cart travel than the north side trails, a government ferry to connect the two banks was set up in 1892; this was renamed the Pakan Ferry and operated until 1972.

Frank Mitchell wrote reminiscences of his boyhood on the river. Living as close to it as they did in Pakan, residents were deeply affected by its seasonal changes. "No one," he wrote, "who saw the flood waters of 1915 could ever forget the sight."

> *The settlement itself, situated for the most part on the highest bank of the river, was not threatened, but the flour mill on the lower level came within a few feet of being swept away. Low lying areas further up river, however, didn't fare as well, judging by the contents of the high water racing by. Besides the*

usual debris from along the shore, there were logs by the thousands from "Walter's Mill" in Edmonton, thousands of feet of lumber, small houses, one big barn, and a granary with a stranded rooster on its roof. This was the river on a rampage after a sudden hot spell melted the snow and ice at its source in the Rockies....

On another spring day before the ice went out of the river, two mission ladies, Miss Weekes and Miss McLoan, arrived at the river in the late afternoon to find they couldn't possibly drive across. This would mean returning seventy miles to Fort Saskatchewan the following day to cross on the bridge. From there they could continue on home to Kola Kreeka Mission at Smoky Lake after two days of travel. So to avoid all this, a friend, Harry Gordon, my brother, Gordon, and I decided we would try to help the ladies in distress. We put long planks and dry dead trees together to made a kind of rough bridge across the twenty-foot stretch of open water that was flowing on either shore. This proved sufficient to hold the ladies. Crossing the horses over was much more difficult as they had to be forcefully led into the icy cold water up to their necks. Dr. Lawford met us on shore with horse blankets and took the horses to his warm barn. The buggy crossed last but not without a thorough ducking also. Without too much loss of time, the ladies went on their way rejoicing, promising they would remember us in their wills....

Crossing the mail, when it was being despatched to Pakan from Andrew to the south, was often difficult and dangerous. I remember once when it was being pushed across the ice in a rowboat when one of the men dropped through the weakened ice. Luckily he was able to grasp the side of the boat and only went in up to his neck. At other times the mail was crossed over in a bucket attached to the pulley of the ferry. At any rate, the mail usually got through according to tradition, and in spite of the river.

Although Mary Ann Hushlak has lived decades in London, England, she travels frequently to Alberta to see her family and especially to her birthplace in Andrew, Alberta, a town in the heart of the Ukrainian bloc settlement just south of the North Saskatchewan river. In her unpublished creative nonfiction, "Safe," she reconstructs tragic events in 1928 when her grandfather was robbed and murdered along a country road as he drove his team and sleigh towards the frozen river, on his way home from Smoky Lake, where he had sold the last of his Fall crop at the grain elevator. The ferryman heard the wild whinnying of the horses and trudged out to help the dying man.

Hushlak remembers another winter river crossing, from her own childhood when she was eleven years old. The "funny Mr. Mitchell" who helps out the ferryman is Frank Mitchell.

A Sunday in early December. This time, we're going on an ordinary visit to my mother's brother's house, the one who lives in Smoky Lake.

The river is frozen. A snow plough has cleared the equivalent of a wide tunnel. Snow sits in folds higher than the car as we drive across. We swerve. From the back seat, swerves and lurches always feel bigger. I don't want us to get stuck in the snow while we're on the river. Even in winter, the swift current rushes deep beneath the ice.

All afternoon, I worry. It's sunny. The sun glistens on the snow. It's so sunny that, as we stroll over to see the new paint colour-scheme in my uncle's barber shop, I wear his sunglasses. I worry that the ice in the river might start to melt. They tell me that river ice is far too thick to possibly melt or weaken in a few hours of sun in one afternoon, let alone, as they laugh, in a week or two.

I keep eyeing the clock. I keep watching the arc of the sun. I want everybody to eat up the Sunday roast quickly.

I want everybody to skip dessert. I don't want to play piano tunes on my uncle's piano. I don't want to tell everyone about all my new pen pals. I don't want the neighbour to bring over his foreign stamp collection. I don't want to wait for the bakery's fresh batch of warm cinnamon buns. I want to get to the river before dark. I want to get back to the other side without needing headlights.

It starts to snow. "Let's go," I say. We do go.

I'm holding my breath. I see the moving shadow of our car in the snow bank. I know that means the sun is very low on the horizon. We reach the ridge just before dusk. We pass the clearing where the Hudson's Bay Company fur-trading settlement used to be and start down the steep hill. It's treacherous. You can see the skid marks from cars that swerved before. We reach the bottom of the hill. The ferry is up on blocks, where, in the summer, the cars wait. It's like the skeleton of a small ship up on a dock with curtains and blankets of snow covering it. I hear the drag of the bumper as we go over the hump of the bank. It takes only a few thumps of my heart and we're across the river. The drag of the bumper on the other side and we're on land. And we shoot up. The road on this side winds and curls its way to the top. You need enough speed to zoom up and, at the same time, you have to slow down enough to make it round the first hairpin bend.

The road is like a skating rink.

There's no sand on the road.

There's not enough traction. We're not making it up to the bend.

We start sliding.

The car is slipping.

We are sliding back. Sliding and skidding backwards and backwards. It feels like a toboggan that could tip over backwards.

We get back to the landing. My face stays scrunched. I have to stay in the car. I'm told to keep the heater on. The ferryman keeps extra bags of sand on hand. He and funny Mr. Mitchell help scatter it. It's pitch black outside. There's only the falling snow and headlights and the dots of flashlights. Their last task is to let air out of the tires. I hear them talking. If the tire surface is wider, there's more for grabbing the road.

I don't want to have to reverse back onto the river, but there's no other way to be able to pick up speed. I don't turn around to see Mr. Mitchell's two flashlights guiding us back. I'm looking down. Out of the corner of my eye, I see the tail lights turning the snow green. And once we're all set, I hear the crunch Mr. Mitchell makes as he climbs into the snow. I see him slip and have to catch his balance on the ice as well. We have to wait for him to get to the start of the hill.

I don't see his signal. I close my eyes as my father picks up speed. I can feel the lurch over the river-bank hump. I can hear the bumper rip and the drag of metal on the gritty ice. I can feel the extra push of speed. I can't bear it. I crawl down onto the back-seat floor. I feel us start going up. I hear the moment the tires start spinning; I hear the ferryman shout "to the left," "to the left"; I feel Mr. Mitchell and the ferryman pushing, the tires spinning, all their weight into that extra push until we make it around the first bend. It's not finished yet. We're not out of the woods yet. I can hear them – Mr. Mitchell and the ferryman – running behind us. The second bend is too near to get up a lot of extra speed. Again, the tires start to spin; again, I can feel them push with all their force and we are clear. We are around the second bend. The road is more level now, the curves more gradual. We won't roll now. We'll be fine now.

I am lying on the floor, stretched out on the back-seat floor. As if I know that if a car were to roll, the safest place is flat. As if I now, also, read the world only through the prism of what is safe. And what is not safe.

Shandro Crossing
Brosseau & Duvernay

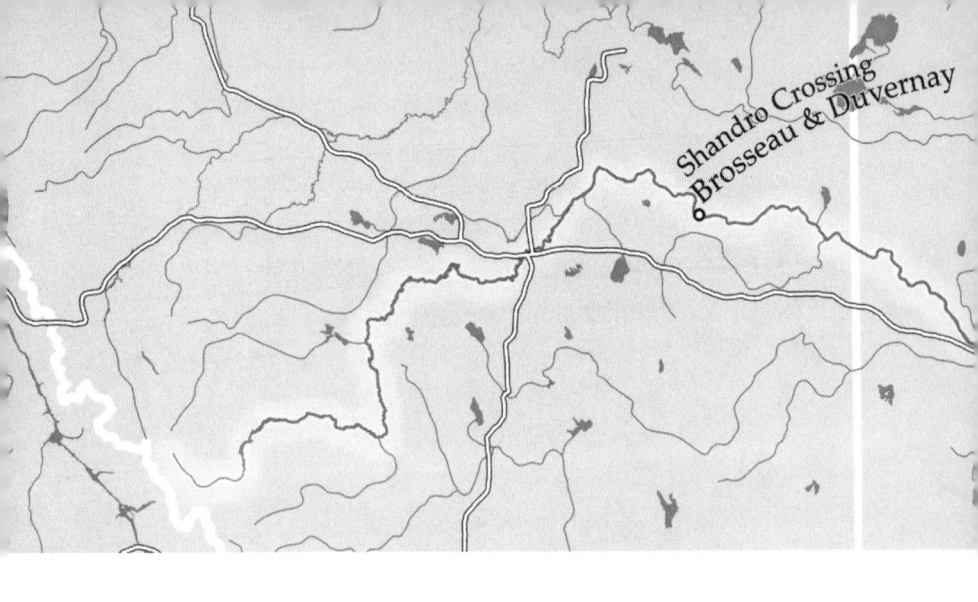

The little settlement of Shandro, which took in all the lands from about present-day Andrew to Willingdon [between Victoria & Duvernay], right up against the south shore of the North Saskatchewan, gave its name to the Shandro Crossing, a ferry landing from 1900 until a bridge went in in 1964. Eventually the craft, operating from ice melt to freeze-up, could carry eight teams of horses, and was just as busy in the summer on Sundays when families crossed over to the north side to pick saskatoons and blueberries. In fact, the Crossing was also a place to go fishing, and to do laundry, and to take out timbers from the banks or, it is told, to hide distilleries of the local moonshine business. – The Shandros: Our Story, 1999

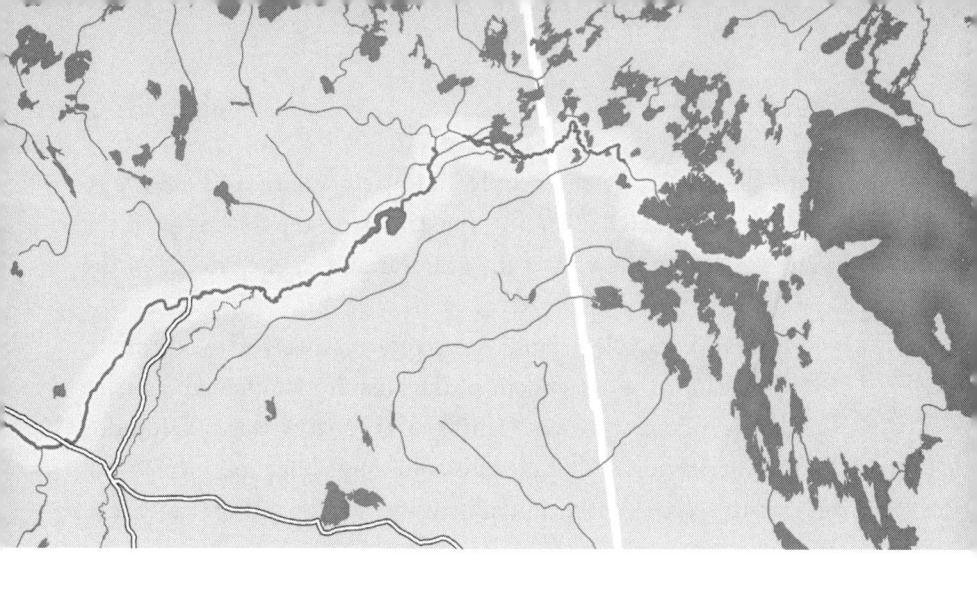

SHANDRO CROSSING/ BROSSEAU/DUVERNAY
Blessed Water

For the young Ukrainian immigrant Maria Hawrylenko in Yuri Kupchenko's 1989 novel *The Horseman of Shandro Crossing*, who takes the ferry at the Shandro Crossing on her way to the homestead, the North Saskatchewan River is a spellbinding sight, "a long, winding path of shining silver" in its deep valley below. That summer, she will labour barefoot in shimmering heat, down near the river, filling pail after pail of saskatoons from bushes black with fruit.

For the Ukrainian homesteaders of Shandro settlement, the river in winter had as important a role to play as when it was flowing clear. Come Christmas time and the Feast of Epiphany, the river played the symbolic role of the River Jordan, in which Jesus Christ was baptised by John the Forerunner (Baptist). The Feast falls on January 19, when the river is, of course, frozen over. Nevertheless, at four o'clock in the morning after Mass and even in the bitterest cold, the people and priest walked a kilometre to the North Saskatchewan for the ritual of the blessing of the waters, marking the end of the old year and the beginning of the new.

Roman Fodchuk paraphrases a 1958 interview with his uncle, Johnny Shandro, a descendent of the Shandro families who settled on the river, and who was Cantor at St. Mary's Russo-Orthodox Church at Shandro, Alberta. This is Johnny's boyhood memory, of an event that took place annually in the Shandro community during the "horse and buggy era."

> *In most rural communities, a cross of straw was laid out on the ice and burned. The ice was then cut and the waters so obtained blessed. Every family took a jar of water home to use in whatever way they considered appropriate. Johnny Shandro described the tradition this way:*
>
> *"At Shandro this was a significant religious celebration, as everyone in the community would go down to the Saskatchewan River where the blessing of the waters took place. The day prior, the church elders would cut a hole in the ice with an ice saw in the shape of a cross. The cross was lifted and placed at the end of the open water cross, to stand free. In the cold winter night, it would freeze solid and present an impressive setting for the 'blessing of waters' service After the ceremony, everyone would take their jars or containers, dip them into the open channel of the cross, take a drink and fill their receptacle with the blessed water. Next everyone would chant the appropriate hymns in unison with the priest and then take their container of holy water to their sleighs." Johnny Shandro recalls marvelling at the long line of horse-drawn sleighs with runners squealing in the sharp ice-cold snow going up the embankment and on their way home. This would form a circuitous snake-like line of approximately a mile long. Some*

of the horses had fancy harnesses with dancing Percherons and ringing sleigh bells creating a wonderful winter postcard scene never to be experienced in the same grand scale again.

Brosseau/Duvernay

April 3/08
The ice has left the river and the ferry is in operation. Mr. Hilaire has built 12 small houses which are occupied by renters...

June 24/08
Saint John the Baptiste Day. Father Chanoire of Edmonton representing Bishop Legal blessed the church. The steeple and bell are still missing....

Jan. /09
Three sawmills are in the area to saw lumber for new settlers.

Feb. 9/11
We still hope to build a convent.

Le Courier de l'Ouest

Founded in 1865 by Father Lacombe, who noted that this had been a camping place the Indians called *Kamabeskutewegak,* "the place where the prairie meets the river," the mission of St. Paul des Cris at Brosseau hoped to persuade the Plains Cree of the area to settle down and farm at this spot on the river rather than the priest having to travel along with them as they followed the buffalo. A community history of Brosseau-Duvernay explains the attraction of this site to the young missionary.

After spending the winter at St. Albert getting his expedition organized, [Father Lacombe] left in early May on a raft down the Saskatchewan River to his New Mission one hundred miles east of Fort Edmonton. The Hudson Bay Company objected to his new plan claiming that it would draw the Indians away from Fort George, which was located close to where Elk Point is today. But the Indians favored the location and that was good enough for Father Lacombe. Likewise the soil was fertile and easy to till on the north side of the river and Father Lacombe was determined to locate there in the hope of getting some of the Metis and Indians interested in tilling the soil as they were doing in St. Albert. He found a large encampment of Crees faithful to their promise of the fall before awaiting for him. They greeted him with enthusiasm, running into the water to pull his raft ashore. On this he and his faithful servant Alexis had fifty bushels of potatoes, seed grain, a plow and other provisions. His brother Gaspard and Noel Courtepatte had conveyed other provisions overland by ox cart a few weeks before, and had a shelter built. As the multitude of Indians looked on with the interest of prospective owners, the raft was unloaded and contents put inside the newly built shelters.

On the following day the young missionary started to plow the land. The women and children flocked behind him, crushing the raw earth with their hands into fine particles. A couple of days after when the ground was prepared, it was the women and children again who dropped the potatoes and vegetables seeds into the rows.

Born in St. Sulpice just outside of Montreal to a farming family, Father Albert Lacombe was entranced at an early age by his teachers' tales of the missionaries in the Northwest, of buffalo hunts and Indian warriors. Ordained an Oblate in 1849, he first reached the Edmonton area in 1852 and served first at the Lac Ste Anne mission east of Edmonton, where he learned to speak Cree. In 1861 he opened a new mission site north of Edmonton, hoping to encourage Indian families to farm, and named it after his patron saint, Albert.

Katherine Hughes's *Father Lacombe: The Black-Robed Voyageur*, appeared in 1911, the first biography of the great missionary. Hughes was able to interview Lacombe and had access to his correspondence and archives.

Lacombe's spiritual gifts have been long appreciated by the communities he served, even taking into account the paternalism of the missionary-aboriginal relationship, but less remembered are his literary achievements. He began by trying to learn to speak Cree on his first mission to Fort Edmonton in 1852.

Eventually, Father Albert Lacombe's parish of St. Paul des Cris included Cree, Blackfoot, Stoney, Sarcee and Métis families. Father Lacombe with Blackfoot men, Crowfoot, left, and Three Bulls, October, 1886.

> *The priest found himself so handicapped by his slim knowledge of Cree that he returned to Edmonton [in 1882] resolved anew to master Cree - "or to blow my head off," as he picturesquely phrases his determination. The inhabitants of the Fort from Rowand down to the youngest dog-runner were mostly Catholic, and he busied himself instructing young and old daily. On Sunday he tried to impress the Sabbath feeling by making the Mass as solemn as possible, and to this end taught the French-Canadians to sing the liturgy of the Mass. Several hours each day were given to the study of Cree, which he describes as a delightful occupation....*

Two years later, he produced the monumental *Dictionnaire de la langue des Cris* [Dictionary of the Cree Language] followed the same year by the *Grammaire de la langue des Cris* [Grammar of the Cree Language] and a New Testament in Cree syllabics. In 1875 he published a Cree-language Catechism, in 1880 a book of prayers in Saulteux, in 1886 the Cree version, and a reader in English and Blackfoot. "No other Christian missionary created such an extensive body of work," literary historian George Melnyk summarizes admiringly. "Looking at these works today, one is overwhelmed and humbled by the extent of his achievement."

Eventually, the parish of St. Paul des Cris included Cree, Blackfoot, Stoney, Sarcee and Métis families, but after the devastation of the 1870 smallpox epidemic, Father Lacombe closed down the mission, founding instead in 1896 a colony for the Métis further north, known as St. Paul des Métis from which present-day St. Paul takes its name. In 1910, the Oblate missionary Rev. Father J. A. Ouellette would write of his journey from Edmonton east by the CNR as far as Vegreville, changing there to stagecoach or freight wagon to St. Paul des Métis via the Duvernay ferry. The village of Duvernay had been established in 1905, opposite the site of Father Lacombe's abandoned St. Paul des Cris mission on the north bank. The river was shallow enough to be forded but, with the influx of homesteaders, Mathias Lambert put the first ferry into operation in 1904, just upstream of the present bridge. Alternatively, travellers could follow the trail beaten by freight wagons along the north shore of the river from Edmonton to Brosseau, in the pathways of Indian and surveyors' trails. The bridge built in 1930 was the first on the North Saskatchewan between Edmonton and North Battleford.

Brosseau is named for Edmond Brosseau, a Quebec-born but Minnesota-raised prospector who searched for gold in California and British Columbia before coming to Alberta, where he traded in Peace River country and ran a store on Jasper Avenue in

Edmonton in the 1890s. In 1903 he sold the store, then loaded a scow with trade goods and floated down the North Saskatchewan until he got to the site of the future Brosseau. Brosseau set up his new store on the south bank, and in time a small settlement, established in 1905, prospered there, until the railway bypassed it for towns further south of the river.

By 1980, the year the dwindled Brosseau-Duvernay community published its history, *Our Crossing: Rivers to Roads,* "the church on the hill rings out the memories of passing time." A pioneer of the district still lived in the old house by the church. "Each day he looks out his front window and sees the sun. He sees the bridge and he remembers the crossing. As he watches the cars speed down the hill across the bridge, he knows it was not always so. There was a time when people stopped at 'Our Crossing.'" Reece Demchuk, who grew up near the settlement, wrote down his recollections.

> *In the early days the North Saskatchewan River was a large river. Through all these years till now it washed away lots of dirt. My father told me that in 1915 the river was so high that wagons loaded with as much as ten thousand feet of lumber chained on were floating downstream. Hundreds of logs, hay stacks, even some houses. A big saw mill hooked the cables at the Myrnam ferry and snapped them.*
>
> *Some nights when the ice would start breaking up there was so much noise that, if we were sleeping, it would wake us up. It was a sight to see, that ice when it started piling up then breaking apart. It would scrape against the banks and move tree stumps around like sticks.*

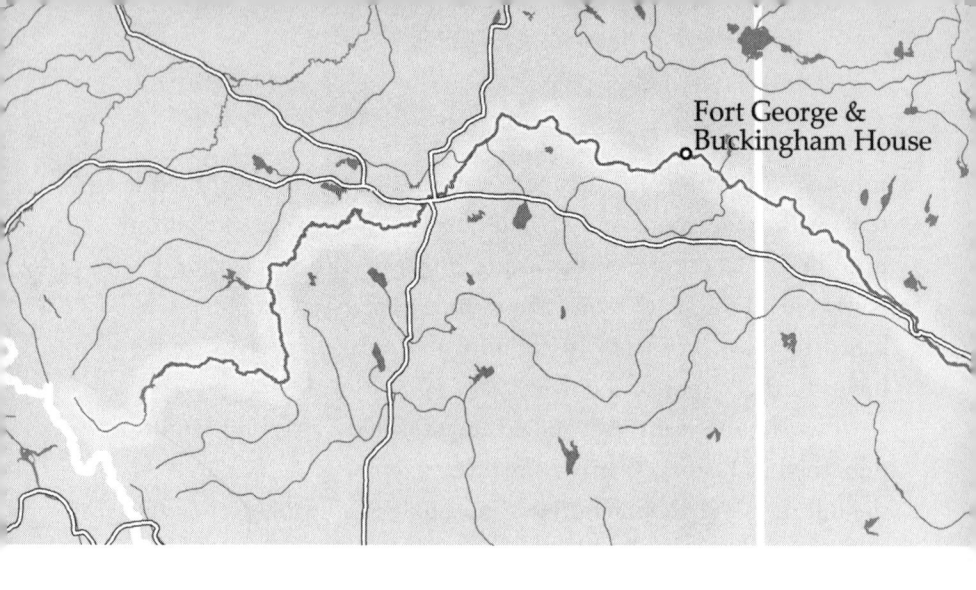

Fort George was built...with about 60 men, in 1792, and abandoned in 1801.... The opposing H.B. Co. post was Buckingham House where [David] Thompson wintered 1793-4.... He was also repeatedly at Fort George after he had left the H.B.Co. and entered the N.W.Co., May 23, 1797, when the entry in his journal is: "This Date left the Service of the Hudson's Bay Co., and [entered] that of the Company of Merchants from Canada – may God Almighty prosper me." In 1799 he found Fort George a fort without doors or windows "and otherwise dilapidated." On September 11 1799 he shut up the place. – Elliott Coues, footnote to manuscript journals of Alexander Henry and David Thompson

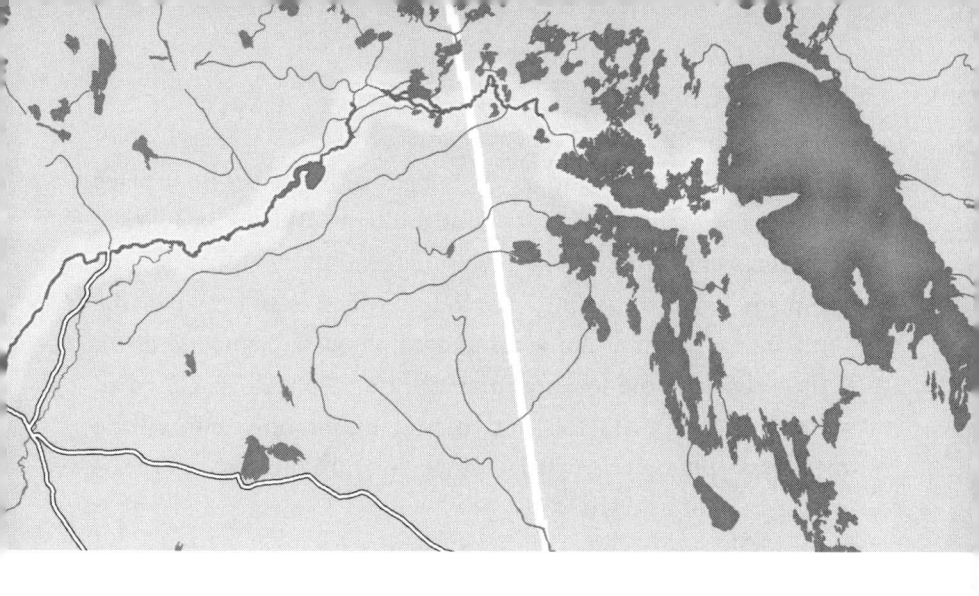

FORT GEORGE & BUCKINGHAM HOUSE
The Region of Plenty

The panoramic view of the great furrow of the North Saskatchewan River valley from the two rival posts high up on the north bank is breathtaking. East and west, you can see the blue serpentine coils of the "swiftly-flowing waters" move among the dense foliage of the valley, exactly the view the people had who used to live and work here, who watched with mounting excitement for the arrival of the spring and fall brigades, upriver with trading goods, down river with furs, and for the canoes of the Aboriginal hunters and middlemen, come to set up camp and do business at the post. Orkneymen greeted them at the Hudson's Bay Buckingham House; Highland Scots, French-Canadians, and Métis at the North West Company's Fort George. The unit of currency was one beaver pelt.

There's almost nothing to see of it anymore except a few cellar depressions, unidentified rock piles, and homely artefacts excavated from decomposed buildings. A walk around the site – the outlines of the posts' foundations suggested by timber floor plans laid by busy archaeologists – winds through parkland bush heavy with the scent of June's wild roses, out onto the "plantation," the camp for Cree and Assiniboine lodges which is still clear of the bush and tree stumps uprooted to accommodate them, and down a little dip past the location of the spring-fed well that used to serve both posts. It's too hot to find mushrooms, but a little meadow of plump yellow lady's slippers – still a protected species – is a treasure of its own.

This is the "region of plenty," as the fur traders knew it, a prodigiously fertile though slender stretch of land wedged between the southern grasslands and northern boreal forest. This is the trench of the North Saskatchewan. Before ever the Europeans came crashing into this country, Swampy Ground Assiniboine and Woods Cree fished and hunted the birds of the river shore, small fur-bearing animals and bigger game in the summer, and hunted buffalo in the winter. When Anthony Henday, on Bay business in 1754, suggested they may like to trade their furs and hides for Bay goods at the posts on Hudson Bay, they could not be enticed from the plains. But when the posts came to them in 1792 – Buckingham House established by William Tomison and Peter Fidler, Fort George by Angus Shaw – everyone was in business.

In subtitling his biography of Peter Fidler "Canada's Forgotten Explorer," James G. MacGregor had hoped to rectify what he felt was the severe injustice of the eclipse of Fidler's reputation. According to MacGregor, "Fidler was one of the few surveyors who laid the framework for all maps of western Canada. He spent years working out the details of the intricate labyrinth of lakes and rivers in northern Manitoba, Saskatchewan and Alberta. He was the first surveyor to map the exact course of most of the North and South Saskatchewan rivers."

MacGregor describes Fidler's return to "the House" in March 1793:

During Fidler's long absence from Buckingham House, Tomison had evidently kept his men busy. Now the well-built fort, made up of the usual trading building, the stores, and the men's houses jammed against the stout stockade which encompassed the whole, had a look of permanence and an air of strength. It had been built not on the first bench back from the river but at the edge of the high plateau, perhaps 150 feet above the water and nearly a quarter of a mile back from it. Behind it lay the belt of dense woods which, extending for half a mile back up the gradual slope, finally merged with the two-mile stand of open pine woods which formed a pleasant park on the sandy soil.

To the west, across the trifling gully in which Tomison had dug his well and in plain sight some hundreds of yards away, stood Fort George, where Angus Shaw and his large staff had built the North West Company's post. Indeed, Buckingham House had been built so that at all times a watch could be kept on Fort George to see who came and went and which Indians traded there.

Immediately in front of Tomison's stockades the bank dropped sharply to a lower bench. From the fort gate Fidler had a clear view of the river far below. Straight downstream he could see for three miles. That way lay Manchester House, 115 miles away, and Cumberland House, the headquarters of the inland trade, five hundred miles away and seven hundred miles beyond that was York Factory, downstream all the way. Upstream from Buckingham House the silent bed of the river was visible for perhaps five miles. The rival forts commanded a good view of the river east and west by which to keep track of any brigades, friendly or rival, that approached along this great highway.

As yet it was a little-used highway, this magnificent river striding along its deep, forested channel three hundred feet *below the surrounding uplands. Up it somewhere lay the Beaver Hills. Farther up, nearly four hundred miles, almost to within echoing distance of the Rocky Mountains, Peter Pangman had gone three years before. The North-westers were already dreaming of a further advance up the mighty river.*

As clerk of the NWC posts on the North Saskatchewan, Duncan McGillivray was expected to keep a business journal of the trade, and our earliest knowledge of the area around Fort George and Buckingham House comes from those journals: he was in charge of Fort George in the winter of 1794-95. He commented on the large herds of bison and deer and the large numbers of moose in the Elk Point area.

As McGillivray's editor and himself a prolific historian of the Canadian West (from the era of Rupert's Land to the founding of the University of Saskatchewan), Arthur S. Morton points out that "the advantage of the Northern Saskatchewan lay in the fact that it ran along the edge both of the wooded belt and of the open prairie. There were many parts of the valley, as they said in those days, a 'strong wood' region, offering a harvest of fur."

Unfortunately, Duncan M'Gillivray does not give us a description of Fort George. We may picture it from the river as a group of rough shanties surrounded by a stockade, on the edge of a fine hummock, overlooking the majestic valley of the Saskatchewan and standing out against the autumnal shades of a belt of "strong woods" a mile deep and twenty miles long. To the east was a gully, immediately beyond which stood the Hudson's Bay post, Buckingham House, likewise surrounded by a strong stockade. A path leads down from each post into the gully to a well there, dug by Mr. Tomison, to supply water sweet and pure to his post, and from which the North-westers were allowed to draw.

The stockade at Fort George had a gate to the south, facing the river, and one to the north leading out to the "strong woods." As one would go up the gully and climb up the hummock and enter the south gate one would see a series of shacks, mud-plastered on wall and roof for warmth. Immediately facing one, would be the Wintering Partner's quarters, larger than the others, just a little more pretentious. Its principal apartment was "the Indian hall" for receiving the chiefs in ceremony – larger at Fort George than the ordinary. Its inner parts were occupied by the Wintering Partner and his "girl," usually a Chief's daughter, the leaders of Society on the Saskatchewan in 1794.

McGillivray's journal ends in the spring of 1795, with a note of satisfaction that 325 packs of furs of 40 kilograms each and 300 bags of pemmican had been shipped out of Fort George that season. His subsequent activities inland are not so well known. He wintered at Fort Augustus in 1796-97 and was back at Fort George the following spring. This post was abandoned when he built upstream on Fort d'Isle.

By about 1800, the area was trapped out and the trading companies moved on further upstream to repeat the boom-and-bust cycle right up to the foothills of the Rockies.

In 1809 Fort George was in ruins, having been abandoned in 1801. Canoeing past it, Alexander Henry marvelled that "only the chimneys are now to be seen." The trade and its traders could no longer make a living here. Burned to the ground, the posts left little sign of their former importance. Only after excavations in 1965, with findings of animal bones, gun shot, and shoe buckles, and from oral narratives of descendants, was it possible to reconstruct a probable description.

The Sense of Loss

By the 1870s, the celebrated buffalo hunter Peter Erasmus had lived long enough to see the disappearance of the herds on which the Indians had depended in this very region: "In July [1870] I joined a small party of six carts and was successful in finding a small herd of buffalo northeast of where the town of Vegreville was later built."

> *Each year I noted the buffalo were getting harder to find. On this trip our scouts covered a radius of twenty-five miles each side as we went south to where we found that small herd. The vast herds that crowded the banks of the Saskatchewan River and crossed over even into the timber country fifteen to twenty miles north of the river were no longer to be found.... I had not believed that the vast herds could possibly be killed in so short a period of time. Only eleven years had gone by and there was now less than one animal for the hundreds that could once be found within a few days' ride of the North Saskatchewan River. The Crees with whom I had talked carried the same tale of the rapid deterioration of buffalo numbers that reached to the borders of the United States. They also told stories, carried from one to the other among the tribes, that great herds of skinny cattle, with horns longer than both arms of a man could reach, were being driven into the prairies of the south border country. Captain Palliser had said, "Vast herds of longhorned cattle from Texas will take the place of the buffalo." I had no doubt now that all the things he and Hector had predicted for this country were about to take place.*

J. G. MacGregor wrote out of a sense of loss too, about the erasure of the earlier Indian names for things under the encroaching language of white people's commerce and settlement. The old names, he contended in *Blankets & Beads*, were "full of meaning" and every detail of landscape was distinguished.

> *Hills were all named, there being Buffalo Hills, Thickwood Hills, Moose Hills, etc., and the ubiquitous Birch Hills and Snake Hills are on either side of the Saskatchewan River near present-day Willingdon. A hundred years ago the view from Snipe Hills took in innumerable buffalo in groups of a hundred or so feeding here and there as far as the eye could reach. Paul Kane, in travelling through the country twenty miles south of Willingdon, says: "We had much difficulty that evening in finding a place to camp away from the immense number of buffaloes that surrounded us, and we found it necessary to fire our guns during the night to keep them away." Today the view from these hills is one of the most remarkable in Alberta for the wide expanse of prosperous farms stretched out west and south of them.*

Alberta author Pam Chamberlain grew up near the river, in a place no one had ever heard of.

North of the River

> "Where are you from?"
> "Tulliby Lake."
> "Oh! My family went there one year for summer vacation."
> "Uh, I don't think so."
> "We took swimming lessons there. There was an ice cream stand on the beach."
> "I don't think that's the same place."
> "Yes, Tulliby Lake. I remember. What an awesome place to grow up!"

"Where are you from?"
"Tulliby Lake."
"Where?"
"Tulliby Lake. You know, north of Marwayne? West of Onion Lake?"
"Sorry. Never heard of it."

"Where are you from?"
"I'm from north of the river."

Tulliby Lake actually refers to an area more than it does to the tiny hamlet of twenty-or-so people, a three-room school, a hall/curling rink/outdoor arena, and a grocery store/gas station/garage/restaurant/post office. Tulliby Lake is a strip of land that ranges from four to eight miles wide, running along the north bank of the North Saskatchewan River, hemmed in on the north by community pastures and then bush. It's about thirteen miles long, stretching from the Onion Lake Reserve and the Saskatchewan border on the east to the west where it is fenced in by secondary highway #897 and the river, both coming down from the north.

The river fascinated me when I was young. The North Saskatchewan was wide and slow. It was second hand, like most of the farm equipment in Tulliby Lake, hand-me-down, like most of the kids' clothes. It was born in the mountains and had introduced itself at Rocky Mountain House. The river had flowed through Drayton Valley, Devon, and Edmonton before it wound its way to us, providing those towns with water and accepting their waste. Factories lined the river in Edmonton and Fort Saskatchewan, and once in a while we'd get a report saying that mercury levels were high and that we shouldn't eat more than three river-caught fish per week. How they came up with that number, we never knew.

The river was an unending source of conversation: "Did you see how high the river is?" or "But the river's so low." Neighbours who had come across would report that there were sand bars showing, that a flock of pelicans or swans had landed, that a fleet of canoes was floating past, or that high water was bringing down huge logs. If the news seemed big enough, we'd all drive down to take a look.

If you listened to the residents of Tulliby Lake while I was growing up in the seventies, you'd suspect that the river divided two continents. We'd hear news of kids doing drugs at bush parties, thieves stealing purple gas from farm tanks, and even more shocking stories, about affairs and divorces and stepmothers, and Tulliby Lakers would dismiss it with a slow, "Yeah, but that was south *of the river," as though that explained everything.*

Most of the men and women of Tulliby Lake were fulltime farmers and parents. They made their own schedules. People usually crossed the river only to buy farm supplies or groceries and to sell cattle or grain. Our family faithfully made the trip to Lloyd[minster] every Friday. Going to town involved shopping for groceries, getting parts, buying feed, and stopping at the library; best of all, it meant crossing the river.

Including loading and unloading, the ferry ride took about ten minutes, or triple that if we pulled up just as the ferry had left our shore and we had to wait for it to complete its trip. That made the trip to town a good hour in those days. Taking the ferry made it impossible to be in a hurry.

The ferry ride was a little vacation in the middle of the drive to and from town. I imagined I was on a pirate ship on the ocean. After all, the North Saskatchewan was the biggest body of water I had ever seen, and I couldn't imagine waves bigger than the whitecaps that formed when the water was rough. I loved it when the wind was up and the ferry pushed hard against the cable that guided it across the river, pulling it taut into a long arc, threatening to snap it. The wind splashed water over the railing, and I leaned out to get wet, imagining myself on a perilous trans-Atlantic voyage.

When the river started to ice up, the ferry was pulled out and we waited for the water to freeze. This might take two weeks, or it might take six, depending on the weather. In the meantime, we made as few trips to Lloydminster as possible, because now going to town meant driving out the west end of Tulliby Lake, over the Lea Park Bridge, past Marwayne, and through Alcurve, which, as Dad always reminded us, added at least *twenty miles*.

Once the ice looked solid enough, one of the ferrymen would walk across the river with an axe, chopping holes and measuring the thickness of the ice. If he found a path where the ice measured at least three inches thick all the way across, he'd put willow branches in the holes to mark the trail. He'd give an okay, with no guarantees, and then it was up to whoever was courageous enough to be first across. During our first trip over the ice-covered river each fall, I hung on white-knuckled to the door handles in delicious terror, imagining the car falling straight through the ice and drowning us all.

When I go home now, I don't need to take the ferry. They pulled it out in 1986 when they built the George F. Bayton Bridge.

The George F. Bayton Bridge is a tall, long arc; you can't see the north end when you drive onto the south end. It's wide and smooth like a highway, so you could easily drive over it, especially at night, and forget that it is *a bridge and that there is a river below*. In the fall, you might not notice if the water's frozen solid yet. In winter, you might neglect to wonder how thick the ice is. In spring, you might forget to check if the river has broken up already. In summer, you might not see that the water is high and full of timber or low enough to reveal sand dunes. In fact, regardless of whether it's fall, winter, spring or summer, nowadays you're across the bridge and over the river in twenty seconds. Below, though, whether or not you remember to look, the river is the same, changing only with the seasons, never slowing down or speeding up.

The North Saskatchewan River flows on past Tulliby Lake. It travels to Frenchman Butte, North Battleford, and Prince Albert; then it merges with the South Saskatchewan and moves on to Nipawin, Cumberland House, and The Pas. Finally it is absorbed by the maze of Manitoba lakes that drain into the Hudson Bay. Ask someone at the end of the river somewhere in Manitoba where the North Saskatchewan has been, and I'll bet you Tulliby Lake won't be on the list. The community, that narrow stretch of land connecting a couple dozen families and their farms nestled between the north bank and northern bush, exists quietly beside the river. With no municipal water supply system, the community takes nothing from the river. With no sewers, logging, mining, factories, or feedlots, Tulliby Lake doesn't make much of a mark on the river. But what an impact that river has had on Tulliby Lake.

Christmas was coming to old Fort Pitt on the North Saskatchewan, still in that year of 1884 an outpost of the white man's civilization, and preparations were afoot to celebrate in becoming manner, according to custom, that time-honoured festival of peace on earth, good will toward men. – William Cameron, *Blood Red the Sun*

FORT PITT
Mistahimaskwa: Big Bear

Fort Pitt Provincial Historic Park contains archaeological remains of two different posts, interpretive panels, and a National Historic Sites & Monuments plaque commemorating Mistahimaskwa (Big Bear) and the signing of Treaty 6.

In the winter of 1829-30, Hudson's Bay Company Chief Factor John Rowand built this post between Forts Edmonton and Carlton to trade in buffalo hides, meat, and pemmican with the Cree, Assiniboine, and Blackfoot hunters of the prairies. When the touring British gentleman James Carnegie, earl of Southesk, dropped by in August, 1859, he described it as situated "within a hundred paces of the river, which is here deep and rapid, free from sandbanks," and cut out of a woods which sprouted a few heroic spruce and fir trees "amidst the eternal poplar." Only half the size of Fort Carlton, it nevertheless attracted, at the time of Southesk's visit, six tents of Woods Cree and some Métis hunters whose dogs, apparently starving, kept the earl awake most of the night "pelting the

Mistahimaskwa's [Big Bear's] response was characteristically plain spoken: "Let your chiefs come like men and talk to us." Group of Plains Cree or Assiniboine people, ca. 1880s.

beasts with sticks and stones...to save our meat and harness from their famished maws."

In 1883, Francis Dickens, son of English novelist Charles Dickens and newly minted sub-inspector in the newly formed NWMP, was transferred from southern Alberta to Fort Pitt. He heard reports of local unrest among Crees and Métis and was made doubly anxious by the poorly defended position of the fort on the river.

In April 1885, Mistahimaskwa (Big Bear) and 250 mounted Indians surrounded Fort Pitt and demanded the surrender of the fort and its inhabitants. The civilians decided to take their chances with Big Bear while the mounted police fled down river to Battleford by scow, the Native warriors then burning the fort to the ground behind them.

Fort Pitt was partially rebuilt in 1886 and closed in 1890.

Travel Arrangements

Sir James Hector, geologist on the Palliser Expedition and a Scot through and through, passed muster even with the redoubtable Peter Erasmus, a mixed-blood guide of many other parts – linguist, buffalo hunter, mission worker, trader. In his memoirs, *Buffalo Days and Nights,* Erasmus recalls his first meeting with Hector in 1858: "I had expected to see a scholarly type, but his athletic appearance and brisk step impressed me very favourably. His handshake was firm and had a hint of strength that captured my interest immediately...a thoroughly pleasing personality that had nothing of that assumed superiority or condescending mannerism that I was beginning to associate with all Englishmen of my narrow acquaintance."

Affable he may have been but Hector was a scientist to the nth degree. Early in his papers relating to the Palliser Expedition, published in London in 1860, he offers this cool description of the great river as he observes and reflects on it at Fort Pitt:

> *This river is usually closed with ice for five months from the second week of November to the second week of April, but of course becomes navigable much sooner than the lakes, which are never clear of ice until June. On the whole it can hardly be considered as a river offering much advantage to steam navigation, on account of its small size in comparison to its length, which need not appear so extraordinary when we consider that it runs through a great extent of level plains, from which it receives no waters, there being a remarkable absence of tributaries. In fact the Saskatchewan does not drain the plains, but traverses the country as a canal fed from the Rocky Mountains, it may therefore be said to have no basin, and consequently the fertile valley of the "Great Saskatchewan, containing an unlimited extent of arable land," really does not exist. The water of the Saskatchewan, except near the moun-*

tains, is very earthy, especially during floods, and helps to give to Lake Winnipeg its expressive name.... From the Forks upwards the river is generally in a deep narrow valley about 200 feet below the level of the surrounding country, and in many parts having precipitous banks. I ascertained the current at Fort Pitt during high water to be two and a half knots per hour, but during spring and fall it would in most parts probably not exceed two miles.

On the heels of the Palliser Expedition arrived a member of the Scottish gentry in declining health, James Carnegie, earl of Southesk, independent traveller of means. Travel arrangements through the Saskatchewan River country having been made by the Hudson's Bay Company, the earl set out in enthusiastic pursuit of buffalo on the American plains – "I was well pleased with our sport among the buffalo, which to my mind could scarcely have been improved" – and later canoed up the Athabasca River, over to the Kootenay Plains, and down the Pipestone River valley to the Bow River about one month after James Hector.

But Southesk was a very different traveller, temperamentally. As historian L. G. Thomas points out, the earl of Southesk "has irritated some of his readers, perhaps because he seems to lack the seriousness of purpose that North Americans regard as the only possible justification" for the large sum of money his expedition must have cost.

On October 17, 1860, the earl and his party tore themselves away from the pleasures of Fort Edmonton – "Wine, well-made coffee, vegetables, cream tarts, and other good things too many to mention" – to sail downstream on the "broad current" of the Saskatchewan to Fort Pitt. Then the weather turned.

October 17th. – *All our arrangements being completed, we embarked in Mr. Christie's own new and roomy boat, "The*

Golden Era," which he had obligingly lent us for the voyage, and by noon were fairly on our way down the broad current of the Saskatchewan River. I felt depressed, almost sorrowful, on leaving Edmonton, where I had been made more than comfortable, through the constant attentions and hospitalities of my kind entertainers, and but little could be gathered from the aspect of nature to chase away gloom and raise one's spirits to cheerfulness. Bright as shone the sun the cold was most cruelly severe, and there was something very melancholy, although not wanting in poetic charm, in the monotonous, incessant flight of legions of ducks, which swiftly and steadily winged their way down the river, perusing their accustomed easterly course in search of more warm and genial habitations. But travellers view things practically; so those who were not rowing brought out their guns, and immense blazing at the ducks went on; seven only, however, were actually secured, for the birds flew high and wild, and those that we merely wounded could seldom be recovered....*

October 18th. – Heavy snowstorm at night. Sleet and snow, with high north-west wind, continued till late in the afternoon. It was awfully cold. Took an oar for a couple of hours to warm myself; pretty hard work tugging at those eighteen-foot poles called oars. River beginning to freeze.

October 19th. – Cold intense: ground covered with snow. The intensity of the cold nearly destroys one's vitality; several times I felt as if going to faint.... The river is very nearly frozen over; unless a change come to-night we shall be ice-bound, and have to walk a hundred miles or more to Fort Pitt, where the horses ought to be.

October 20th. – Snow in the night, frost in the day. River blocked with great masses of ice: boat closed in....

October 22nd. – Intensely cold night; blankets sprinkled with hoar-frost, notwithstanding the shelter of the tent; could

> not put my head out from under the buffalo robe without positive pain....
>
> October 23rd. – *Passed an uncomfortable night, feverish, and suffering from a bad cold in the head and throat. Weather continues frosty and intensely cold: river quite frozen over. Much depressed at the thought of staying another week in this miserable place, and, after that, two months' hard travelling to Fort Garry in snow and wretchedness. This detention completely upsets all plans. My travels hitherto have often been wearisome enough, but formerly I had hope and novelty for consolers. Now, all chance of sport is at an end....*

Only a decade later, another winter traveller, William Francis Butler, having struck northwest over high-rolling plains from the Battle River towards Fort Pitt, became lost, tricked by the broken terrain and deep-sunken river valley, with no track to guide him and his party. But his Cree companions "went straight as an arrow over hill and dale and frozen lake," not stopping, as Butler did, to stare in awe at a show of meteors in the pre-dawn sky: when day broke, he was alone and several kilometres behind. When he caught up with the others, they made the decision to take the advice of the Métis, Daniel, who knew a shortcut. "So much for the plan," he wrote. "Now for the fulfilment."

> *We entered the region of the Red Deer Hills at about two o'clock in the afternoon, and continued at a very rapid pace in a westerly direction for three hours.... It wanted yet an hour of sunset when we came suddenly upon the Saskatchewan flowing in a deep narrow valley between steep and lofty hills, which were bare of trees and bushes and clear of snow.... The valley here was five hundred feet in depth, the slope being one of the steepest I had ever seen. At the bottom of this steep descent the Saskatchewan lay in its icy bed, a large majestic-*

looking river three hundred yards in width.... The Frenchman led the way riding, the Hudson Bay officer followed in a horse-sled, I brought up the rear on horseback.... The night got later and later, and still no sign of Fort Pitt.... I called out to the Hudson Bay man that I had serious doubts as to Daniel's knowledge of the track, but I was assured that all was correct.... After some time the Frenchman returned and declared that he had altogether lost his way, and that there was nothing for it but to camp where we were, and wait for daylight to proceed. I looked around in the darkness. The ridge on which we stood was bare and bleak, with the snow drifted off into the valleys. A few miserable stunted willows were the only signs of vegetation, and the wind whistling through their ragged branches made up as dismal a prospect as man could look at. I certainly felt in no very amiable mood with the men who had brought me into this predicament, because I had been overruled in the matter of leaving our baggage behind and in the track we had been pursuing. My companion, however, accepted the situation with apparent resignation, and I saw him commence to unharness his horse from the sled with the aspect of a man who thought a bare hill-top without food, fire, or clothes was the normal state of happiness to which a man might reasonably aspire at the close of an eight-mile march, without laying himself open to the accusation of being over-effeminate.

Watching this for some seconds in silence, I determined to shape for myself a different course. I dismounted, and taking from the sled a shirt made of deer-skin, mounted again my poor weary horse and turned off alone into the darkness. "Where are you going to?" I heard my companions calling out after me. I was half inclined not to answer, but turned in the saddle and holloaed back, "To Fort Pitt, that's all." I heard behind me a violent bustle, as though they were busily engaged in yoking up the horses again, and then I rode off as hard as my weary horse could go. My friends took a very short time to harness up again, and they were soon powdering along through the wilderness. I kept on for about an hour, steering by the stars due west; suddenly I came out upon the edge of a deep valley, and by the broad white band beneath recognized the frozen Saskatchewan again. I had at least found the river, and Fort Pitt, we knew, lay somewhere upon the bank. Turning away from the river, I held on in a south-westerly direction for a considerable distance, passing up along a bare snow-covered valley and crossing a high ridge at its end. I could hear my friends behind in the dark, but they had got, I think, a notion that I had taken leave of my senses, and they were afraid to call out to me. After a bit I bent my course again to the west, and steering by my old guides, the stars, those truest and most unchanging friends of the wanderer, I once more struck the Saskatchewan, this time descending to its level and crossing it on the ice....

It was ten o'clock when we reached the closely-barred gate of this Hudson Bay post, the inhabitants of which had gone to bed.

The Mind of Mistahimaskwa

As lieutenant-governor of the North-West Territories (1872-76), Alexander Morris oversaw the introduction of the first form of responsible government there. He became passionately interested and involved in Aboriginal affairs, and in the diplomacy of the negotiations of Treaties 3, 4, 5, and 6 with the Native leaders.

The treaties were the means by which the transfer of Aboriginal land to the Crown could be effected peacefully and consensually. Thirty-five thousand Indians lived in the territories scheduled to be opened up for settlement, and it was hoped they would acquiesce in their loss of its use. They drove a hard bargain, extracting promises from the Crown that medicine would be supplied as needed on the reserves, and that in the event of "any pestilence" or "general famine" Crown officials would come to their rescue. On the other hand, they were already hungry from the loss of the buffalo herds and sickened by the white man's pox.

Of the chiefs, Mistawasis (Big Child) didn't sign the treaty until 1879; Mistahimaskwa (Big Bear) refused to sign until 1882 when the buffalo hunt failed and his people were starving; Pitikwahanapiwiyin (Poundmaker) signed but with deep suspicions ("From what I can see and hear now, I cannot understand that I will be able to clothe my children as long as the sun shines and water runs").

Novelist Rudy Wiebe works exhaustively with historical documentation to re-imagine – some would say mythologize – the worlds of his protagonists. His first knowledge of Mistahimaskwa (Big Bear), for instance, came from reading William Bleasdell Cameron's memoir of the events of 1885, *Blood Red the Sun*, in which Mistahimaskwa is sympathetically portrayed as non-violent and tormented by the passions of the people around him, including some of his own young warriors.

The negotiations of Treaty 6 were conducted at Forts Carlton and Pitt in August and September 1876. The Cree had been sounded out by the missionary George McDougall; he knew they were opposed to "the running of lines, or the making of roads through their country, until a peaceful, orderly settlement between them and the Government had been effected," as Commissioner Morris records. By and large, the Aboriginal leaders who most readily accepted the terms of the treaty were Christians, and the missionaries who served among them worked as mediators between the Crown and the Cree. Mistahimaskwa's response was characteristically plain spoken: "Let your chiefs come like men and talk to us." As Rudy Wiebe recounts in his novel *The Temptations of Big Bear*, Rev. George McDougall sent his son, John, also a Methodist missionary, to be party with them at the negotiations.

> *So what can anyone, Big Bear included, think I would say at the treaty at Fort Pitt in 1876?... The prayers that concluded every meeting I had with the prairie bands in 1874 – they prayed in their fashion as fervently as I; most whites find it impossible to imagine how deeply every Indian action is rooted in his, albeit almost completely false and most tragically limited, faith in The Great Spirit – were so movingly answered. The Queen's law had come, what could I say?*
>
> *Acting both for the Canadian government and the church, my father had instructed me to attend the treaty.... In accordance with the treaty timetable sent me, I was at Fort Carlton in late July. After waiting a week, the message came that the commissioners would be one month delayed. Chief Bearspaw of the Stonies was with me and I wanted very much for him to understand about the treaty with the Crees but now there was nothing for it but return to Edmonton and return later. Bearspaw rode back six hundred and sixty miles, while I could come only to treaty for the upper river banks at Fort Pitt. When I arrived September 2, on the hills and along creek ravines stood the lodges of at least one thousand Cree. Perhaps a thousand more could have been there, and those the most savage who lived on nothing but buffalo and Blackfoot raids, the ones with Big Bear who most needed the highest official explanations, but governments never explain their delays. The final results of this one were seen in 1885....*
>
> *But I prepared myself. I made careful note of all the Governor said and on September 8 when a messenger came to my tent, asking me to come to the Indian council, I was ready with a prayer on my lips.... Rarely, not even the many times I*

have preached the Gospel, have I felt the weight upon me as I did then, looking around the motionless faces of that dark council tent.

Five years after the signing of Treaty 6 at Forts Carlton and Pitt, the First Nations on the reserves allotted them were in despair. For the first time in memory no buffalo had showed up north of the U.S.-Canada border, and their first farming efforts had failed. Even when crops were good, as on Pitikwahanapiwiyin's (Poundmaker) reserve in the Battleford area, there was no local flour mill. Stringent – sometimes pitiless – Indian agents doled out meagre food rations. Famine loomed over the nations who had, in good faith, signed treaties with the Crown for mutual benefit. Instead they found themselves eating gophers and dogs and dressing in rags. Non-treaty Indians, such as Mistahimaskwa's (Big Bear's) band, were denied rations altogether. Petitions landed on deaf ears. Into this brew of discontent, the Métis followers of Louis Riel stirred their vision of a combined Indian-Métis effort to secure land tenure from the Canadian government and even a provisional government.

On April 14, Mistahimaskwa, who was appalled by the killing of white settlers at Frog Lake and hoped to prevent further violence, accompanied 250 mounted Indians who surrounded Fort Pitt and demanded its surrender from the gloomy and moody commander, Inspector Francis Dickens (Charles Dickens nicknamed him "chicken stalker"). It wasn't much of a prize, consisting of six sturdy buildings arranged in a square inside a rickety stockade. Nevertheless, the warriors wanted it; commanding the ridge overlooking it and the North Saskatchewan, some 100 metres wide at this point, they effectively had the inhabitants trapped. Samuel "Fighting Sam" Steele – who thought of Mistahimaskwa's band as a "bad bunch" and "bad medicine" who should never have been left "without at least 100 well-armed and mounted men near them" – takes up the narrative:

In the meantime Dickens continued to strengthen the post, and a scow was being built by the carpenters of the Hudson's Bay Company, when on April 13 a large body of Indians appeared on the rising ground to the north of the post.... Big Bear demanded the surrender of the arms and ammunition....

Later on in the day [HBC factor] Mr. McLean went out again and was taken prisoner, and constables Cowan and Loasby and Special Constable Quinn, who had been out to ascertain what had occurred at Frog Lake, came upon the Indians, who lay between them and the fort. Young Cowan, a fiery, hot-headed lad, in charge of the party, decided to ride through them.... Cowan and his horse were shot, and the Indians rushed forward and drove the muskrat spears into the poor fellow's body, tearing them out again to increase his torture.... The party eventually arrived safely at Battleford.

While these events were transpiring Quinn had gone round to the Saskatchewan, moved along in the shelter of the cut bank until the fort was between him and the Indians, and galloped into it to find to his horror that it was in their possession. He was seized and would have been put to death, had he not said that he was a friend of Mr. McLean, who had done a good turn to the leader when he was in a scrape some years previously. This saved his life....

The day after our arrival before the ruins of Fort Pitt, I sent scouts across the river and to the north and east of our bivouac....

On the afternoon of the 26th Big Bear's trail to the north was found, and I was directed to proceed in pursuit to locate the whereabouts of the enemy.

In their revision of the same events, historians Blair Stonechild and Bill Waiser dispute the "bloodthirstiness" of the Cree:

Another aspect of the situation that is often overlooked is that the Cree offered the occupants of the fort a peaceful resolution to the crisis. These were the same so-called villainous Indians who had committed the atrocities at Frog Lake and now had a virtual stranglehold on defenceless Pitt. Yet instead of attacking, they allowed the police a chance to escape. Far from being on a bloodthirsty rampage, the Indians showed incredible restraint and only engaged the scouts because they appeared to threaten their safety. The Cree demonstrated their true temper when two of McLean's daughters, Kitty and Amelia, drove out in a wagon to check on the well-being of their father, just after the shooting incident, and returned unmolested....

Now, with the death of ten people behind them and Fort Pitt in ruins, the old chief and his followers had been transformed into some of the vilest criminals the young dominion had ever known.

Glen Sorestad's poem *Windsong* "records" the mind and prayer of Mistahimaskwa (Big Bear) at the end of his days, foreseeing, too, the ruin of all hopes at the battle of Batoche on the South Saskatchewan.

Windsong

The tiger lilies still explode
in wild dashes of orange
forcing up through the tangle
of golden rods and brown-eyed susans,
crowded into their last stand
between grainfields and roadsteads
in the land of disappearing fences.
The wind scurries in and over each fiery lily burst with its secret,
with its promises and its lies.

Big Bear heard the wind at Fort Pitt;
it told him not to sign the treaty.
His horse stood patient and listened.

> *the grandmother's men can not know*
> *what the wind says they do not know*
> *the cry of the wind as the last buffalo*
> *sank to its knees on the bloody grass*
> *they can not hear the wind voices*
> *whispering over the flaming lilies*
> *whispering of the people's final hunt*
>
> *all they hear is the shrieking*
> *of the iron horse on the steel*
> *the rattling sound of silver coins*
> *with the grandmother's head on them*
> *the white man's talk of land and ploughs*

Only his people hear the wind voices
murmuring their warning through poplars.
Big Bear heard the voices and listened,
listened with the lilies on a hill
above the twisting South Saskatchewan
where there was no barbed wire
and there were no more buffalo.

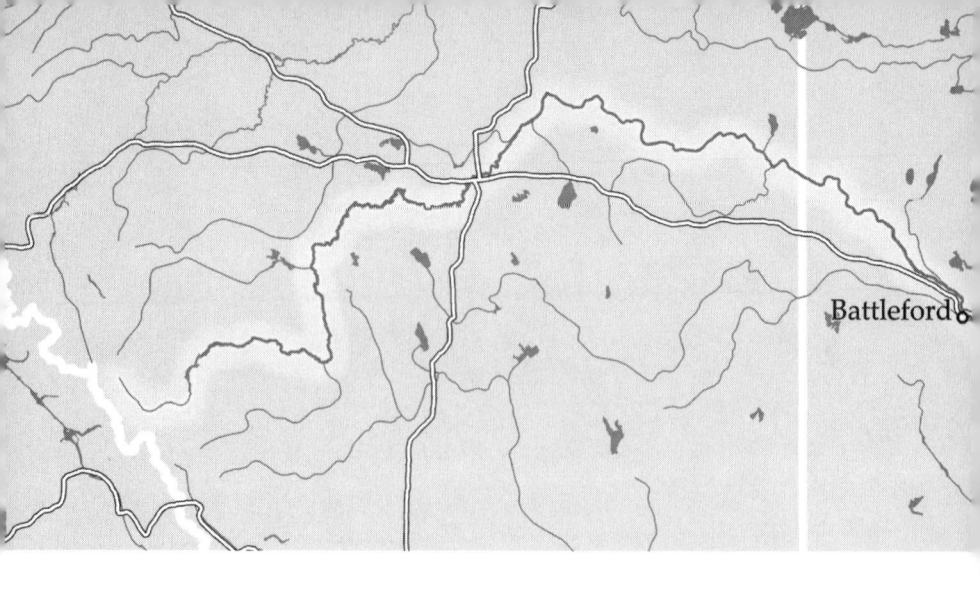

At first it had seemed so romantic, an adventure. Her betrothed, a young man from Parkdale, Ontario, had gone west seeking his fortune. Had he not strategically placed himself at what promised to be the gateway to the Territory, the hub of commercial activity and capital of the North-West Territories, Battleford?

She is walking in the new upper town just then being built and to which people are moving from the flats on the south side of the Battle River where it floods each spring. By relocating on higher land between the Battle and Saskatchewan Rivers, residents hope to escape the hazards of floods, and by being next to the Mounted Police barracks, the increasing resentment of the thousands of Crees that surround them. – Mel Dagg, "The Women on the Bridge"

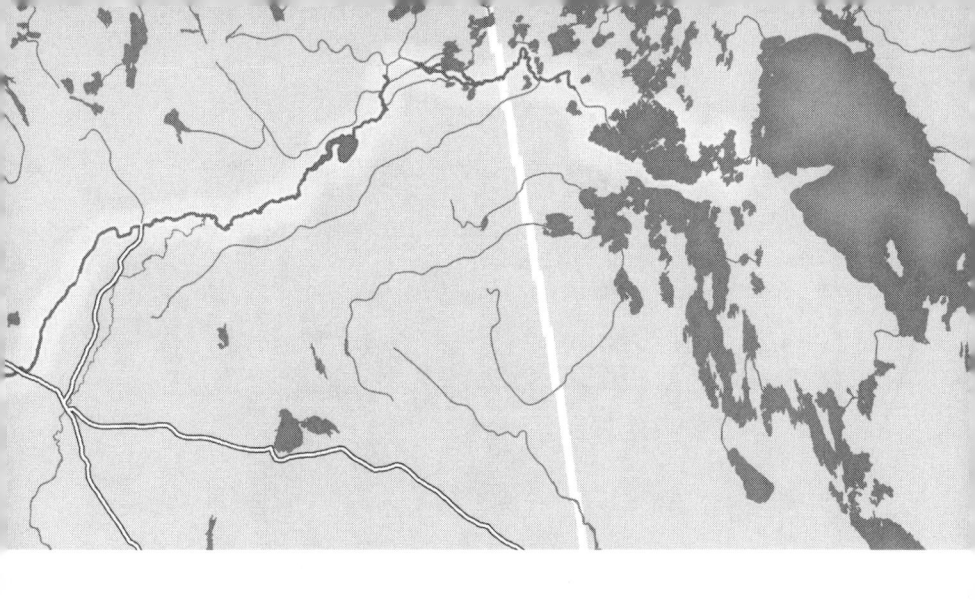

BATTLEFORD
Untold Stories

Now an urban community of more than 14,000 residents, the Battlefords – North Battleford and the Town of Battleford – are slung in the Battlefords River Valley, a superb landscape of riverine and parkland panorama created by glaciation and continual erosion and the wear and tear of the North Saskatchewan and Battle rivers. Besides their modern cultural attractions, such as the art gallery devoted entirely to the celebrated work of Cree artist Allen Sapp, the regatta, and a fiddle and harmonica contest, the Battlefords are also home to the historic site of Fort Battleford, which was established in 1876 as Battle River Post, an outpost of the North-West Mounted Police in the North-West Territories. In this same year, the town of Battleford was declared its capital and the NWMP became involved in the negotiating and signing of Treaty 6. But, in spite of the solemn promises of the treaty, there was disagreement among the parties. Métis settlers, bumping into government surveyors and their rigid rectangular

> "We were once a proud and independent people and now we can get neither food nor clothing, nor the means necessary to make a living for ourselves... The treaty is a farce enacted to kill us quietly." *Cree woman with horse, cart and dog about to cross bridge*

grid system, were anxious about land rights to their lots along the rivers. Indians, confined to reserves and told to farm with little instruction and few resources, began to starve, while the CPR and Hudson's Bay Company scooped up enormous parcels of fertile land to sell to homesteaders. Towns grew and commerce with them. In March 1885, armed Métis and their Indian allies skirmished with the North-West Mounted Police in the Métis town of Duck Lake and won. Saskatchewan River country was soon in an uproar.

Although the decision had been made in 1883 to move the capital of the North-West Territories to Regina, a substantial detachment of the NWMP remained at the fort, and, under pressure of events, grew from 12 men and 16 horses to 200 men and 107 horses. After the battle of Duck Lake, on March 26, 1885, some five hundred white residents of nearby Battleford barricaded themselves in the fort, fearing imminent Indian and Métis attack. Instead, hungry residents of neighbouring reserves – whom Indian agent John Rae, refused to meet – looted the deserted village's homes and stores. Then came news of the killing of nine white people at the village of Frog Lake at the hands of the war chief Kapapamahchakwew (Wandering Spirit), and of the survivors spirited away to the camp of Mistahimaskwa (Big Bear) as war hostages.

The hostages eventually escaped or were released. In July 1885, Big Bear surrendered to authorities in the charred ruins of Fort Carlton. At Fort Battleford in November, eight Indians, tried without counsel, were convicted of the Frog Lake murders and executed in a mass hanging and their bodies removed to a common grave behind the fort in a sandy ravine overlooking the North Saskatchewan. Now, however, they have a proper grave "in the beautiful gully where the hillside levels off to the water," in the words of poet Walter Hildebrandt: a black granite headstone erected within the sacred circle formed by the wheel of bare poplar poles of a ceremonial lodge, their names in Cree and English.

Fort Battleford was decommissioned in 1924 but, thanks to the interest of local residents in the historical importance of the post, a few buildings were preserved. The site was turned over to the Government of Canada in 1951 to be administered as a National Historic Site.

In spite of the agreements made in 1876 between the signatories of Treaty 6 that dealt with payments and material assistance to the Indian bands settled on reserves, by the winter of 1884-85, life had become very hard on the reserves near Battleford. "We made Treaty with Queen Victoria," Cree elder Keyam reminded his interviewer, Edward Ahenakew, "and the idea was that we should have sufficient land to live quietly, unmolested, and molesting no one." Instead, a tight-fisted Department of Indian Affairs and imperious Indian agents held back or even reneged on promised farming assistance and on food supplies when the agricultural programs failed; rations were reduced in federal budget cutbacks;

Indians on the reserves were on the edge of starvation. In the 1880s, the average death rate on the Battleford reserves was 58 per 1,000 people; by comparison, that in Winnipeg in 1890 was 15.7 per 1,000, according to historians Blair Stonechild and Bill Waiser in *Loyal Till Death: Indians and the North-West Rebellion.*

In a letter to the Minister of the Interior in Ottawa, 1883, Cree chiefs at Fort Edmonton explained, "We were once a proud and independent people and now we can get neither food nor clothing, nor the means necessary to make a living for ourselves... The treaty is a farce enacted to kill us quietly."

Perspectives on the events of March-April 1885, in Battleford, town and fort, vary according to who is telling the story. When it had been decided that Chief Poundmaker, with his followers, would negotiate on behalf of all bands in the area with the Indian agent at Battleford for better rations, they were frustrated in their plan when they found the town deserted, the residents having taken refuge inside the palisades of the fort. Against Poundmaker's orders but sensing an opportunity, a few of the Cree and Assiniboine looted and burned some of the town's stores and houses, a job completed by the scroungers and looters among the Canadian soldiers who arrived a month later, the fearful citizens still huddled in the fort.

From the point of view of the townspeople, they were under a state of siege, by groups of Indians who pillaged their property and set their houses on fire while they watched helplessly from the stockade of the fort.

BLOOD RED THE SUN

Safely holed up at Prince Albert, NWMP Constable John George Donkin nevertheless records his colourful impressions of events in Battleford, presumably from an informant: "Poundmaker had let loose his hordes from among the wooden coulees of the Eagle Hills...and a career of pillage and bloodshed had been begun. They had sacked the village of Battleford, and gutted the Hudson Bay stores, and had burnt the whole, indulging in wild orgies and dances around the flames."

The Alberta Field Force, under the command of General Thomas Bland Strange, arrived at the scene of the Frog Lake killings on May 23, 1885. They buried the bodies (the gravesite can still be visited) and pushed on to Fort Pitt in pursuit of Big Bear's band, followed by Sam Steele's Scouts. Some of the band managed to escape to the United States; the rest surrendered to the soldiers who caught up with them. Those charged with the Frog Lake murders came to trial at Fort Battleford in September, 1885, were found guilty and sentenced to hang.

William Bleasdell Cameron, a survivor of the Frog Lake murders and one of the hostages taken into Big Bear's camp, wrote a memoir, *Blood Red the Sun,* first published in 1926 as *The War Trail of Big Bear,* forty-one years after the events. It was something of a best-seller, hitting all the high spots, including his eye-witness account of the hanging of the Indians at Battleford who had killed his friends at Frog Lake. In the memoir, he revisits the day of the executions in the stockade at Fort Battleford, the largest mass hanging in Canadian history. An admirer of Big Bear, whom he called "a great statesman," Cameron senses there is something tragic in this climax to a drama of oppression and violence.

> *As I entered the square the death chant of the condemned red men, a weird, melancholy strain, came to me from the guard-room. A group of Cree and Assiniboine Indians sat with their backs against the blacksmith shop in the open space before the scaffold. The authorities, hoping it would have a salutary effect, had allowed a limited number to view the executions.*

Small knots of civilians conversed in low tones inside the high stockade about the fort; everywhere was that sense of repression always freighting the atmosphere of tragedy. The curtain was about to rise on the final act in the shocking drama which opened eight months before at Frog Lake.

Suddenly the singing ceased and a hush fell upon the men gathered about the square.... Sheriff Forget appeared, dressed in black and carrying in his hand the warrants of execution. A Roman Catholic priest and a clergyman of the Church of England followed. Next came the prisoners, eight in all, their hands bound behind their backs. They marched in single file, a policeman before, another following, and one on either side each of the doomed men. They stepped almost jauntily, dressed in their new suits of brown duck. The weights had been removed from their ankles. Round their shaven scalps were the black caps ready to be drawn over their faces. Immediately in front of them walked Hodson [the Ft. Pitt cook]. Intense silence had fallen upon the square, the only sound the measured tramp of the sombre procession.... The time was up. The strapping was completed; they were bound hand and foot. A deathly silence fell. Hodson stepped up to Miserable Man, drew the black cap over his face and adjusted the noose. He turned to Manichoos and repeated these final preparations. A moment later he was engaged with Walking the Sky, who stood next Wandering Spirit. The war chief turned his head and watched him with the detached air of one who has an idle but no personal concern in an interesting proceeding. Then the black cap dropped over the face of the war chief himself and the rope settled about his lean, sinewy neck.... A hush fell over all as Hodson stepped behind the still line of dark heads and stooped to draw the bolt. There was a sharp sound of grating iron, the trap dropped and eight bodies shot through it. A sickening click of dislocated necks, and they hung dangling and gyrating slowly at the ends of as many hempen lines. A few convulsive shudders and all was over.

I drew a long breath and stepped forward with the remainder of the jury to view the bodies. The tension was past. I had not felt it greatly during the preliminaries, but that awful pause just before the drop is something I am not likely ever to forget.

The bodies were dropped into rough wooden boxes and buried in a common grave on the hillside below the police barracks, overlooking the broad wild valley of the Saskatchewan.

Part autobiography and part history, *Prison of Grass* by Métis scholar Howard Adams was published in the charged political atmosphere of 1970s Canada when "Red Power" movements of the late 1960s had demanded entrenched Aboriginal rights, self-government, and cultural autonomy. As reviewer Barnett Richling summarized Adams's achievement in 1992 in *Canadian Dimension*: "Adams' book stands as an early and valuable commentary on the connections between historiography and colonial context and as a challenge to the political 'truism' that history belongs to the victor alone."

A case in point is Adams's review of the events of 1885. In *Prison of Grass*, Adams lists the "several significant victories" of the Native resistance over "white colonizers." By the end of April, 1885, he writes, they had captured three forts – Pitt, Carlton, and North Battleford (presumably referring to the looting and burning of the town) – though they would lose the war:

> *Even though internal dissension weakened Big Bear's force, federal troops that chased him for several weeks did not succeed in capturing him. Big Bear surrendered on July 2. From the trials that followed this conquest, eight Indians were judicially murdered, and 20 were given jail sentences of from two to 20*

years. Big Bear and Poundmaker were sentenced to three years each. Every member of the Indian nation heard the death-rattle of the eight heroes who died at the end of the colonizer's rope and they went quietly back to their compounds, obediently submitting themselves to the oppressors. The eight men who sacrificed their lives at the end of the rope were the champions of freedom and democracy. They were incomparable heroes, as shown by their last moments.

According to Saskatchewan poet Don Kerr, "Walter Hildebrandt celebrates talkers, the dispossessed, the history of the West, his own life, the outliers, in poems that are themselves the speaking voice...."

In his poem, "Fort Battleford's History," published in 1986, Hildebrandt exposes the real significance of a national historic site one hundred years after its trauma.

Fort Battleford's History

The new men of the Empire are the ones who believe in fresh starts, new chapters, clean pages; I struggle on with the old story, hoping that before it is finished it will reveal to me why it was that I thought it worth the trouble. – J. M. Coetzee

I drive each year
to Fort Battleford
to tell guides
the history that has made it
a site of national significance

Most don't know what the Cree tell
believe what is written:
that the history

of the fort is honourable
its significance
in the grand architecture
of the Gothic Revival details
on the Commanding Officer's Residence

The full history of this fort
lies in the stories
that remain
untold
stories of the eight Indians
hanged within the
stockaded fort
now lying
next to the
Battle River
underneath an unmarked
slab of cement
surrounded
by a metal chain
I am impatient
with history
that will not
tell their story
wary of the academic
historians who
write about the
past so their sons
can live comfortably with it

We know about the good intentions of
Christian-minded people yet
little of the starvation

Big Bear knew and spoke but
few listened

We have learnt
almost nothing in 100 years
I drink in a bar divided
have spent the day
explaining you cannot
rely totally
on what
has been
written
Tomorrow
I will
take them down
to the
common
grave
along the
river bank
beyond
the police
fort
in the beautiful
gully
where
the hillside
levels off
to the water
where
the concrete
slab
lies

unmarked
surrounded
only by
a
chain
fence

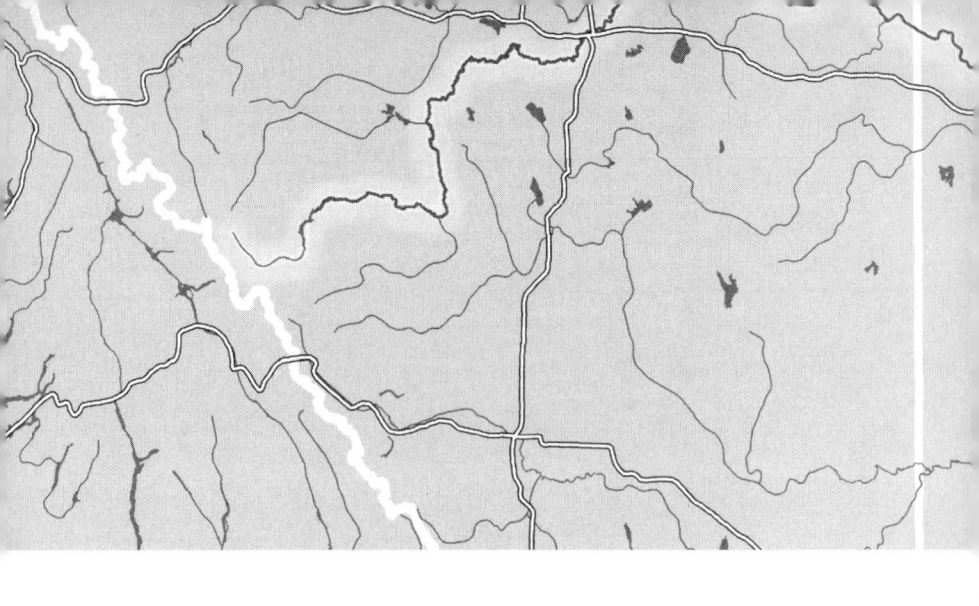

The arches are impressive, but are also humble in their simple, even-textured concrete. There are no ropes and cables, no towers or fanciness. Just simple, perfect rainbow arches. Three of them. – Ellen Arrand, *quoted in Myrna Garanis, "Gracing the Space"*

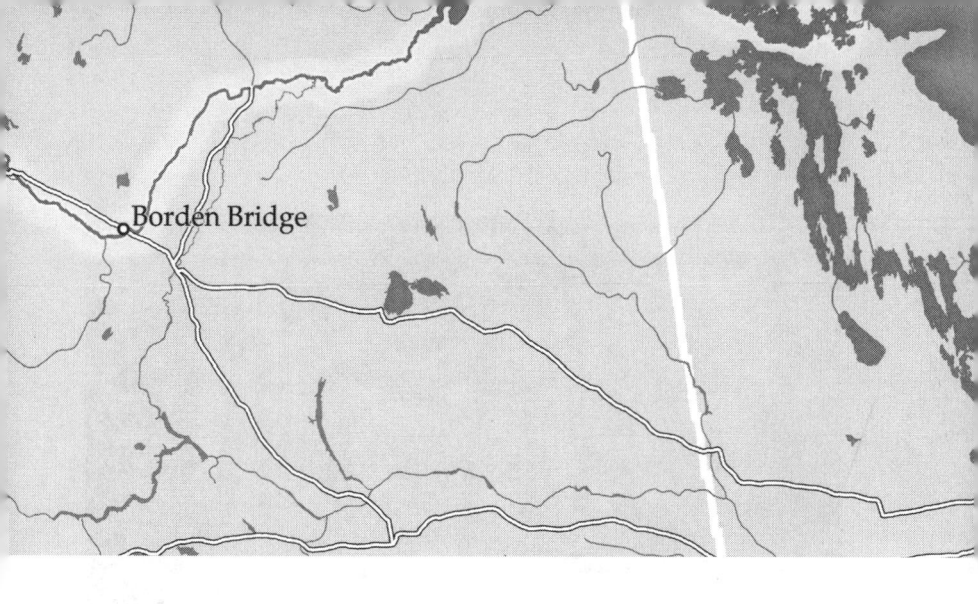

BORDEN BRIDGE
Gracing the Space

As you cross the North Saskatchewan River on the highway (43 kilometres to/from Saskatoon) at the big dip where it veers north again to Fort Carlton historic site and Prince Albert, you see upstream from the current bridge (basically a spanless, asphalt extension of the highway roadbed) the lovely concrete arches of the original bridge, now disused. It was built in order to give unemployed workers a job for a few weeks during the desperate years of the Great Depression. A University of Saskatchewan professor of engineering, Chalmers Mackenzie, drew up the blueprints in 1934, choosing concrete over steel trusses in order to provide even more jobs for local labourers, mainly farmers, who managed to move 60,000 tonnes of concrete in wheelbarrows, often working in freezing river water up to their shins.

Sixty years later, Ellen Arrand, the granddaughter of the bridge's general contractor, Richard J. Arrand, returned to Borden to learn the story of the bridge's construction from the people who

The original Borden Bridge. 7,000 people attended its official opening in 1937.

could still tell it. "I sit on the old vinyl couch [of the hotel] and think about the little I yet know of this place," she writes in a fictionalization of her own story, *Public Works, Private Souls*. "There used to be one store and a post office at the river crossing. And the Henrietta ferry at Ceepee. A typical sight, I had read, was to see the heads of horses and oxen in the river as they had fallen off the ferry and had to swim to shore." From the bus window, she had a good, long view of Borden Bridge: "The arches are impressive, but are also humble in their simple, even-textured concrete. There are no ropes and cables, no towers or fanciness. Just simple, perfect, rainbow arches."

Myrna Garanis's mother grew up in the Langham district of central Saskatchewan, not far from the Borden bridge. On her many trips to see her parents, retired in Saskatoon, Garanis has become obsessed by the bridge. She has also seen the bridge in family photographs and has tried in vain to convince her very elderly mother to retrieve them and tell their story. She will have to make do with her own.

Gracing the Space: Borden Bridge

Sometimes even a rank amateur can get off a truly fine shot, which this one is, of the original three-arched Borden Bridge, 40 kilometres west of Saskatoon. My son Taso and I still argue as to which of us was behind the lens when we captured it on 35 mm. Its middle bow string arch was once the longest in North America. Now Borden Bridge is no longer used. Barricaded off. Despite the barricades, despite the dearth of river beneath it, this 1930s make-work bridge continues to grace the space it occupies. Those who travel the Yellowhead regularly count on its familiar shape, how it snugs into a covey of harmonious hills.

To call its replacement a bridge is to defame the original. The new basic crossing, a couple of kilometres into the valley east of Borden town, is simply an extension of highway over water; flat and spanless. A letdown stretch running parallel to the true Borden Bridge, perhaps 100 metres north of it. We were determined to omit it from any photographic version, which wasn't easy.

Almost home. Borden Bridge, the almost-home bridge. Depending where you think home is. East of the bridge, or west of it. I've lived west, in Alberta, for nearly forty years. But every few months, family ties draw me back, more often dutifully than joyfully, strangling ties you might even say....

[My parents] married in 1938, deciding they could wait no longer for the depression to end. The bridge construction must have impinged on their lives, if only peripherally. The building of Borden Bridge created employment during the worst years of the depression: over two years of work for upwards of 50 crew or contracting farmers with horses to haul rocks. Though my mother's parents lived only ten miles away, that was a considerable distance in the 1930's. Too far for my

grandfather's horses. Neither he nor his offspring were involved in bridge work, though they too could have used the money.

My mom and dad and their families were among the crowd of 7,000 at the opening ceremonies for Borden Bridge in May of 1937.

I recall seeing another photograph of the bridge somewhere in my parents' albums. My father, all suited up — not for hockey. He's looking very eligible, very handsome, casually leaning against one of the brand-new pillars. He's alone. The photo undated. My younger son, the present-day chronicler, resembles his grandfather at that age, tall and dark, assured. I wish I could lay my hands on that old photo.

* * *

There are other photos I'd like to retrieve from that jumble of pre-Kodak moments in my mother's cache. Or perhaps it's the memories I want to reassemble, revisit. My dad's family grouped around a picnic table on the eastern bank of the river. There were once tables and a pleasant campground just under the bridge. It was a mutually-convenient meeting place for the two "sides" of the family. The city-dwellers would come out to meet up with relations still living in the country. My father's mother, Carrie MacSorley, would be at the white wooden table, apron on. I don't remember her without it. Uncle Bill in perpetual bib coveralls, and who else? Likely Ivan and Mae, favorite uncle and aunt, although that may have been another summer, another picnic, another photo/memory. The family took a lot of pictures when I was growing up. Mae and I would have been saskatoon berry picking over on the southeast side of the bridge. I would have been in high school. Those were good years for berries, unlike last summer with its lineup of empty dugouts along the roadsides, so similar to the Dirty Thirties.

R. J. Arrand's Borden Bridge has stood unused for decades. A bridge put aside. Too narrow for today's traffic; unable to accommodate the big rigs that criss-cross the two provinces. The bridge is a bit of unexpected scenery at the end of a six or seven-hour drive from Edmonton. The surprising poetry of bridge engineering language from Arrand's book resurfaces for me each time I cross the North Saskatchewan at Borden:

"The idea of the cofferdam is that the piles will fit into each other tongue and groove style so that the cofferdam, when drained will be water tight. Excavation can then occur. Even strutted and waled it is a dangerous operation as the dynamic force of the river water is much more powerful than anything as static and immovable as a cofferdam.

"In fact the secret of longevity in a bridge is that it is never static. With the bow string arch the bridge will be in a constant dynamic state – the concrete compressing down on itself, the tension of the steel rods." (Excerpt from R. J.'s diary, November 30, 1935).

Bridge language stays with me, steels me for what lies ahead. Borden Bridge stays with me. So many pillars to lean against.

Two things strike the new-comer at Carlton. First, he sees evidences on every side of a rich and fertile country; and, secondly, he sees by many signs that war is the normal condition of the wild men who have pitched their tents in the land of the Saskatchewan.... This is the Fertile Belt, the land of the Saskatchewan, the winter home of the buffalo, the war country of the Crees and Blackfeet, the future home of millions yet unborn. – William Francis Butler, *The Great Lone Land*

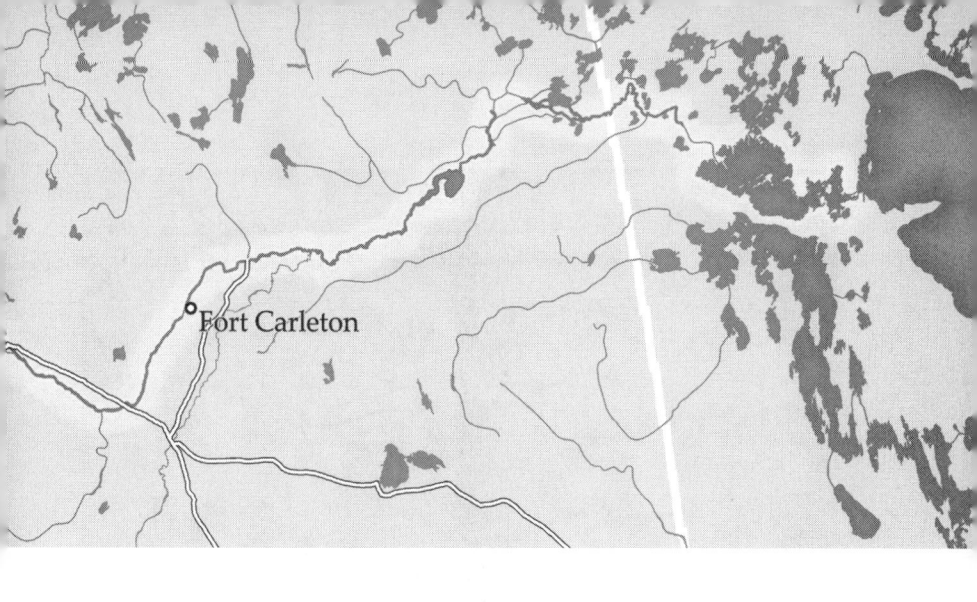

FORT CARLTON
The Fertile Belt

The Hudson's Bay Company trading centre Fort Carlton, a short hike up from the North Saskatchewan River landing dock, operated from 1810 to 1885. At Fort Carlton Provincial Park, the visitor sees a handsomely reconstructed stockade, a fur and provisions store, trade store and spartan clerk's quarters, and, outside the palisade, a tipi encampment (operated jointly with Beardy's and Okemasis First Nation), which represent the fort in the bustling 1860s. If Fort Carlton had a Golden Era, it was the 1860s. The young missionary John McDougall was there in 1862, recording the busy scene of boatmen and hunters, draymen and freighters who converged on this hub of prairie transportation and commerce. He marvelled at the "buffalo-skin lodges and canvas tents [that] dotted the plain in every direction." Twelve years later, the era was over. Chief Factor Clarke reported in the spring of 1874 that "I am leading a dog's life of it now. Freemen, settlers and Indians are all starving and after putting past the

"In accordance with my instructions, I proceeded with as little delay as possible to Carlton, in the neighbourhood of which place I met with forty tents of Crees." Fort Carlton Provincial Park.

quota for D[istrict] we have just 23 bags Pemmican left, all hands are coming to us and as I can't supply them I get many a threat and a curse."

In 1876, representatives of the Crown and of the Plains and Woods Cree negotiated and signed Treaty 6 at Fort Carlton and Fort Pitt. In exchange for giving up claims to 310,000 square kilometres of land, the First Nations were promised land settlements and material and medical assistance, and withdrew to designated reserves. The way for European settlement of the Northwest and its opening up to the plough had been made. "In days gone by the buffalo was our wealth and our strength, but he has left us.... The buffaloes are gone," said Chief Mistawasis, chief of the tribe known as Sak-kaw-wen-o-wak, who would sign Treaty 6 for his people at Fort Carlton.

The concluding event at Fort Carlton came in 1885 when Cree Chief Mistahimaskwa (Big Bear), after months of resisting final treaty settlement on a reserve, surrendered to police stationed at the post, now just charred remains after the Cree attack in the North-West Rebellion. "The view was very beautiful," wrote Treaty Commissioner Morris in his report of 1880, as though looking on it for the last time before the surveyors arrived. "The hills and the trees in the distance, and in the foreground, the meadow land being dotted with slumps of wood, with the Indian tents clustered here and there...." Now you can buy a postcard with a view down onto the reconstructed fort with its four bastions and its parking lot and educational tipis, with the fields hidden behind a horizon of bush, and the river a muddy ribbon drifting majestically along the shallow valley bottom. The atmosphere in summer is hot and drowsy, the historic park landing down at river's edge tranquil to the point of stagnation – the river water so undisturbed you can see the fair reflection of wispy cirrus clouds on its glassy surface – and you realize that the fur trade empire of the Northwest has become a charming picnic site.

According to the journal that the artist Paul Kane wrote while on a westward journey to the Pacific in 1846, he and his companions arrived within a kilometre of Fort Carlton by canoe on September 7, "in a most ragged and dirty condition." They may have been thousands of kilometres from "civilization" but this was no excuse not to make a presentable showing of themselves to the fort's citizens. "This consisted chiefly of a thorough washing," he wrote. "Some, indeed, put on clean shirts, but few, however, could boast of such luxury." Before entering the stockade, he took a look around. He had arrived, he realized, at that particular place in the great Northwest where the line of forest meets the plane of prairie. It was also a flashpoint between competitive bands of First Nations hunters.

"Instead of dense masses of unbroken forest, [the country] presents more the appearance of a park."

The country in the vicinity of Carlton, which is situated between the wooded country and the other plains, varies much from that through which we had been travelling. Instead of dense masses of unbroken forest, it presents more the appearance of a park; the gently undulating plains being dotted here and there with clumps of small trees. The banks of the river rise to the height of 150 or 200 feet in smooth rolling hills covered with verdure. The fort, which is situated about a quarter of a mile back from the river, is enclosed with wooden pickets, and is fortified with blunderbusses on swivels mounted in the bastion. This fort is in greater danger from the Blackfeet than any of the Company's establishments, being feebly manned and not capable of offering much resistance to an attack. Their horses have frequently been driven off without the inmates of the fort daring to leave it for their rescue. The buffaloes are here abundant, as is evident from the immense accumulation of their bones which strew the plains in every direction.

Expeditions

In 1857-58, Fort Carlton was the winter quarters of the members of the Palliser Expedition, who were exploring the Canadian plains for the Royal Geographical Society in London. Here they were engaged in recording hourly readings of changes of the magnetic declination and the air temperature as well as six-hourly readings of the barometer and self-registering thermometers, while all around them bustled the life of a trading post.

In the General Report which introduced the expedition journals, John Palliser writes panoramically and elegically of the terrains of the fur trade enterprise – from the Laurentian Shield to the Rocky Mountains – soon to be transformed beyond Palliser's recognition. For the moment, however, he has the land to himself, as he surveys the North Saskatchewan River on its passage across the alluvial flats, "which form the finest quality of land in this part of the country," winding from side to side in its valley that varies in depth from 30 to 100 metres. So transported is he by the agricultural potential of the land that, even at Fort Carlton, he has emptied it of its denizens and filled it with cattle herds.

> *Wherever the banks of the valley slope gently back to the higher prairie level, as at Fort Carlton, there are to be found the most desirable spots for settlement. By inspecting the map it will be observed that the general course of the river is bounded by hills which sometimes recede to a considerable distance. These hills rise two to four hundred feet above the general level, and skirting along their base there is often to be found areas of land of fine quality, while the whole distance, sometimes equal to 30 miles between the hills and the river, is fine grazing land, and as it all lies within the limit of the partially wooded belt of country, there are "bluffs" that will afford shelter to stock.*

> *The richness of the natural pasture in many places on the prairies of the second level along the North Saskatchewan and its tributary, Battle River, can hardly be exaggerated. Its value does not consist in its being rank or in great quantity, but from its fine quality, comprising nutritious species of grasses and carices, along with natural vetches in great variety, which remain throughout the winter sound, juicy, and fit for the nourishment of stock.*

On the heels of the Palliser Expedition, James Carnegie, the earl of Southesk, a diarist of "Travel, Sport and Adventure, During a Journey Through the Hudson Bay Company Territories in 1859 and 1860," assembled a travelling outfit of seven well-armed and experienced guides and hunters at Upper Fort Garry and arrived at Fort Carlton, via the Assiniboine and Qu'Appelle river valleys, in July 1860. He was obsessed, like Palliser, by the need to "travel and shoot things," to acquire trophies for his Scottish manor. But he took the time to write of his impressions and reactions to this challenging new environment, the northwestern parkland, which he seemed to prefer, under cover of his tent, to the house of the fort's factor: the next morning he was rewarded with a fine view of...an English park!

> *On the 24th we camped at a wooded creek, a few miles beyond the Elbow of the North Saskatchewan. The river at this place has hardly half the breadth or water that the South Branch possesses where it makes its great Elbow; the banks of the former are more wooded than those of the southern stream, but neither so wild nor so roughly and picturesquely broken into heights. In the neighbourhood of our camp rose a fine spring, but it was too strongly flavoured with iron ore to be useful for ordinary purposes.*
>
> *The next day we made an early start, travelling for some miles before breakfast, and by the afternoon we had arrived at*

Carlton, and encamped ourselves near the river a few hundred yards from the Fort.

Mr. Hardisty, the officer in charge, at once came to welcome us, offering every assistance in the most kind and obliging manner. He stayed a while at my tent, and we had tea together, after which he returned to the Fort, – where, by his hospitable invitation, I might have had a room, but as our stay was to be but a short one, I preferred remaining under my own canvas. As things turned out, it was a bad arrangement; for, presently, a set of drunken Indians pushed into the camp, prying everywhere, and making themselves quite at home, and between this intrusion and the savage attacks of the mosquitoes it was long before we could settle ourselves comfortably for the night....

All my horses, excepting the Bichon, whose worn-down hoofs required a set of shoes, having first been swum over to the better pasturage on the other side, we crossed in the skiff, and then proceeded on our way through a fine grazing country of undulating character, diversified with many small lakes and poplar groves, and covered with grass of the richest description abounding in different kinds of vetches. Looking back towards the Fort, the opposite banks of the river seemed like an English park, rising after the first steep ascent in gradual slopes luxuriantly clothed with wood, disposed by nature in groups and gladed masses, as if some skilful hand had been cutting the forest into forms of symmetry.

William Francis Butler made *his* trip through this same country ten years later in the winter of 1870-71, a quarter-century after Paul Kane. He followed what was by then the overland fur-trade route by way of Fort Ellice, Fort Carlton, and Fort Pitt, Victoria settlement, and Fort Edmonton, reporting on conditions among the Native peoples of the Northwest and the best way to secure government authority over them. Butler was struck by the area's fertility, clearly an echo of the Palliser Expedition's assessments, reported first in 1859.

> *Like all things in this world, the Saskatchewan has its poles of opinion; there are those who paint it a paradise, and those who picture it a hell. It is unfit for habitation, it is to be the garden-spot of America – it is too cold, it is too dry – it is too beautiful; and, in reality, what is it? I answer in a few words. It is rich; it is fertile, it is fair to the eye. Man lives long in it, and the children of his body are cast in manly mould. The cold of winter is intense, the strongest heat of summer is not excessive. The autumn days are bright and beautiful; the snow is seldom deep, the frosts are early to come and late to go. All crops flourish, though primitive and rude are the means by which they are tilled; timber is in places plentiful, in other places scarce; grass grows high, thick, and rich. Horses winter out, and are round-carcased, and fat in spring. The lakeshores are deep in hay; lakelets every where. Rivers close in mid-November and open in mid-April. The lakes teem with fish; and such fish! fit for the table of a prince, but disdained at the feast of the Indian.*

Treaties

Ottawa was far more interested in the agricultural potential of the North-West Territories than in its diminishing provision of furs, hides, and pemmican. The end of the nomadic hunting and seasonal trapping economy was signalled by the flourishing community around the Presbyterian mission near Isbister on the North Saskatchewan – which would soon become Prince Albert – and a permanent Métis settlement, Duck Lake, on the South

Saskatchewan. But the transition to a new economy would be painful. Native populations faced disease and starvation in the wake of the extermination of the buffalo herds and encroachments on their traditional lands. Company men worried that a restive population of hungry and landless Indian tribes would fall upon helpless settlers to pillage them of their property. As W. J. Christie, chief factor in charge of the HBC's Saskatchewan District and eventually a treaty commissioner, wrote to the secretary of state in Ottawa in 1871: "I think that the establishment of law and order in the Saskatchewan District, as early as possible, is of most vital importance to the future of the country and the interest of Canada, and also the making of some treaty or settlement with the Indians who inhabit the Saskatchewan District."

Several Plains Cree chiefs themselves sent a message via Christie to His Excellency Governor Adams George Archibald, "our Great Mother's representative at Fort Garry, Red River Settlement" as quoted by treaty negotiator Alexander Morris in his book, *The Treaties of Canada with the Indians of Manitoba:*

Messages from the Cree Chiefs of the Plains, Saskatchewan, to His Excellency Governor Archibald, our Great Mother's representative at Fort Garry Red River Settlement.

1. The Chief Sweet Grass, The Chief of the country.

GREAT FATHER, – *I shake hands with you, and bid you welcome. We heard our lands were sold and we did not like it; we don't want to sell our lands; it is our property, and no one has a right to sell them.*

Our country is getting ruined of fur-bearing animals, hitherto our sole support, and now we are poor and want help – we want you to pity us. We want cattle, tools, agricultural implements, and assistance in everything when we come to settle – our country is no longer able to support us.

Make provision for us against years of starvation. We have had great starvation the past winter, and the small-pox took away many of our people, the old, young, and children.

We want you to stop the Americans from coming to trade on our lands, and giving firewater, ammunition and arms to our enemies the Blackfeet.

We made a peace this winter with the Blackfeet. Our young men are foolish, it may not last long.

We invite you to come and see us and to speak with us. If you can't come yourself, send some one in your place.

We send these words by our Master, Mr. Christie, in whom we have every confidence. – That is all.

Alexander Morris was lieutenant governor of the North-West Territories from 1872 to 1876, and chief negotiator of land treaties for the Crown. In his book, *The Treaties of Canada with the Indians of Manitoba,* he includes an account sent to him by Rev. George McDougall of preliminary discussions in 1875 with the Cree chiefs about their grievances and their hopes for a successful treaty.

Morleyville, Bow River, Rocky Mountains,
October 23rd, 1875.
to his honour Lieutenant-Governor Morris.

SIR, – *In accordance with my instructions, I proceeded with as little delay as possible to Carlton, in the neighbourhood of which place I met with forty tents of Crees: From these I ascertained that the work I had undertaken would be much more arduous than I had expected, and that the principal camps would be found on the south branch of the Saskatchewan and Red Deer Rivers. I was also informed by these Indians that the Crees and Plain Assiniboines were united on two points: 1st. That they would not receive any presents from Government until a definite time for treaty was stated. 2nd. Though they deplored the necessity of resorting to extreme measures, yet they were unanimous in their determination to oppose the running of lines, or making of roads through their country, until a settlement between the Government and them had been effected....*

In a word, I found the Crees reasonable in their demands, and anxious to live in peace with the white men....

The topics generally discussed at their council and which will be brought before the Commissioner are as follows in their own language. "Tell the Great Chief that we are glad the traders are prohibited from bringing spirits into our country; when we see it we want to drink it, and it destroys us; when we do not see it we do not think about it. Ask for us a strong law, prohibiting the free use of poison (strychnine). It has almost exterminated the animals of our country, and often makes us bad friends with our white neighbours. We further request, that a law be made, equally applicable to the Halfbreed and Indian, punishing all parties who set fire to our forest or plain. Not many years ago we attributed a prairie fire to the malevolence of an enemy, now every one is reckless in the use of fire, and every year large numbers of valuable animals and birds perish in consequence....

All of which is respectfully submitted.

In his memoir, *Years in Canada: Reminiscences of the Great North-West,* published in 1915, Colonel Samuel B. Steele recounts the vivid impression made on him of the preparations and rituals leading up to the treaty negotiations themselves. As chief constable in the NWMP Swan River Barracks (at Livingston, Saskatchewan), he had been put in charge of making arrangements for the large police contingent that was needed at the negotiations at Fort Carlton.

On August 18 at sunset we arrived at Fort Carlton. We found there a very large number of Indians of different bands in one huge camp with the tents in a great circle. Near at hand many traders had assembled to get the benefit of the large sums of money that were to be paid to the Indians at the conclusion of the treaty.

The first day's proceedings were over when we arrived. The commissioners for the treaty were the Hon. Alexander Morris, Lieutenant Governor of Manitoba and the North West Territories, the Hon. W. J. Christie, and the Hon. James Mackay [sic]; the two latter were well known in the country, had been born in it and spoke the Indian languages with ease and fluency.... The secretary of the commission was Dr. Jackes, of Winnipeg; the interpreter, a dignified plainsman named Peter Erasmus.

The council tent was pitched on an eminence about a quarter of a mile from the Indian camp, which contained upwards of 2,000 redskins. These assembled soon after the arrival of the commissioners, firing rifles, beating their tom-toms, dancing and yelling, the whole bank chanting to the accompaniment of their drums.

When quite ready they advanced in a semi-circle, preceded by a large number of mounted warriors giving an exhibition of their magnificent horsemanship. These braves had been painted by their squaws in the most approved Indian style, some like zebras, others like leopards, each according to the skill and fancy of the artists. It was a fine show, well worth coming many hundreds of miles to see. Nothing so fine or barbaric can be seen nowadays; the exhibitions one sees at fairs and shows being a mere sham and disgrace to the red man.

The Indians gradually approached in the same semi-circle to within 50 or 60 yards of the Council Tent, where they halted and began the "Dance of the Stem." This was commenced by the chiefs, medicine men, councillors and musicians coming to the front and seating themselves on robes and blankets spread there for the purpose. The bearer of "The Stem," which was a gorgeously adorned pipe with a long stem, walked slowly along the same semi-circle of Indians and advanced to the front. He then raised the stem to the heavens, turned slowly to the four cardinal points and, returning to the group on the robes in front of the Council Tent, handed it to one of the young warriors, who commenced a slow chant, at the same time performing the stately dance, accompanied by the musicians and the singing of the men and women in the semi-circle. This was repeated by the other men, the main body steadily advancing. The commissioners then left the Council Tent to meet them, the horsemen still performing their wonderful feats. The bearer of the pipe of peace presented it first to the Lieutenant Governor, who gently stroked it several times and passed it to the other commissioners, who repeated the ceremony. This when repeated meant that the friendship of the Indians had been accepted....

"This country lasted long with only Indians here..."

Edward Ahenakew is best known now for his collection *Voices of the Plains Cree*, an account of tales related to him by Chief Thunderchild in 1923, recorded in his journal, and finally published in 1973, as edited by Ruth Buck.

Thunderchild resisted signing Treaty 6 until 1879. He had had a dream – but had not believed it – that "there would be white men everywhere, overwhelming this land. Today I see it," he told Ahenakew. "I love this land greatly, and what is still the Indian's I am resolved to hold fast. For that I pray much."

Thunderchild's Conclusions

It seems to me that since we have been fenced into reserves, the Cree nation has shrunk, that there are fewer of us. The white men have offered us two forms of their religion — the Roman Catholic and the Protestant — but we in our Indian lands had our own religion. Why is that not accepted too? It is the worship of one God, and it was the strength of our people for centuries.

I do not want to fight the white man's religion. I believe in freedom of worship, and though I am not a Christian, I have never forgotten God. What is it that has helped me and will help my grandchildren but belief in God?

He looks upon the wrong that is done on earth, and knows what would correct it. But we ourselves must find the way and do it.

I remember old Indians who were afraid of guns, even of metal knives.

In the days before my father, the Hudson's Bay Company had a wintering post at Battleford, but there was too much fighting there between the Crees and the Blackfoot, and so the Company went down the river and built Fort Carlton. They gave the Indians one boatload of goods for the use of the Saskatchewan River. That was soon past and forgotten.

This country lasted long with only Indians here, and then the white man came, and they came with might. That was permitted by God. Yet see how they treat the nation that is weaker. Surely our nation is not to be wiped out. In the days that I remember, an Indian would prepare himself to go on a long and difficult journey. So must all be ready for this road of life.

With the settlement of First Nations bands on reserves and the decline in hunting and trapping, Fort Carlton's importance in the economy and culture of the North-West went into severe decline, so much so that only a skeleton staff remained after 1880. However, it enjoyed – or endured – a brief importance again during the violence of the North-West Rebellion in 1885, when, under the leadership of the visionary Louis Riel, Métis in nearby Batoche took up arms in an effort to settle land grievances with the federal government.

Take Me to the River

Most summers when he was growing up in the 1950s, writes Lloyd Ratzlaff, "there came a Sunday when the church announced its intention to baptize." His own call came at age fourteen when all his male friends, including his cousin who fished with him in the river, declared themselves ready to be "candidates" for baptism. Lloyd didn't want to be left out and so also declared his readiness to the Mennonite Reverend. In preparation, his grandfather read from the German New Testament and concluded: "So if they ask you why you want to be baptized in a river, you tell them, 'Jesus was baptized in a river too.'"

That was it. Two generations after the incineration of Fort Carlton in 1885, after its brief role as jailhouse of Chief Mistahimaskwa (Big Bear) who surrendered to the four last policemen on duty there, and after its final abandonment by the Hudson's Bay Company, the upstream waters of the North Saskatchewan served as a baptismal font for a teenaged boy, then flowed on past the ghosts.

> *Well, get on with it, down to the river. An old rhythm-and-blues tune begins playing in my head:* Take me to the river, wash me in the water....
>
> *That baptism at fourteen wasn't just a few drops of water on the head of a baby in a blanket, wrapped in the consoling*

arms of parents still silly with adoration. It was wading through mud into waist-deep water, kneeling so your chin just cleared the river, and being ducked under a swift current that threatened to carry you off and deposit you on a sandbar downriver somewhere near Fort Carlton. Yes we'll gather at the river, the people sang to us, where bright angels' feet have trod.

Here it is. A little field, and the rock where the deacons pitched the tents, one for the girls, one for the boys. I sit on the rock, take a draft of water, settle into the placid flow of the river....

Over there where the grass slopes down, the deacons had erected a handrail cut from green poplars to help us into the river. The onlookers gathered round while we candidates waited here by the tents. At the appointed hour a hymn was sung – Trust and obey For there's no other way To be happy in Jesus but to trust and obey – and we waded through the mud, steadied by the rails, and out in to the current, I at the head of the line behind the minister. The black and white photos of this occasion show us taken in ascending order of size: how small I look there at the head of the line wearing another of my father's loathed haircuts, how much deeper the water is for me than for the others.

We baptized forwards, not backward as certain other denominations did. The men of the church had debated the issue exhaustively, whether the death of Christ was more authentically pictured by the forward *dunk, in token of his head's slumping forward on the cross when he gave up the ghost; or by the* backward *dunk, in token of his being laid on his back in the sepulchre. Forward was the right way, they had discerned. I wanted very much to think trusting and obedient thoughts as I entered the river, but I hadn't yet learned to swim and I feared suffocating under the muddy water; then as I knelt, and the bottom of the river shifted under my knees, I prayed that the current at my back wouldn't sweep me away — hadn't we heard so many warnings about the undertow and sharp drop-offs in that North Saskatchewan River?*

And the new church! Built in 1872, it consisted of 80 logs, 150 planks for the floor, and 350 boards for ceiling and sheeting. Twenty bushels of lime went into its plaster. It could seat 120 people, and needed to, for the Prince Albert mission was gaining fame throughout the plains to the south and usually there were Natives camped in the vicinity, on one occasion up to 250. Separate services were held in the Cree language and in English, with regular attendance at each of 50 and 70 people, respectively. – Victor Carl Friesen, *Where the River Runs: Stories of the Saskatchewan and the People Drawn to its Shores*

PRINCE ALBERT
Gateway to the North

Called a "Gateway to the North" at the geographical centre of Saskatchewan, Prince Albert is dramatically situated in the deeply eroded trench of the valley and up on the bluffs of the North Saskatchewan River, where boreal forest, aspen parkland, and prairie grassland meet.

According to oral history, Woods Cree settled in the vicinity of today's Prince Albert National Park during the mid-nineteenth century but travelled through the area much earlier. Today, there are several First Nations communities in the area. That fully half of Prince Albert's ethnically mixed population is Aboriginal, speaking Cree or Dene, is directly related to the history of the fur trade there: the North Saskatchewan was a natural transportation artery west and into the Athabasca region, and fur traders and Native trappers were eager to do business.

After Henry Kelsey in 1692 and La Vérendrye in 1741 made the initial explorations, the French built a trading post at Fort-à-la-

"Prince Albert is a trim little city on the south bank with one main street facing the river and a great wealth of trade in furs and lumber..." River Street, Prince Albert, Saskatchewan, ca. 1912. Postcard view, looking west, with bridge in background.

Corne (down river from Prince Albert) in 1753, which was followed by as many as thirty more posts all up and down the river. In 1776, explorer Peter Pond set up a trading post on the north shore of the river just west of the present city site. Soon an overland trail was established as well, west to east, connecting Fort Carlton, Fort-à-la-Corne, and Cumberland House.

In 1808, the North West Company sent Alexander Henry the Younger from Pembina Post on the Red River to the Saskatchewan River (on his way he met David Thompson at Cumberland House), where he made notes of river travel in early September, passing "the forks" of the north and south branches of the Saskatchewan River, then steadily upriver toward the site of the future Prince Albert in 1809. "From that time till 1811," fur trade historian J. G. MacGregor summarized, "when [Henry] crossed the mountains for the last time, bound for Astoria at the mouth of the Columbia [he drowned in the Columbia River in 1814], he travelled every foot of the [Saskatchewan] river either in a canoe or by land."

The settlement of Prince Albert – an old Indian camping ground – was given its name by the man considered its founder, Rev. James Nisbet, who, along with a party of settlers from the Red River colony in Manitoba, moved here as Presbyterian pastor among the Cree in 1886 and presumably wished to honour Her Majesty's consort, Prince Albert, in London, in time-honoured colonial fashion. Within fifteen years, Ottawa opened a land titles office, hundreds of settlers were cropping the land, and entrepreneurs were operating a grist mill and sawmill. Without a railway line until 1891, however, all provisions and machinery had to be brought in by wooden cart along a spur of the Carlton Trail.

In the wake of the 1885 North-West Rebellion and the abandonment of troops at Fort Carlton, a North-West Mounted Police post was set up in Prince Albert – "probably the best system ever devised for keeping order in a very extensive and sparsely populated country," according to Elliott Coues, American editor of traders' journals. In the early 1900s the area had a bit of an economic boom with rail service from the south, the influx of new homesteaders, and the opening up of the forests to the logging industry.

While working in Prince Albert National Park for the Dominion Park Service in the 1930s, conservationist Archibald Stansfield Belaney, a.k.a. Grey Owl, wrote three of his most popular books, including *Sajo and the Beaver People* (1935). Many of the facilities and roads and trails in the park were completed in that same period by inmates of the relief camps that operated there.

BODIES AND SOULS

In Centennial year, 1967, several Canadian publishers launched series of travel books that sent Canadian writers off from sea to sea to sea. Macmillan of Canada's *The Traveller's Canada* series included Edward McCourt's *Saskatchewan*. In 1967, Prince Albert

"Here, on the south shore of the North Saskatchewan, settlement has an end." Seaplane at Prince Albert, Saskatchewan, on the North Saskatchewan River, ca. 1938.

was still the jumping-off spot for tourists driving north on gravel roads to the fishing lakes of Saskatchewan whose far northern areas were going to be inaccessible except by water or air for some time to come. McCourt zeroes in on the town's founder, the Rev. James Nisbet.

Prince Albert's founding father was a Presbyterian missionary, the Rev. James Nisbet, born in Glasgow and a graduate of Knox College, Toronto, who in 1866 at the age of forty-three left his parish of Kildonan and journeyed west with his family to bring the word to the Indians of the North Saskatchewan. The mission he established became the centre of a large Indian settlement; and Nisbet, believing it to be a vital part of a missionary's work to feed the hungry and clothe the naked, worked with enormous enthusiasm to grow cereals and vegetables in a land where cultivation had never extended beyond the occasional garden-plot on the grounds of a trading-post. In 1869 the Prince Albert Mission produced one thousand bushels of grain and four hundred of potatoes. The next year Nisbet was charged by the Manitoba Presbytery, whose members obviously preferred starving Christians to well-fed heathens, with spending too much time on the bodies of his Indians and not enough on their souls. The charges were eventually dropped, but neither Nisbet – a slight, frail man – nor his devoted wife seems to have recovered from this shock of having their zeal for the faith called into question. Both died in 1874 within a few days of each other.

"I do not think," John Donkin wrote in his memoir, *Trooper in the Far North-West*, "that anyone, since Butler wrote his 'Great Lone Land,' has thrown light on the hidden phases of existence in this vast abode of desolation." He was writing as a member of the North-West Mounted Police (which had been formed partly on Butler's recommendation), with whom he had enlisted in Winnipeg in the portentous year of 1884. That December he arrived in Prince Albert, no longer the frontier mission of the days of Rev. Nisbet, who had died in 1874, but a municipality of substance, if still a bit uncouth.

> *Prince Albert consists of a long, straggling settlement, stretching along the right bank of the North Branch, beginning at a distance of thirty miles from the Forks of the Saskatchewan. A trail passes from the town through a country rich in grassy hollows, lakelets, and clumps of trees, to the Hudson Bay Ferry on the South Branch, about twelve miles distant. There is a considerable population of Scotch half-breeds on the outskirts, and the first germ of this colony was a Presbyterian mission. The women are excellent laundresses, though their charges would strike astonishment into the minds of the female professors of the art at home. The uniform settled rate is ten cents for each article that passes through their hands, whether it be a sheet or a pocket handkerchief. A large lumber-mill now stands here, and logs are rafted down the stream. The residence of the Hon. L. Clarke, the Chief Factor of the Hudson Bay Company, was a many-gabled house of painted frame-work, with a wide verandah, standing in an enclosure, which could scarcely by any stretch of courtesy be termed "grounds." Near to this, by the river, rose the glittering tin spire of the church, attached to the Convent and the Roman Catholic Mission. A long straggling street of wooden stores fronted the wide Saskatchewan, which at this point is studded with lovely islands....Many of*

> the "moccasin aristocracy" – as we dubbed the French half-breeds, in barrack parlance – lived in huts for the winter, on the north side of the river, a quarter which was named Chicago. When the warmth of spring enabled them to emerge from their foul-smelling dens, they migrated in canoes, with tent and teepe, to the open spaces in the town, and went in for mild labour, such as a little wood-chopping, for the citizens. There was also a camp of thirty lodges of Téton Sioux, in a glade of the forest on the northern side. As they were simply refugees from the United States, after the Custer massacre, they were not treaty Indians. That is to say, they received nothing from the Dominion Government in consideration of lands surrendered by them. They were consequently in winter often on the very verge of famine. After a donation of scraps from the barrack-kitchen, they would indulge in a pow-wow of wild hilarity, and the beating of the tom-tom, mingled with piercing yells would sound across the snow-robed river far into the night, and their strange forms would be seen dancing round the ruddy camp-fire....

Aboriginal and Métis grievances may have been settled, by negotiation or military campaigns, but the newly arrived homesteaders to the territory soon had grievances of their own. They accused the Canadian government of operating the territory solely for the benefit of eastern Canadian business to the detriment of local interests. (Many local land investors lost large sums of money in 1882 when the CPR route was diverted from Prince Albert to Regina.) Others complained that, with civil servants arriving from the East, local residents were without political representation.

In a stringent editorial in May 1884, the Prince Albert *Times* forcefully condemned the "greedy, grasping, overbearing" performance of the Dominion and warned that the central authorities "need not look for friends" among the settlers, Métis, and Indians.

Two weeks later a protest meeting of white settlers, English-speaking half-breeds, and French-speaking Métis gathered in Lindsay schoolhouse near Prince Albert, and in July 1884, five hundred residents of Prince Albert turned out to hear Louis Riel speak.

"Till the last note of the music had died away…"

While the North-West Rebellion was fought further south, Trooper Donkin remained in Prince Albert. Rumours and panic raged after the Métis rebels cut the telegraph wires in March 1885. In due course, the army arrived. On May 20, Major-General Frederick Middleton, the "short and portly" commander of the Canadian militia which, just days earlier, had been victorious in the decisive battle of the rebellion in Batoche, the Métis capital, marched into Prince Albert looking rather bedraggled, according to Donkin:

> *On May 20th General Middleton's column marched into Prince Albert, arriving about noon, having performed the last eighteen miles that morning, with only half an hour's rest. The scarlet of their tunics was a dingy purple with exposure to all the storm and sunshine of their march, and the smoke and work of battle. Their war-worn features were bronzed with weather and over this "shadowed livery of the burnished sun," the dust of the trail had spread a coat of black….*
>
> *An immense transport train followed the infantry. This, of course, is a necessity in such a country as this. Civilians were hired for this duty with their teams; being paid at the rate of ten dollars (2l.) per diem, with forage and rations thrown in.*
>
> *Boulton's scouts and the Intelligence Corps, who formed the rear-guard, were a fine body of young fellows, the majority*

> *being old countrymen. They wore slouch hats and the general garb of the western plains, and were armed with repeating rifles....*
>
> *General Middleton pitched his camp upon a level plateau, near the residence of Mr. Lawrence Clark. What a luxury it was to us poor exiles to hear the bands discoursing the latest tunes at night while the headquarters staff were at dinner. There was an enclosure roped off; and on the outside were gathered the military, and the rank, and beauty, white and dusky, of the Prince Albert settlement. Every one was there. The broad river looked lovely in the evening light; the green islands with their rich foliage mirrored in its still bosom. A small bear was tied in front of the General's tent. At the first signal of the drum this shaggy little ball of cinnamon-hued fur would stand upon his hind-legs, and dance wildly till the last note of the music had died away....*

Indian prisoners had been brought into the barracks at Prince Albert, but otherwise the community was restored to its previously bucolic pleasures – bathing in the river, for example – and, come autumn, the entire countryside was a panorama of colour.

> *The Indian summer came in all its glory in September. It is much earlier here, in the north, and lasts for a month generally. A luminous mist floats over all; and everything seems bathed in the tranced calm of one long summer's evening. The hideous mosquito has received his* quietus *from the nightly frost. The poplars and birch-trees begin to change their worn green garments for all the splendour of their autumnal robes of russet, and bronze, and red. The roads are dry and hard, and over lake and bush, open space and mighty forest, over broad river and sere and yellow marsh, lies the quiet slumber of the fall. One splendid afternoon, a comrade and I sallied forth for*

a ramble over the ridge to the south-east. When we reached the summit a scene lay spread beneath us beyond all words of mine. Prince Albert, to the left, nestled in its amphitheatre of copsewood; its white toy-like houses peeping out from amid their embroidery, and the great river rolling gently by, with gem like islands on its gleaming breast. To the north and east stretched the primeval forest, all golden and olive; like a vast ocean of colour, its billows spread sleeping and dreamlike. Such a sight can never be forgotten. Here, on the south shore of the North Saskatchewan, settlement has an end. Beyond, as far as the desolation of the Coppermine and Great Mackenzie Rivers, beyond fertile meadows of the Peace River Valley, beyond the wild Lac la Ronge, as far as the moss-clad beach and lichened rocks of the Artic [sic] Ocean, stretches the unknown.

Almost twenty-five years after the Rebellion, Agnes Laut and companions canoed down the North Saskatchewan, excited by all the sights on view from their perch on the river. Already the narrative about the Canadian West was thought of as legend even though the North-West Rebellion was still a vivid memory and thousands of settlers were just moving in. At the great bend of the river as it turns to Prince Albert, she saw the fields of grain and big frame and brick houses of Doukhobor settlements and how their gardens sloped to the water:

> *Nightly you can see the Russians coming down to examine their fish weirs, or punting in and out among the fowl. Herds of cattle dot the hills. Happier faces we did not see among all the settlers of the West. A gold dredge plies industriously on this part of the river for Prince Albert people; and indeed, if you try some of the river silt on any of the gravel bars in your frying pan, you get minute specks of gold.*

> *Prince Albert is a trim little city on the south bank with one main street facing the river and a great wealth of trade in furs and lumber....*
>
> *I confess the wealth that interested me most there was the wealth of legend about the Old West. Here, as at Edmonton and Battleford, dwell many of those delightful and vanishing types of old-timers who have seen the West transformed from a boundless hunting field to a checker-board of barb wire fences. They have lived the kind of things that other people read about — these old frontiersmen — and some of their experiences make the finest spun inventions of fiction seem very flaccid indeed.*
>
> *Beyond Prince Albert the Saskatchewan takes a great swing north-east through the true wilderness primeval.*

Agnes Laut's "old-timers" have long-vanished, and it has become the task of storytellers after them to keep the materials intact. In *Descent Into Lima*, poet Bruce Rice travels to Peru and back to Saskatchewan. In the poet's words, "the poems explore questions of vision and displacement. I gobbled up books on archaeology when I was a kid growing up in Prince Albert, Saskatchewan, on the 'pine tree line.'"

From that collection, the poem "Enough," whose narrator stands by the river falls near Prince Albert, names a string of markers of this place: the forest trees, the antediluvian river fish, the shifting river bed, and the La Colle Falls hydroelectric dam 64 kilometres downstream, abandoned in 1913.

> *It would be enough if I could name the oily blue smudge of the spruce, arches only we could get under. If I could map those miles of forest from end to end, describing as I went the loom of its darkness. It would be enough, if I could see the flesh of the creature that lived on the iron-stained bones I pulled from the bank. If I could tell my father where his words went as his*

voice travelled into the loam, explaining itself to layers and layers of time as he spoke, more to himself than me. If I could swim the brown river, finding the sandbar as the feared depth shifted – falls down river, the silenced turbines of a half-built dream. If I could summon the heron that flew by night to the valley I never descended, where it slept in the tree by a stream the muskeg drank up. It would be enough, to see the way a clearing sees before the deer arrives, to see a little further through the dark. To know why when the knife sliced my hand to the bone I wound it in the scrap of a shirt, washed the knife and told no one. If I could say why secrecy is necessary. Why blood must be traced to its human home. Why the winds hump and swell through the spruce. And that blue. If it could be picked up and moved, a sea could not hold it.

At half-past two P.M. we arrived at the North Branch, coming upon it suddenly and finding ourselves in its waters almost before we were aware of its proximity. The temperature of the South Branch was 67°, of the North Branch 62°; an important difference at this season of the year. It is perhaps a fair standard by which to estimate the climatic character of the regions of country through which these rivers flow. The water of the South Branch is yellowish-brown in colour, and turbid; of the North Branch a shade lighter in colour; the one more resembled the waters of the Mississippi, the other those of the St. Lawrence. – Henry Youle Hind, *Narrative*

The Forks

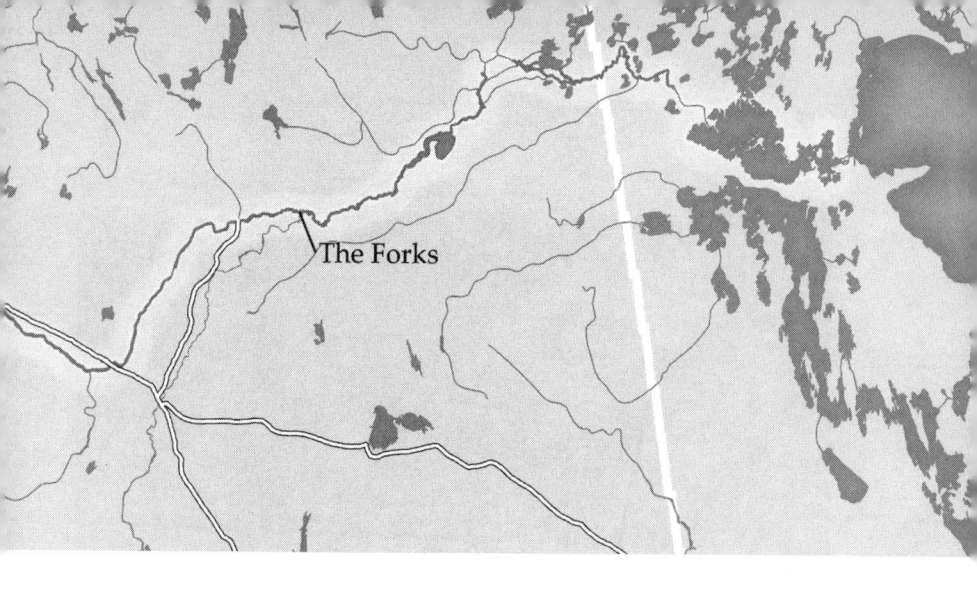

THE FORKS/FORT-À-LA-CORNE
What a Highway!

The French were the first on the Saskatchewan. In 1755, when Anthony Henday came visiting in a flotilla of sixty canoes on his way to St. George's Day celebrations further upstream, the Chevalier Louis-François de la Corne, governor of Fort St. Louis, had already been there two years and had grown the Saskatchewan valley's first crop of wheat, a prescient harvest.

From Henday's journal: "The Governor came with his hatt in his hand, and followed a great deal of Bowing and Scraping, but he neither understood me nor I him..., he treated me with 2 Glasses Brandy and half a Bisket." They sipped and munched just downstream from The Forks, the juncture of the North Saskatchewan and South Saskatchewan rivers where the two branches form the Saskatchewan proper.

This isn't a "forks" at all, it's a confluence, but "the forks" makes sense once one realizes that all the Saskatchewan's travellers in historical times came upriver, paddling their way deep into fur coun-

"The main Saskatchewan, or Ki-sis-kah-che-wun, as the natives call it, is a noble river, sweeping in magnificent curves through a valley about one mile broad, and from 150 to 200 feet deep." The Forks

try. This included the Cree (known as the River People on the upper North Saskatchewan), who emerged from their original eastern woodlands to move westwards, in tandem with the fur trade and its traffickers, driving the Blackfoot ahead of them. You can walk down to the confluence easily, far down along a trail zigzagging through a luxuriant stand of deciduous trees, out on to a lip of mud flat, right there at the crotch of the two branches. Just below, Chevalier de la Corne built Fort St. Louis in 1753. It was a natural site for a post: from the "branching" of the north and south streams of the Saskatchewan River, hunters and trappers had clear access to the woods and plains.

Realizing the competitive advantage the French traders now had on the Saskatchewan, the directors of the Hudson's Bay Company in London, whose posts were still stubbornly anchored around Hudson Bay, called for volunteers to go into Saskatchewan country, direct to the Indians and their traplines. In 1754 Anthony Henday (a convicted smuggler with a skill for making nets) volunteered. The HBC hired him as a labourer, outfitted him, and sent him off from Hudson Bay with a canoe and a band of Indians who guided him to the Saskatchewan, to the foothills and then back, when the North Saskatchewan had thawed and the fur-laden canoes were aimed downstream to the Bay. Writer Marjorie Campbell, in *The Saskatchewan*, lyrically recreates the journey:

> *It was a great moment for a mere servant of the Hudson's Bay Company paddling with his Indians in so vast an array, down the wide reaches of the river, under the high banks with the clear blue sky above. Spring was in their blood. Tall trees and shrubs made the islands pleasant. The waters were fast. Even though the canoes were low and heavily laden, paddling meant little more than steering. They carried food in abundance, pemmican prepared during the winter, fresh moose, and red deer venison. They carried a vast wealth in beaver and marten from the woods Indians, fox and bear and wolf from the prairies.*
>
> *The trip downstream was swift and comparatively easy. In an amazingly short time they came to another great river which the Indians identified as the Waskesew, the south branch of the Saskatchewan. Just below the mighty confluence stood the French post of La Corne. Henday's flotilla of canoes spread along the shore and Henday went to call on the governor of the French post. Perhaps he wanted to show off to these Frenchmen, to let them see his vast wealth in furs. Perhaps it was the longing to speak to another white man, for he had not seen a white man for almost a year. The French, too, were eager to welcome him....*
>
> *There were but six men in the small, primitive fort, and they lived up to the French tradition of friendship with the Indians. In time the brandy did its work, as the French had intended. Next day there was more, ten gallons in all, adulter-*

ated with water. Ten gallons of brandy, even when adulterated with Saskatchewan water, went a long way. So did the trading between the Indians and the French. Henday noted that, when intoxicated, the Indians "traded cats, Martens & good Parchment Beaver skins." The French turned down the less valuable wolves and dressed beaver.

"I am certain he hath got above a thousand of the best skins," wrote Henday ruefully.

At the beginning of August 1808, Alexander Henry and his party of three men, plus baggage and dried provisions, set their canoe into the Red River, headed for Lake Winnipeg and the mouth of the Saskatchewan, en route upriver to the fur trading grounds. August 31 they camped at the spot on the Saskatchewan River "where the French formerly had an establishment called Fort St Louis...where some years ago were still to be seen remains of agricultural implements and carriage wheels. Their road to the plains is still to be seen, winding up a valley on the S. side." Coues, the ever-vigilant editor, weighs in with a footnote to alert us to the fact that this *old French fort* St. Louis is the same as Fort La Corne, à la Corne, or de la Corne, below the Fort St. Louis of the North West Company.

On September 2 at 9 a.m. they arrived at the forks.

At eleven we proceeded up the North Branch, which here comes from the N.W. The stream is much contracted between high banks on both sides, the current is stronger than below the forks, rapids are more frequent and some of them dangerous, requiring the utmost exertion of the men at the line and in the canoe with the poles. The course of the river is more crooked than below the junction of the two streams, and the descent much greater. We met an Indian who had killed a buck moose, about a mile from the river. I dispatched eight men for the meat, which I divided among the canoes and paid for in liquor. At sunset we camped at Sucker creek, having performed a great day's journey. The track along the beach has become very bad for the men at the line; the bank comes in close to the water's edge at many places, which are obstructed by heaps of earth and wood daily sliding from the upper part of the shore. At such places cold springs issue and form miry rivulets, into which the men sink knee-deep. Wherever the beach is broad, in turning the low bottoms, the shores are covered with loose round stones, which makes tracking laborious....

"A pattern of neatness, order and comfort..."

Full of enthusiasm about Canada's agricultural potential once it expanded into the Northwest, Henry Youle Hind was an eager if underqualified participant on two expeditions dispatched by the legislature of Upper Canada, one to Red River settlement in 1857, and another in 1858, under his own leadership, to the country west of Red River and to the Saskatchewan River to explore the resources of the area.

Like so many canoeists before him, Hind is mightily impressed by the sight of the forks of the Saskatchewan's two branches, north and south. They flow swift and green, reflecting the bush on their tranquil surface, and seem equally broad and powerful, equally muscular – but in fact the south is a few metres wider. In Hind, emotion mingles with stern scientific enquiry.

The main Saskatchewan, or Ki-sis-kah-che-wun, as the natives call it, is a noble river, sweeping in magnificent curves through a valley about one mile broad, and from 150 to 200 feet deep. We paddled rapidly round eight points, making a distance of sixteen miles in three hours, and towards evening sighted Fort à

> la Corne, with the Nepowewin Mission on the opposite or north side of the river. As the description of the Saskatchewan and the valley in which it flows at Fort à la Corne applies equally to the river between it and the Grand Forks, it is unnecessary to incur the risk of needless repetition by enumerating the features of each of the eight points or bends we passed, and of the valley through which the river flows. At Fort à la Corne we made measurements of its leading dimensions, a section of the bed of the river, ascertained its rate of current, examined the cliffs, points, and flats, which are so curiously reproduced at every bend, which will be amply sufficient to illustrate the most interesting and important features of this noble stream between the Grand Forks and a short distance below Fort à la Corne; from that point the country begins to assume a different aspect, and will require an independent notice.
>
> The Saskatchewan opposite Fort à la Corne is 320 yards broad, twenty feet deep in the channel, and flows at the rate of three miles an hour. The main depth of the river is fourteen feet, but it is in the memory of those living at the fort, when it was crossed on horseback during a very dry season.

Presently, he also comes to the site of the Nepowewin mission, established by Reverend Henry Budd, first Native Canadian to be ordained in the Anglican church in North America, which he assesses for its agricultural potential, and muses on the consequences for Native culture.

> The valley of Long Creek, five miles south of the Nepowewin, appears to furnish a very large area of land of the best quality, and will probably yet become the seat of a thriving community, while the Nepowewin will remain a mere fishing station or landing-place. But when these events take place, the wild Indians will have passed away, and the white race occupy the

soil, yet it is to be hoped that the descendants of some of those heathen wanderers who have here the opportunity of hearing of Christ and His kingdom, may find a permanent home near the Nepowewin, so long distinguished for the medicine feasts which are celebrated in the pine woods crowning the banks of the Saskatchewan, and whose remains in the form of painted idol posts, I saw almost within sight of the mission station, on the opposite side of the swift flowing river....

These were the images of Manitou the Indians invoked during the celebration of important ceremonies. The features of a man were roughly carved on each post, and smeared with patches of vermilion and green-coloured paint over the cheeks, nose, and eyebrows. When decorated with fresh paint, feathers, strips of leather, and a painted robe of elk, moose, or buffalo skin, these idols inspire the most superstitious awe among the untutored savages who carve and ornament them. But the awe of many becomes terror, and the superstition absolute idolatry, when illumined by fires at night, and invoked as the representatives of all-powerful Manitou, the whole assemblage jumping in time to the wild song and monotonous drum of the conjurors....

In September 1853, newly ordained Anglican priest Henry Budd moved from Paskoyac (The Pas) to Nepowewin, where he cleared a small piece of ground on the river bank opposite Fort à la Corne and built his mission. He laboured here with his wife and family until 1867, teaching, preaching, performing weddings and baptisms, and growing potatoes.

"Mr. Budd's house, garden, and little farm," writes Hind, "is a pattern of neatness, order and comfort, yet it is difficult to say whether the prospects of this mission are favourable or otherwise." Hind was very struck by the tenacity of the First Nations' spiritual practices even in the midst of an Anglican mission district. He quotes from Rev. Budd's own journal (itself written with a style and attitude indistinguishable from any Victorian gentleman's), "the progress and continuances of these annual idolatrous ceremonies." Budd's entries for April, for example, tell of a feast:

> April 2nd. – *The feast has commenced betimes this morning, and the drum has had no rest the whole last night. The dance does not commence until there have been some long speeches put forth, and the feast is over.*
>
> April 3rd.: Lord's day – *The Indians have been dancing and drumming the whole of yesterday and last night, and this very likely will continue for some time yet.*
>
> April 4th. – *The Indians are still carrying on their dance and feasting: they are preparing some more places for dancing in. Their great dance, the goose dance, is not yet commenced. This dance is repeated every spring and fall, in honour to the gods for preserving the Indians.*

"What a highway..."

William Francis Butler was reluctant to leave the Northwest, and leaped at the opportunity to stay on when Lieutenant Governor Adams George Archibald asked him to travel through the newly acquired western territory and report on conditions. Butler set out on October 24, 1870 for Edmonton, continued to Rocky Mountain House, returned to Edmonton, and set out for the journey back to Red River by dog team in the dead of winter.

Although Butler was travelling the Saskatchewan a century after Anthony Henday, he was still apprehensive about the rigours of the country, especially in winter. In January 1871 he came to Fort à la Corne, where he had a break, waiting for the mail. Eventually, he stood at the great confluence of the north and south branches of the Saskatchewan River, faced north, and had a vision.

At the "forks" of the Saskatchewan the traveller to the east enters the Great Sub-Arctic Forest. Let us look for a moment at this region where the earth dwells in the perpetual gloom of the pine-trees. Travelling north from the Saskatchewan River at any portion of its course from Carlton to Edmonton, one enters on the second day's journey this region of the Great Pine Forest.... Some 500 or 600 miles to the north this forest ends, giving place to that most desolate region of the earth, the barren grounds of the extreme north, the lasting home of the musk-ox and the summer haunt of the reindeer.... Into the extreme north of this region only fur trader and the missionary have as yet penetrated....

This place, the "forks" of the Saskatchewan, is destined at some time or other to be an important centre of commerce and civilization. When men shall have cast down the barriers which now intervene between the shores of Lake Winnipeg and Lake Superior, what a highway will not these two great river systems of the St. Lawrence and the Saskatchewan offer to the trader!... It is not too much to say, that before many years have rolled by, boats will float from the base of the Rocky Mountains to the harbour of Quebec. But long before that time the Saskatchewan must have risen to importance from its fertility, its beauty, and its mineral wealth.... So must this great valley of the Saskatchewan, when once brought within the reach of the emigrant, become the scene of numerous settlements. As I stood in the twilight looking down on the silent rivers merging into the great single stream which here enters the forest region, the mind had little difficulty in seeing another picture, when the river forks would be a busy scene of commerce, and man's labour would waken echoes now answering only to the wild things of plain and forest.

"He [Nor'wester James Finlay] came up here with 4 canoes and next year went down to Canada and his returns in furr being so great that the clear profits of that year enabled him to live very gentelely all the remainder of his life and he never more visited the interior – not the least remnant of the house to be seen. – He was the first person from Canada that ever wintered so high up the country, except Colonel St. Luke La Corne, under the old French government who built a Kings post a few days higher up in 1756 or 7." – Peter Fidler, in *Peter Fidler: Canada's Forgotten Explorer*

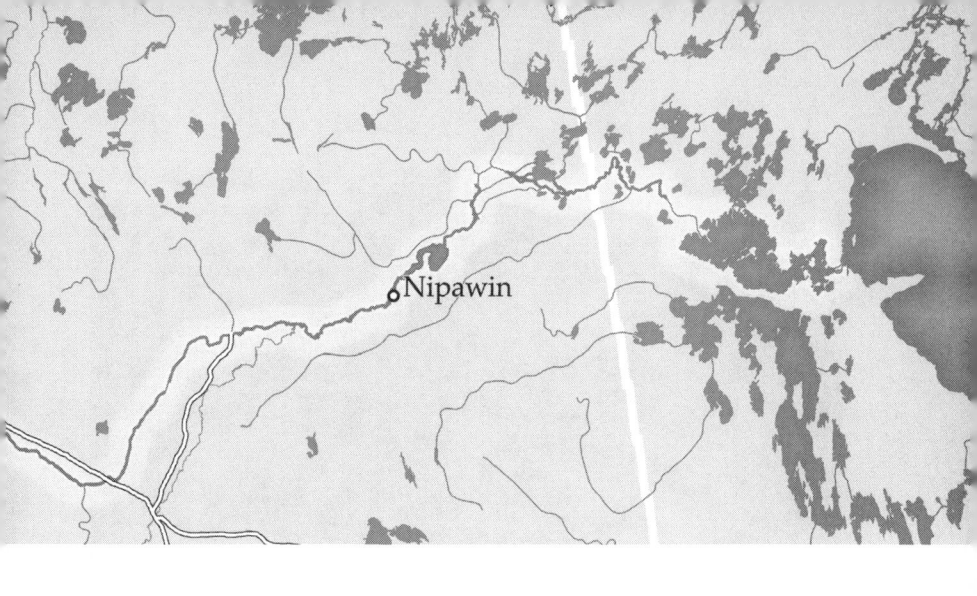

NIPAWIN
Between Farmland and Forest

Nipawin got its name, by official account, from the Cree word *nipawin,* meaning "a bed, or resting place." This designation originally applied to an area along the river that has since disappeared under Codette Lake, created, along with Lake Tobin, when SaskPower constructed the E.B. Campbell (formerly Squaw Rapids) Dam in 1963 and the Francois-Finlay Dam in 1986.

From here again, farmland stretches south, parkland and forest north.

Around the turn of the twentieth century, settlers homesteaded in the area, lumbering and farming. Unlike the canoeists and York boatmen of the fur trade, the settlers were stymied by the river, for them no longer a highway but an impediment on the trail to their homesteads. From the 1860s to World War II, provincial ferry services took them across the river, to be replaced in turn by a flurry of bridge-building after the war.

Saskatchewan River at Nipawin.

Norman Kilgour was the head ferryman at the Nipawin crossing of the Saskatchewan during the 1920s and 1930s. Saskatchewan writer Lionel Hughes wrote his story in 1999.

> "Mr. Kilgour filled two positions, that of head ferryman and cook," wrote George Evans in the Nipawin Journal, *1952. Evans worked with Kilgour on the ferry in the spring of 1927.* "He was nearing 70 years of age," said Evans, "and was as hard and tireless as a man made of steel. He had worked for the department long enough to be entitled to a pension, but kept refusing the pension, preferring to work for his living."
>
> The ferries came to Saskatchewan during rapid growth and frontier enthusiasm which is always fertile ground for legend. But the dangers of river crossings in spring runoff were real and the sacrifice of personal safety to get people across the water was not uncommon.
>
> In the spring of 1928, Kilgour, Evans and another assistant risked a rapidly rising river to get one last load of horses and a

Model T across. A massive spruce tree, carried whole in the quarter-mile wide current, smashed their ferry.

"With her front end foundering and her stern rising," wrote Evans, "the deck of the ferry soon had a sharp incline. The forward slope of the deck was now proving too much for the horses and they were sliding down against the big chain across the end of the ferry. With the weight all thus piled on the front end, the ferry took one tremendous shudder. I saw the stern lift so high the rowboat tied there stood straight up on end. With one mighty bound the ferry boat came up out of the water like a cork released from an air gun.

"We now took stock of our predicament and found we were headed straight down the broad Saskatchewan River, destination unknown, and with no means of controlling our craft."

Nipawin shrivelled and died when the railway bypassed it in 1924. The modern town "sprang into being overnight," according to writer Edward McCourt, following the end of the First World War. This new site was close to the railway and in 1928 the CPR built a "million dollar bridge" over the Saskatchewan River which is still in use.

In an earlier, more romanticized era of historiography, Duncan McGillivray, fur trader and author, was described as a man's man, "bold, ruthless and brooking no opposition," in the phrase of James G. MacGregor, a popular historian of the fur trade, writing this in the 1940s, perhaps a little tongue in cheek. Although McGillivray's *Journal* covers only the winter 1794-95 that he spent at Fort George, his editor, Arthur S. Morton, places him in the context of the whole trade enterprise of the time, especially the hot rivalry among companies for deeper and farther penetration of the Northwest and access to the Indians who trapped and hunted there. The first English-speaking fur trader, James Finlay, appeared on the Saskatchewan in 1767, followed in indignant haste by the Hudson's Bay Company's Matthew Cocking in 1772-73, who canoed up the Saskatchewan at least as far as Nipawin, "where the natives wait for their friends." At this point, like Anthony Henday before him and Duncan McGillivray after, he got out of the canoe and onto a horse, to travel overland along routes laid by Indian hunters and trappers.

The HBC was still trying to lure trappers and traders to their posts on Hudson Bay – a policy finally broken when the London-based company sent Samuel Hearne to establish a post at Pasquia (The Pas) – and so Nipawin became linked with the idea of river-borne leave-takings and returns, as McGillivray noted in his journal.

> *Indians hunted beaver as far west as within sight of the Rockies and descended the Northern Saskatchewan with their families to Nipawi. Here at "the place where one stands and waits," as the name signifies, on the edge of the prairies where the food supply was abundant, the families were left to await the return of their lords, or perhaps they drifted to the Carrot River Valley where Hendry's Indians found their people. On the return from the Bay the dusky traders, once more with their wives and children, wandered across the prairies, hunting, drumming, dancing and feasting in a land of plenty all the way to their wintering grounds in beaver country, far up the Saskatchewan.*

A Tedious Strip

Alexander Henry (the Younger), in charge of the trade for the North West Company in the territory of the Saskatchewan, was travelling in August 1808, the first of storied journeys that would see him travelling "every foot of the river" by canoe and overland by 1811, keeping a journal the whole time, full of incidents. He was an excellent reporter, with a point of view all his own.

They had pushed off into the mouth of the great river on August 20 and proceeded by poling to the first rapids, then towing their craft through the 2-kilometre-long Grand Rapids, and reaching Cumberland House by August 26. Two days out of Cumberland House they were tracking and poling again, averaging about 40 kilometres a day. They would soon travel past "Nepawee," one of several dizzying early variations on the theme of today's Nipawin – Editor Coues lists them all: Nipawi, Nipawee, Nepiwa, Nepoway, Nepoin, Neepoin, Nippewean, Nepowewin. "The word is said by some to mean 'wet place.'" Under these guises, it had been long in the lexicon of traders and adventurers; according to Alexander McKenzie, the French had a post there, Nipawi, "long before and at the conquest of Canada in 1763."

Henry, however, found this strip of the river road "tedious":

> Aug. 30th. *Early this morning we were off, and I had the satisfaction of taking a comfortable nap without any noise to disturb me; the canoe glided on as if under easy sail. The bowman and steersman had only to keep her straight against the current, which was done with the greatest facility; those at the line endured the greatest labour. The line was from 40 to 60 fathoms long, and frequently fouled among the stones and driftwood, which added much to their toil and trouble. The bank, or range of high land on each side, which runs parallel with the river, confines the view on either hand; and this, with the nearly straight course of the river, whose bends are at a considerable distance apart, gives a far from pleasant sameness to the prospect; while the strong current we have to stem renders this part of the voyage very tedious. On the tops and sides of some of the hills are small spots of ground, free from wood. The*

> *country in general appears to be thickly wooded, but the growth is small, particularly on the N. side. At noon we passed the old establishment at the Nepawee, which stands of the S. side. Here, I am told, the plains are at no great distance from the river; indeed, we now frequently see barren spots on that side, the banks appear to increase in height, and the current augments in velocity [Nepowewin and other rapids]. At sunset we camped at an Indian tent. The family had gone out for the meat of a moose, which they soon brought in and gave to me in return for liquor, which kept them intoxicated all night. We find amusement in fishing with hook and line in the eddies, when the men stop to rest and light their pipes, as they frequently do in the course of the day.*

One hundred and fifty years later, Edward McCourt and his wife Margaret followed the old fur trade route by automobile. Their destination was the still utterly remote site of Cumberland House, but they stopped en route from Prince Albert to have a look at modern Nipawin.

> *The modern town of Nipawin sits on a high bank commanding a fine view of the Saskatchewan River, which here is a majestic stream running deep and swift, for the two great branches, North and South, after pursuing their independent ways for a thousand miles or more, have at last joined forces some fifty miles above the town. The approach to the town from the north must be made over an horrendously narrow bridge; but it is worth while making the crossing several times for the sake of the superb up-and-down-river views which almost any point on the bridge provides.*
>
> *The business section of Nipawin could be interchanged with the business section of almost any other town of comparable size in Saskatchewan and no one would notice the dif-*

ference. *The main street is wide, windswept, lined on both sides with conventional small-town shops and business places – a bit drab in the daytime, neon-lit, gaudy at night.* It may be, though, that more of the frontier spirit, the old genial pioneer bonhomie, *survives in Nipawin than in most Saskatchewan towns. Although we consider ourselves inured to the strange sights and shocks one encounters in Saskatchewan small-town restaurants, my wife and I were a little taken aback when our Nipawin waitress, a not unattractive creature in a loosely assembled sort of way, sat down at our table with us – her feet hurt she said – and smoked a cigarette while we wrote out our order. The restaurant is, we admit, entirely justified in describing its atmosphere as 'friendly and informal'.*

The residential part of Nipawin is the town's chief charm. Nipawin is young even for Saskatchewan, but the houses, oddly enough, are reminiscent of an earlier day. Many of them are two-storeyed; nearly all are set in spacious well-treed grounds encompassed by splendid lawns and gardens. Nipawin is, in fact, a town that enjoys the best of two worlds. The forest is here unobtrusive, unimpressive, providing natural windbreaks and shelter belts; and the great plains begin to assert themselves just across the river. Plains that grow some of the finest wheat in the west–evidenced in the large-scale production of seed grain, one of Nipawin's most profitable enterprises.

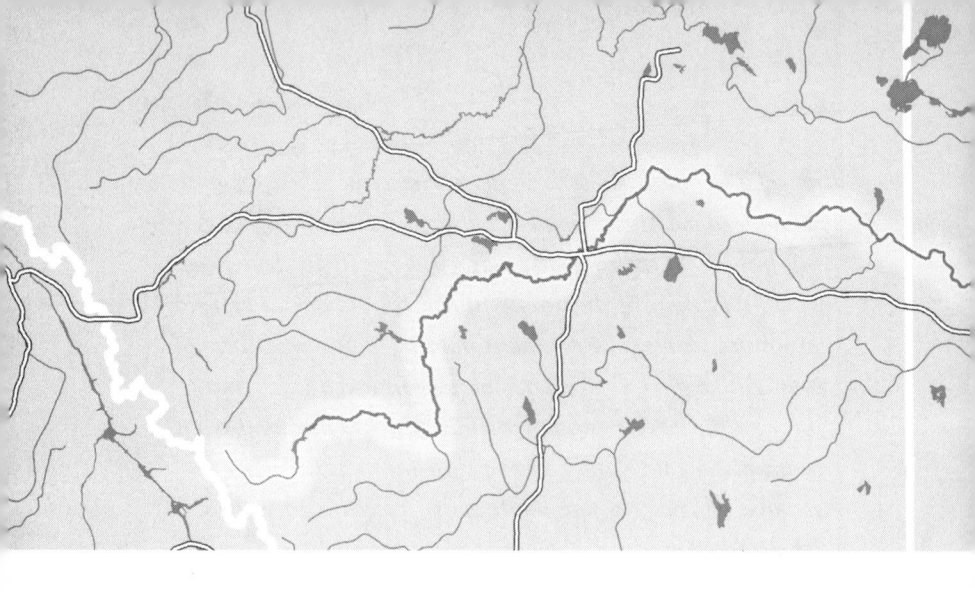

Cumberland House enjoyed its finest hour from 1818 to 1821 when Governor William Williams made the post his headquarters. In 1820 Sir John Franklin and the members of his first expedition spent part of the winter at the post, and so, nearly thirty years later, did the men of the first search party sent out to try to solve the riddle of Franklin's fate. The fortunes of Cumberland House declined rapidly from the mid nineteenth century on as a result of the opening up of more convenient trade routes father south, but it has precariously survived to the present day.... – Edward McCourt, *Saskatchewan*

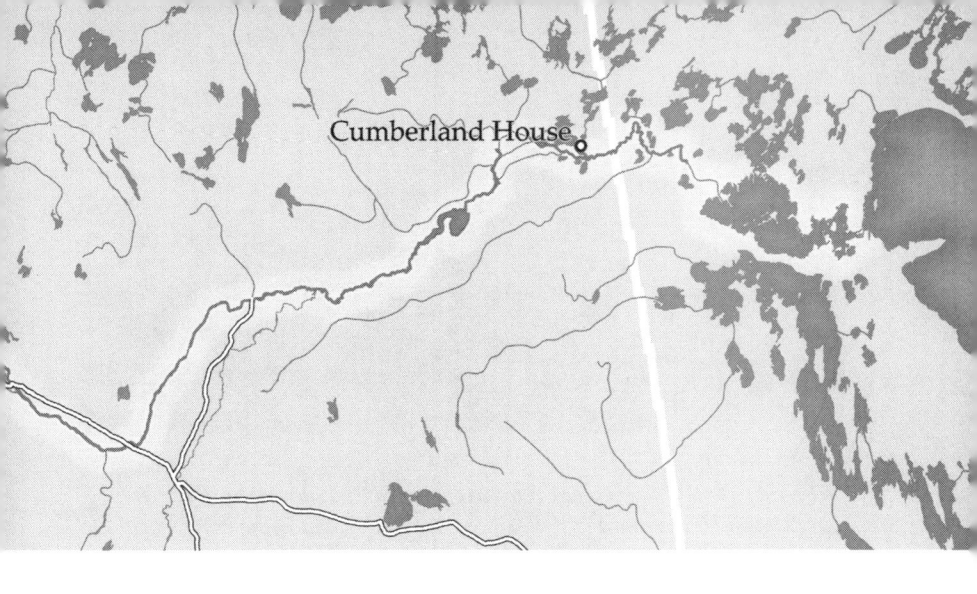

CUMBERLAND HOUSE
A Strategic Location

Cumberland House/Waskukikun (or Waskahikanihk, "at the house") is located on Pine Island, on the southern edge of the Canadian Shield, in the Saskatchewan River delta – the largest fresh-water delta in the world – 300 kilometres east of Prince Albert on Highway 123 and 90 kilometres from The Pas.

The oldest continuously occupied settlement in Saskatchewan, its population of 1,506 includes 836 residents of the northern village of Cumberland House and 670 members of the Cumberland First Nation. That population dropped to zero for over a month in 2005 when the river flooded the town and forced the residents to camp out in a Prince Albert college gym.

Sharing the location with the posts of some 150 independent traders (known as "pedlars"), Samuel Hearne established Cumberland House in 1774 as a Hudson's Bay Company trading post and pemmican depot for the fur brigades on what was known as Pine Island. This, the HBC's first inland trading post, was strate-

"The chop-chop of axes echoed through the woods and across the small, shining bay. Samuel Hearne's men were clearing a 'spot of Ground to Build a Log Fort for the present." View of Cumberland House, Saskatchewan, ca. 1875. Henri Julien, artist, sketched for the North-West Mounted Police. This sketch was published in Canadian Illustrated News, June 12, 1875.

gically located on the confluence of two major fur trade highways – the Saskatchewan flowing from the Rockies and the Nelson draining into Hudson Bay – and at the border of three tribes.

For the preceding one hundred years the HBC men had kept huddled close to the shores of Hudson Bay, waiting for the trappers to come to them from far inland. The far more intrepid Nor'Westers from Montreal had the jump on them by "brazenly heading upriver and inland" from the 1760s, to take their trade straight to the customer-trappers, the Cree and Chipewyan of the Saskatchewan country.

Within twenty years, the two mercantile rivals had hopscotched all the way upriver to the abandoned site of Fort St-Louis/à la Corne at the Forks. The trail tramped from there back to Cumberland House is one of the earliest of the trade.

Cumberland House was in operation until 1794, when a new one was built to the west. In 1778 its importance was superseded by the establishment of Norway House at the northeast end of Lake Winnipeg, a more direct route to the Bay. Nevertheless, with the establishment of a post by the North West Company at Fort Lac des Boeufs in 1790, inter-company rivalry continued strong for another couple of decades as long as the muskrat resource held out. By 1811, the HBC had 320 men inland compared to the NWC's 1,200 – an over-extension of supply lines that forced the Nor'Westers into a merger with the HBC in 1821. With the official merger of the NWC and HBC in 1821, posts were downsized or closed entirely

Smallpox struck in the 1780s and in 1839; fur-bearing animal stock plummeted after 1820.

Cumberland House was, from its beginnings, a Métis community. In 1773, for instance, Samuel Hearne married Mary Norton, a Métis woman. His successor, Matthew Cocking, had three Aboriginal wives. These women proved a godsend to the men because they could "Make, Mend, Knit snowshoes etc for us during the winter." The "etc" could have included moccasin manufacture and food provisioning. The men worked as York boat freighters and packers until steamer service arrived toward the end of the century.

It was here that Rev. Henry Budd, an Anglican and the first Métis (his father was Indian, his mother Métis) to be ordained in western Canada, inaugurated a school in 1842; in the 1850s children were being taught to read and write in Cree syllabics; in 1853 a Métis woman, Jane Ross, helped translate the Bible. Père Ovide Charlebois founded St Joseph's Roman Catholic Mission in 1875 and built a permanent one-room log schoolhouse.

The steamer *Northcote,* launched in 1874 from Grand Rapids at the mouth of the Saskatchewan on Lake Winnipeg, was the first of the some half-dozen steamers to ply the river between Fort Garry and Fort Edmonton. The HBC used it to bring supplies to Cumberland House, where they were transferred to York boats and canoes. Although the events of the 1885 Rebellion had no direct impact on Cumberland House, the *Northcote,* which had carried munitions to the Canadian army in the Northwest, beached here permanently.

The *Northcote* had an auspicious send-off, as witnessed by Rev. Budd in The Pas, and described in *Saskatchewan History Along the Highway:*

"...the people of all ages and sexes were no less excited at the sight of the boat, the first boat of its kind to be seen by them all their life; in fact, the first steamboat going in this river since the Creation." End view of the steamboat Northcote, stranded at Prince Albert, Saskatchewan, ca. 1906. Photo collected by Sir Edmund Walker, General Manager of the Canadian Bank of Commerce in 1906 during a tour of the Prairie Provinces.

They blew the whistle so loud they made the very cattle rear up their heels, and took to full gallop with their tails up in the air at full speed into the woods. But not only the cattle but the people of all ages and sexes were no less excited at the sight of the boat, the first boat of its kind to be seen by them all their life; in fact, the first steam boat going in this river since the Creation.

The *Northcote* carried some 50 tonnes of freight on its first trip to Edmonton in 1882, returning down river with over 6,500 kilograms of fur for the HBC. She came to an inglorious finish, however. Reinforced against rifle fire, she steamed in from Prince Albert to be deployed at the siege of Batoche in 1885. But the rebels had expected this and stretched a ferry cable across the river which tore off her smokestacks, mast and spars. She beached on a sidebar, and there she lay until the following year when the HBC mercifully towed her to Cumberland House. Falling river levels meant she could not navigate the Saskatchewan and so she was stripped of paddle wheel and boilers (now in Cumberland House Historic Park together with the 1890s stone-walled powder house) and burned.

When the Squaw Rapids Dam (now known as the E.B. Campbell Dam) was constructed 80 kilometres upstream in 1962, the lower water levels in the delta adversely affected plant and animal life; the marshlands became stagnant and the fur-bearing animal population was severely depleted. Traditional trapping declined precipitously, along with the community's self-sufficiency. And in 1969 commercial fishing on the river was banned because of mercury contamination.

With the building of a bridge to the island in 1995, the community no longer needed to make canoe or ferry trips to the mainland. It was the end of many eras.

Roughing It in the Bush

Blankets and Beads: A History of the Saskatchewan River was James G. MacGregor's first book. He was a consummate researcher and lay historian who did not play fast and loose with data and facts to make an effect. All the same, he had a lyrical side, most obvious when he stood back from the documentation of his subject to muse about its importance or to re-imagine it. Thus, he puts himself on a headland looking down idly at the current of the Saskatchewan "as it winds around the foot of the hill, the gulls circling so effortlessly back and forth over the surface of the stream."

He sees in his mind's eye the explorer's or trader's canoe down there, on a most remarkable journey, from Hudson's Bay Company posts in Alaska (rented from the Russians) and traplines and posts along the Mackenzie, to Cumberland House in the summer, then almost immediately back to the west, upriver to Fort Edmonton, and beyond.

As the voyageurs travelled up the Saskatchewan in August, the high water would have subsided, and the current would be more gentle, so that the voyageurs would have less tracking to do. We can imagine the brigade, of which the otter skins formed part of the load, travelling from shortly after daylight – and daylight comes early in August on the Saskatchewan – to dusk, eighteen and sometimes twenty hours a day. We can picture them waking at daybreak on a rainy morning and looking out to see the rain pelting and hissing on the surface of the river, and making everything on the banks slippery with the sticky river mud. Surely nothing is more cheerless than being waked under these circumstances at three o'clock in the morning.

A hot cup of tea, and a big breakfast of fried buffalo or pemmican does much to cheer their spirits before the crews get into wet boats to begin pulling at the oars against a stubborn current. Hour after hour they continue rowing, sitting in their wet clothes, the only variations being the periodical crossing from one side of the river to the other to avoid the swift currents, the easy rowing for a while in quieter water, and the welcome halt every hour for a few minutes to smoke. It was in this way that distances came to be measured as so many "smokes". Towards noon, we can imagine the rain stopping, and thus giving the men some respite. But the dark clouds would go scudding across the sky and light mist would rise from the surface of the river, which was warmer than the surrounding air.

An hour before dark, the men would begin to watch for a camping place – some recognized spot on the shore where other parties had camped year after year as evening overtook them – where there would be some shelter and some dead dry wood. Little time would be spent in eating and getting ready for bed. The officer in charge of the brigade would serve out a tot of rum. That, and soothing sleep would soon banish from the minds of the exhausted voyageurs the miseries of aching muscles and the memories of a day in the rain.

Samuel Hearne joined the Hudson's Bay Company in 1766 when he was twenty-one years old. Eight years later, in 1774, after two arduous journeys across the Barren Lands to the Arctic Ocean on a fruitless search for the northwest passage with the Chipewyan guide Matonabbee and his band, he was sent to the Saskatchewan to build the company's first post for inland trade, which was named Cumberland House.

At Cumberland House, he and his companions set about hunting, fishing, cutting timber, and building a log shack caulked with moss and thatched with grass. Marjorie Campbell imagines the scene.

> *The chop-chop of axes echoed through the woods and across the small, shining bay. Samuel Hearne's men were clearing a "spot of Ground to Build a Log Fort for the present." September had arrived and Hearne was well accustomed to the early winters and late springs at York Factory up on Hudson Bay. Though far inland now he was taking no chances of having to spend the winter without shelter.*
>
> *Tents had been pitched on Saturday, following the careful search for a suitable site. On Sunday Hearne had his men at work helving axes. Sunup Monday saw them felling timber for the "log tent" on the south side of Cumberland Lake, close by the short portage to the "Theiscatchiwan" River; it took Hearne, like everyone else, a little time to get on to the spelling of that word....*
>
> *He was soon trading with the first Indians to arrive at the post. On Monday, while the men were felling timber, eleven canoes of Grass River Indians came and pitched nearby. Hearne was able to procure some moose meat and a few beaver from them. The Indians accepted a little tobacco, and after a couple of days' stay returned to their families. They were the forerunners of many who were to come right up to the present day.*

Hearne and his men had shelter to winter-over at Cumberland House, but now they were faced with hunger. In the dead of the cold and snow, there were no more berries, let alone fish and game birds. Author Ken McGoogan, in a recent biography of Samuel Hearne, describes their predicament.

> *By mid-January 1775, Hearne and his crew were surviving on a daily ration of one handful of the dried, beaten meat he called* thewhagon *and four ounces of other meat. Three weeks later, the Englishman observed that this scanty subsistence, so different from the normal allowance at a company fort, "is so alarming to my men in general, that it is with the greatest difficulty I can persuade them from thinking that entire famine must ensue."*
>
> *Partridges, rabbits, and fish had all but vanished. Yet Hearne, having survived long stretches on nothing but water and tobacco, remained sanguine: "I'm not without hopes of some relief before long as I daily expect some Indians in." Two days later a Cree hunter arrived to report that a dozen of his companions had killed five moose and were hauling in the meat.*

The pemmican that so much cheered the weary voyageur makes an appearance in the journals of Alexander Mackenzie, who passed by the House en route to the Barren Lands.

Born in Cumberland House in a family of fourteen descended from generations of mixed marriages, Agnes Carriere grew up learning how to fish and trap, to smoke trout and moose meat, to bake bannock with bear grease, to tan hides, and to dance around the kitchen stove to the tunes from her father's violin. In an interview published before her death in *New Breed* magazine in an issue featuring the Métis elders of Cumberland House, Agnes Carriere describes how to make pemmican.

"I would give anything to eat Pemmican today", Agnes begins, sharing her recipe. First you need to dry the moose meat by flattening it and drying it slowly over a low fire. Then you pound it to break it apart and put it in a clean canvas bag. She recalled then how her mother-in-law would chop the moose bones and drop them into a pot of boiling water, distilling the bone marrow, tallow, and the milk white moose lard would float to the top of the broth. Once cooled, you could just scoop the moose lard from the mixture. You would take the cooled moose lard and add it to the pounded moose meat, kneading it until it was all mixed together nicely, adding raisins for sweet. You keep the mixture aside for a while so the moose lard can get hard again and then you cut it up into squares for later feasting.

The oldest continuously occupied settlement in Saskatchewan, Cumberland House was, from its beginnings, a Métis community. Cree half-breed, John Thomas, fishing, at Cumberland House, n.d.

A hundred years after its establishment, Cumberland House was still a busy place, the destination of fur brigades travelling back and forth on western and northern routes, of adventurers, and of scientists, all of them in need of provisioning, or clean clothes, or a night out on the town.

John Arnot Fleming, surveyor and topographer, accompanied Henry Youle Hind as his assistant on the expedition in 1858 to the Assiniboine and Saskatchewan rivers. Fleming led his own small party down the Saskatchewan River from Fort à la Corne to the Red River settlement by way of the Grand Rapids of the Saskatchewan and of Lake Winnipeg, enduring much bad weather and near starvation. (His account is included in Hind's report of 1859.)

> As the day began to wane we drew up our canoe on a low boulder-promontory of this fast-flowing river, and were soon reclining upon the polished and rounded pavement, beside the ruddy and cheerful blaze of a fire of driftwood. The stillness of night gradually crept on, until nothing was heard but the rippling and surging of the water over the smooth boulder-stones at our feet. The Saskatchewan or "the river that runs swift" is truly well named, for even upon the smoothest and deepest parts of the river, long lines of bubbles and foam, ever speeding swiftly but noiselessly by, serve to indicate the velocity with which this mighty artery courses unceasingly onward, swelling as it goes, with the gathering of its many wide-spread tributaries, to mingle its restless and muddy waters in the Arctic seas.

Fleming and party had 330 kilometres to travel to Cumberland House. On August 13 they found themselves in the marshland of the river delta where the rushes grew so thick and the river stream so shallow that they got out of the canoe and pushed it along to a dry strip of ground behind Cumberland. At the House he was able to stock up on pemmican and flour, and order a new canoe, "for which I had to wait, as it was not quite finished." While passing the time, he idly surveyed the site, pleased to note that the ten acres of barley and potatoes, rhubarb, cabbage, peas, and carrots under cultivation within the post's palings, were "looking well." He examined the storehouse with its machines for the pressing and packing of furs and for making pemmican.

Sir John Franklin slept here, on his first overland expedition to the Arctic in 1819; and the surgeon and naturalist attached to it, Sir John Richardson, left a sun dial in the garden.

On his winter trek up and down the Saskatchewan River in 1870-71 – a prodigy of effort in a few short months between Fort Garry in Red River country, Fort Edmonton, the Rockies, and back again to Fort Garry – William Francis Butler had his fair share of gruelling circumstances. Having got his wind back at Fort à la Corne, and having finally received some news about war and revolution in Europe (newspapers had been delivered to the fort by a courier from Norway House on Lake Winnipeg who had still to go on to Fort Carlton), Butler was full of impatience. The frozen river would be his highway to Cumberland and beyond.

> *To cross with celerity the 700 miles lying between me and Fort Garry became now the chief object of my life. I lightened my baggage as much as possible, dispensing with many comforts of clothing and equipment, and on the morning of the 23rd January started for Cumberland. I will not dwell on the seven days that now ensued, or how from long before dawn to verge of evening we toiled down the great silent river. It was the close of January, the very depth of winter. With heads bent down to meet the crushing blast, we plodded on, oftentimes as silent as the river and the forest, from whose bosom no sound ever came, no ripple ever broke, no bird, no beast, no human face, but ever the same great forest-fringed river whose majestic turns bent always to the north-east. To tell, day after day, the extreme cold that now seldom varied would be to inflict on the reader a tiresome record; and, in truth, there would be no use in attempting it; 40° below zero means so many things*

impossible to picture or to describe, that it would be a hopeless task to enter upon its delineation. After one has gone through the list of all those things that freeze; after one has spoken of the knife which burns the hand that would touch its blade, the tea that freezes while it is being drunk, there still remains a sense of having said nothing; a sense which may perhaps be better understood by saying that 40° below zero means just one thing more than all these items – it means death, in a period whose duration would expire in the hours of a winter's daylight, if there was no fire or means of making it on the track.

Pleasurecraft

Travel on or along the Saskatchewan River would never be so gruelling again. Industrialization began with the steamboat. In the spring of 1974, Ted Barris and his wife Jayne MacAulay began a research trip that would take them across almost 20,000 kilometres to do interviews with almost a thousand prairie residents and to pore over archival photographs and journals, in order to tell the tale of the steamboat era on western Canadian rivers, including the Saskatchewan.

The Saskatchewan River was hard on the steamboat. The flat-bottomed paddlewheeler was thwarted 320 kilometres upriver from Grand Rapids, for instance, by the shape-shifting of the river's channels near Cumberland. Water left the main channel and flowed northward into the streams and swamps that fed Cumberland Lake, directing current away from the "old" Saskatchewan. "To be marooned up the Saskatchewan River became a genuine fear among rivermen in 1882," writes Barris, "the very season the Saskatchewan fleet appeared ready to steam into high gear."

Blocked in 1883 by the rapids below Prince Albert known as Cole's Falls, the captain of the *Marquis*, the flagship of the Saskatchewan fleet, simply dumped the cargo of farm machinery on the shore and turned back for Grand Rapids.

Even later, in 1904, during the river cruise era, passage along that stretch of the Saskatchewan could still be dangerous. A fastwater design built in 1904, the *Alberta* was a "staunch craft," with a sternwheel that rotated at 24 kilometres per hour. But when *Manitoba Free Press* correspondent J. S. Evans travelled on board, down river from Prince Albert in June 1908 (passing Agnes Laut in her canoe?), he got a terrible fright from the rocks at the upper end of the white water of the Grand Rapids cataract, the Missi-pawwis-te-guk. Barris quotes from his report: "A procession of hungry, jagged rocks, every one of which had horns, tusks and a complete set of double-teeth, upper and lower, passed by the side of the boat with horrid rapidity. So close were they, that I thought every one of them would tear the boat to pieces."

But it was not all grim en route, relates Barris:

> "When we docked there at Cumberland, we anchored out from the shore and pulled the gangplank in, because the dogs would get up on the boat and eat everything on it. Those huskies were starvin'; you could throw them a big bar of that hard soap, or a leather shoe, and they'd eat it." Crewman [on the Alberta] Jimmy Soles had grown up with river steamers, the logging industry, the Prince Albert settlement, and the Saskatchewan River tradition.

Just before the '85 conflict, Joseph Soles had rafted his family the six hundred river miles from Medicine Hat to Prince Albert; in 1893, when he was six, Jimmy had fearfully clutched his mother's hand as the *Marquis* whistle bellowed at the Prince Albert pier; at eight, he had lost his mother and learned to pull his weight at the

Log boom at Knudson's Mill on the Saskatchewan River, near Cumberland House, Saskatchewan, 1949.

family's Steep Creek homestead; and by the time the Hudson's Bay Company had launched the *Saskatchewan* from the Goshen bank [of Prince Albert], Soles had driven logs on every major prairie river. So when he joined the *Saskatchewan* crew, Soles brought with him invaluable experience. He also brought a sense of fun.

> "We danced at every place we stopped downriver – The Pas, Cumberland, Chemahawin, Cedar Lake – if we were going to be there overnight, we had a dance.... The Indians called them fiddle dances," mused Soles, who called at all the dances "especially if I knew I didn't have to get up 'til about noon the next day.... Oh those square-dances.... The first trip I made with the Saskatchewan, we had a dance at Cumberland and there was an Indian fellow playin' the fiddle. He had a fiddle alright, and a willow bent with horse hair on it. And he could only play one tune, Little Brown Jug. We danced to that all night."

Agnes Laut was relieved and grateful for the hospitality at Cumberland House as she came near to the end of her epic canoe trip downstream from Edmonton in 1908. There was still free-running water through the marshlands – "quaking silt soft as sponge overgrown with muskrat reed and goose grass, there were not even *low* banks. There were *no* banks at all." As far as the eye could see there was nothing but reeds and waterways, waterways and reeds. And then it started to rain.

Mighty glad were we on the morning of Saturday, August 29th, to see the tuft of a lone lob-stick rise above the mist marking the site of Cumberland Lake fur post. With a rasp of the keel on the pebbles and a howling welcome from the husky dogs in all the keys of a grand orchestra gone on a drunk, we landed in a storm of rain that almost blew us off our feet. The fort is built on an island that runs out like the fingers of a hand. We had landed on the point farthest from the Hudson's Bay House. A tramp through the woods did not lessen our sopping wetness, though it was impossible to add to it – like the sponge, we had reached our full absorptive limit. Dripping from hats to boots, we entered the little Hudson's Bay store and presented our water-soaked letters of introduction for the manager.

Guests at a house three hundred miles from anywhere, without warning of mail or wire, are no light consideration for a housekeeper where help cannot be hired; and a child had been born that very morning in the home of the manager.... The mother heard that two women had arrived and would not rest till we came across to the house. That gives an idea of what Hudson's Bay Company hospitality means. You can liken it to nothing but that of old baronial lords, who welcomed to their hearth all comers who were not enemies.... Two hours later, dry and glowing warm, we sat down to such a dinner of wild game as money could not buy in the hotels of New York or London; and that dinner was prepared by little girls not fourteen years of age.

Only two white families live at Cumberland House, so that the fort more closely resembles the old-time fur post and shows fewer innovations than any other on the Saskatchewan....

The third morning at Cumberland House we awakened to a rose-pink sunrise and blue waters calm as glass. It was not a scene one can quickly forget. The whole reserve seemed to be afloat on the lake like freed prisoners. There were the blue company canoes with white band round under gunnels. There were the red birch canoes of the Indians banded in tar, paddled by tousle-headed urchins and happy-faced women in colored shawls, and bronzed hunters out for a crack at the ducks on the near swamps. We glided away from the fort, waving to the children on the shore far as we could see them, and followed down Tearing River over riffling rapids for the main Saskatchewan.

"We glided away from the fort, waving to the children on the shore far as we could see them..." The front gates at the Hudson's Bay Company post at Cumberland House, Saskatchewan, 1900.

Until 1966 Cumberland House could not be reached by road, but that summer Edward and Margaret McCourt drove in, sharing the roadway, still under construction, with "assorted items of road machinery of appalling dimensions and power" apt to crush them into the roadbed. But it was the Saskatchewan River that awed them.

> *And close at hand and often visible through the forest screen flows the river – a broad, dark, and splendid stream, a little subdued, to be sure, by the Squaw Rapids Dam, but still an impressive spectacle in a world where all things are shaped to a godlike scale.*
>
> *And it is here that, to the man who has wandered widely over Saskatchewan, the omnipresence of the great river at last strikes home. Omnipresent is the right word to describe a river which, like a deity, is everywhere and at the same time isolated, remote, non-involved. For no matter where one encounters the Saskatchewan – even in Saskatoon where it [the South Branch] splits the city in two – or on what terms, it seems to have little concern with the affairs of men. It goes its remote and lonely way, drawing farther and farther away from all settled places, until, out of an almost uninhabited wilderness, it empties at last into the vast reservoir of Lake Winnipeg more than twelve hundred miles from its source.*

More than two centuries after Alexander Mackenzie, who passed by the House en route to the Barren Lands, Maxwell Finkelstein travelled in his wake: "Two days hard paddling up the North Saskatchewan River, past endless marshes that look like they belong more in Africa than in northern Saskatchewan," brought him to a current of the Saskatchewan and fellow canoeists "canoeing a continent."

It's July 29. Todd, Chris and I head up the shallow Tearing River, one of three outfalls of the North Saskatchewan from Cumberland Lake. Brenda, Eric and Kumar take the main channel in the motorboat, to Cumberland House, where they will wait for me. The Tearing River is the route that Mackenzie took. Today, it is very shallow and rocky, another result of the Squaw Rapids Dam. In Mackenzie's time, much more water came down this channel. We cheer at the first piece of granite – a harbinger of the Canadian Shield....

Where the Tearing River spills over a small boulder dam at its outlet from Cumberland Lake, Chris and Todd head north. I sit on the rocks and watch them grow smaller....

I head west, along the shore of Cumberland Lake, to the community of Cumberland House. I can see the radio antenna only a few miles away. The south shore of Cumberland Lake is a vast marsh, and I paddle mile after mile along the rushes and see no town. The radio antenna faces to the east. I keep paddling, until I round a point and can see the main channel of the North Saskatchewan. I turn back and paddle along the shore again, all the way back to the Tearing River (that's a total of about 25 km, or 15 miles). I turn back to the west and begin poking my way along the rushes. I have not gone too far when I see a motorboat pop out of the bulrushes. It is Brenda, Eric and Kumar. They're wondering what's taking me so long.

"We thought maybe you had stopped for a nap," Brenda says.

"No," I shrug. "Just lost again in the prairie marshes."

"That pole with the gull sitting on top," says Eric, "is the marker for the channel."

"Oh, man," I say, exasperated, "I passed that gull twice already."

We head down the Bigstone River to Cumberland House. In Mackenzie's time, it was on the shore of Cumberland Lake, in full view of arriving brigades. The town is in the same place, but the lake has moved in the last two centuries, so that the settlement is hidden in the alluvial plains and marshes between Cumberland Lake and the Saskatchewan. Most of the change has occurred since the building of the Squaw Rapids Dam. Without the annual summer flood, Cumberland Lake is disappearing, quickly filling in with silt dumped by the Saskatchewan to become a vast marsh.

October 27, Monday. Today the slaughtering of the Cattle commenced, we killed today a cow and an Ox for our share; leaving one Cow still to kill tomorrow. The Ice floating in large fields. Shut up 7 Pigs.

October 28, Tuesday. Sent two men across the river to go and kill the young Cow of Isaac Bignell's, and bring over the meat. The rest of the day they were cutting up Yesterday's meat.

October 29, Wednesday. The weather keeps cold, and the river floating down large fields of Ice. We are preparing for the winter as well as we can for now the winter has come and no mistake about it....

November 2, Sunday. The people are still crossing but it is rather dangerous yet as they cross in canoes and large pieces of Ice floating in the river.... – The Diary of the Reverend Henry Budd 1870-1875

THE PAS
Where the River Narrows

The city of The Pas was originally named after the Cree W'Paskwayak, meaning "where the river narrows," or "like a wooded narrows," which evolved into Opasquai, then Pasquai, then *Le Pas,* and finally The Pas. It now comprises three distinct communities: the town of The Pas, Opaskwayak (Swampy) Cree Nation, and the rural municipality of Kelsey.

Once the Hudson's Bay Company opened York Factory on Hudson Bay in 1684, the river systems in the north and northwest became the shipping lanes of the fur trade, with canoes travelling from the prairies and boreal forests to York Factory to trade with the company. The area on the Saskatchewan River delta and its confluence with the Pasquia River was a site of annual feasts of the Swampy Cree and Ojibway and a traditional meeting place of Native trappers and English and French fur traders. Henry Kelsey travelled with Indian trappers returning inland from the Bay as

"In The Pas we edge through pedestrians and traffic. We've moved dramatically from a world of timber, through waterfowl and trapping country, across farmland, and into this." Dog races – 7 miles an hour, 200 miles non-stop – at Le Pas, Manitoba, ca. 1915.

early as 1690. Wave upon wave of explorer, adventurer, and trader, collaborating with the Woodland Cree in the business of exporting fur to Europe, followed in his tracks.

In 1734 French fur traders from Montreal arrived by canoe at Lake Winnipeg; by 1741, Louis-Joseph Gaultier de La Vérendrye, son of Pierre, had located the confluence of the Saskatchewan, Pasquia, and Carrot rivers; between 1743 and 1750, the French operated Fort Paskoyac on the Saskatchewan River and Fort Bourbon near its mouth at Cedar Lake, both in today's The Pas area. In response, the HBC began sending its men farther inland, skipping The Pas to build Cumberland House. (The company did return to The Pas in the 1870s to build a steamship port.)

Alexander Henry the Elder arrived at the mouth of the Saskatchewan on October 1, 1755, ascended the river and found at The Pas a Cree village of some thirty families. His nephew,

Alexander Henry the Younger, working for the North West Company, sailed into the mouth of the river in August 1808 on his way to Cumberland House.

By 1846, artist Paul Kane was enjoying home-made bread baked from the wheat raised at Devon Mission, established in 1840 by Anglican Rev. Henry Budd, whose first concern was the building of a school for Cree and Métis adults and children. The Catholic mission, established in 1887, built a hospital.

Eighty-seven families frequented the site in 1870. In 1876, the Canadian government bought the townsite from the Cree band, who moved across the river to a reserve set aside under Treaty 5.

At the beginning of the twentieth century, the settlement was able to take advantage of the mining, logging, and commercial fishery that opened up in the north. Linked to the Canadian Northern railway line, The Pas could advertise itself as "The Gateway to the Great Northland," a trans-shipment point between Aboriginal communities, mines, and lumber camps and the growing commercial centres to the south. The town of The Pas was incorporated in 1912. In the 1970s, a government-sponsored pulp and sawmill complex was built, now owned by Tolko Industries Ltd.

The annual Trappers' Festival began in 1916. Northern Manitoba's biggest Indian Days has been celebrated annually since 1971; in 1994 the Opaskwayak Cree Nation was the site of the first-ever Cree Nations Gathering. Money from a land claims settlement was invested in a hotel, high school, hockey arena, and the region's largest shopping mall.

"Then up ye river I with heavy heart did take my way…"

On July 10, 1690, Henry Kelsey, who had spent most of his life on Hudson Bay, travelled down the Hayes River from Hudson Bay on his astonishing journey to the western plains. His job was to "call, encourage, and invite, the remoter Indians to trade with us," as authorized by the Governor of York Factory, George Geyer. En route, he camped with his Native guides near present-day The Pas, a site he named Deerings Point, for Sir Edward Deerings, then deputy governor of the HBC. By way of a journal of his travels, he wrote a ninety-line poem, one of the very first strictly literary exercises in Saskatchewan River country.

Jon Whyte not only reproduced Kelsey's dogged lines but wrote his own, interlinear commentary on them as a kind of counterpoint: two poets, same landscape, some three hundred years apart.

Speaking to himself, he speaks to us

In sixteenth hundred & ninety'th year
I set forth as plainly may appear
Through Gods assistance for to understand
The natives language & to see their land
And for my masters interest I did soon
Sett from ye house ye twealth of June

Out of isolation

Then up ye river I with heavy heart
Did take my way & from all English did part
To live amongst ye Natives of this place
If god permits me for one two years space

Seekwan
and the trumpeter swan returns
the long-beaked whimbrel shores to summerhome
curlews whisper in the lengthening dusk and dawn of
spring

as seekwan is noise again
nostril twitching odours from the snow's melt
the sun felt is seekwan
beneath the daily climbing sun
seek wandering
eyes rise
to the blunt horizon
it is
spring rivulets creeks flooding anew rivers flowing
forcing their ice to pack, crush, melt, overflow,
rumbling the heart stirring in the bosque of
seek wondering
spring in the spring of birds and their song returning
buds, birds, cubs, calves, fawns and dawns warm
and incredible in the sparkle, ooze and hues of green,
seeping, washing waters and the rotting mosses' reek
seek wander
and be born again beyond
the sun setting lustwandering
no time for rest
stir, step, stride, walk, wander, follow, pursue,
sequent seekwan

Between the tangent drawn aslant the dream's nivation
of sense: the way things seem: locus of history about
a centre
a vision forming landscape
a manner of seeing
in the current of circumstance
by the south branch of the middle road

French-English Relations

Lawrence Burpee, editor of *The Journal of Anthony Henday,* points out: "As Henday is the only British explorer or trader known to have visited Fort Poskoyac, or indeed any of the French forts west of Lake Superior, up to the close of French rule in Canada, his description of the fort, with his account of meeting with the French traders, is of exceptional value." A succeeding generation of explorers constantly refer to the ruins of the old fort; even as late as 1808, some traces were visible to Alexander Henry the Younger.

Paddling up a river emptying into Moose Lake, Henday finally reached the Saskatchewan River, or Keiskatchewan as he spells it, and the following day came to "a French house," Fort "Basquea" (Paskoyac) at the mouth of the Pasquia River. This place, now known as The Pas, he admitted had been "long a place of Trade belonging to the French." No hard feelings: he was invited to stay for tea by its commandant, Chevalier de La Corne. A year later, he stopped again.

> *22. Monday. The Musketoes are now intolerable, giving us neither peace day nor night; paddled 14 miles up the River West, when we came to a French house. On our arrival two Frenchmen came to the water-side, and in a very genteel manner, invited me into their house, – which I readily accepted. One of them asked me if I had any Letter from my Master, and where, and on what design I was going inland. I answered I had no letter, and that I was sent to view the Country, and intended to return in the Spring. He told me the Master and men were gone down to Montreal with furs; and that they must detain me till their return. However they were very kind; and at night I went to my tent, and told Attickashish, or Little Deer, my Leader, that had the charge of me, who smiled and said they dared not. I sent them two feet of tobacco, which was very acceptable to them....*

From her vantage point writing in the late 1940s, Marjorie Wilkins Campbell reflected on the long and confusing history of the name of the Pasquia.

Probably the next time fur traders stopped at the Pasquia fishing grounds they found another Indian village or no village at all. The Indians frequently moved their camping grounds, sometimes following game, sometimes for sanitary reasons, or because of a mere whim. But the mouth of the Pasquia, like that of the Carrot not far to the west, is a natural choice for tenting or townsite. For many years The Pas mission gave the place its name, combining a French and an English word. When the railway finally threw a huge bridge across the Saskatchewan on its way to Churchill on Hudson Bay, Le Pas or The Pas – it is given both French and English spelling by the Canadian post office – became one of the most northerly and important towns in the country. It has been called Fort Pascoyac, Basquea, and Pasquia. Probably it got its name originally from the Chevaliar du Pas who was with La Vérendrye; in some early records the river is referred to as La Rivière du Pas.

With both French and English being used all the time and both mixed with a certain amount of Cree, words were easily confused. The old Hudson's Bay Herald *claimed that English settlers had naturally translated du Pas into "of the Pas." Du Pas might have been a better name for the town, Le Pas, "the step," having no particular meaning, and The Pas even less. But there it is, on all the maps, on railway timetables and airway schedules. The town's most enterprising newspaper, the* Northern Mail, *chose to place itself in The Pas, Manitoba.*

Alexander Henry the Younger, employed by the North West Company, first arrived on the Saskatchewan in 1808, in charge of the fur trade in that territory. On August 20, 1808, he had his first view of the river – whose every flow and eddy he came to know from repeated travels until 1811 – when he entered its mouth, poled up to the Grand Rapids, and canoed through its tedious delta marshlands.

On August 23, at daybreak, the weather was fine and clear, but he could see a gale forming directly ahead. Coues adds in a footnote that in 1775, Alexander Henry the Elder (1739-1824), uncle to Henry the Younger, travelled this same waterway on his way to the prairies, and wrote of coming upon "the Pasquayah village" of thirty circular tents and a chief "who obtained rum by show of force, after a stormy conference."

> *We renewed our search for a channel, and after a tedious spell of hauling the canoe over mud, into which the men more than once sunk up to the middle, we made an entrance, up which we proceeded. At eleven o'clock we found a spot of dry land, called Pine Island, where we put ashore for a much-needed breakfast, after the disagreeable night and morning we had passed. The country appeared to be the same as below – a continuous marsh on every hand, though wood is seen at a distance on both sides. Having refreshed ourselves, we embarked and stemmed the strong current, soon coming to where the banks began to be covered with willow and other wood; but the same marshy country continued. To all appearance the banks are overflowed annually, about mid-summer, in consequence of the melting of snow on the Rocky mountains, and this inundation makes mud into which one sinks knee-deep. We shot a number of wild fowl during the day – outardes, ducks, pelicans, and some pigeons, of which we saw great numbers; and at sunset we put ashore to camp. During the night we heard dogs barking up the river.*
>
> *Aug 24th. At an early hour we were upon the water. We soon came to a tent of freemen, but only stopped to learn who*

they were. At eleven o'clock we entered the main channel of the Saskatchewan, and soon after reached the Pas. This place may be called the first real dry land we have found since we left Lac Bourbon.

"The most solemn vows..."

In 1837, Reverend Henry Budd was a teacher in a parish school in Red River, and was moved as schoolmaster to Cumberland House in 1840. His stay there was brief: a few months later he was in The Pas at Devon Mission, where he laid the groundwork for future mission work in the North. He was ordained the first-ever Native Canadian Anglican priest there in 1853. "The most solemn vows that man can make to God on earth are now upon me," he recorded in his journal, "...and the eyes of my countrymen are daily upon me."

In 1950, writer Lyn Harrington visited The Pas and its Anglican church, St. Andrew's, then a hundred years old and serving only a fraction of its earlier congregation. Recalling that Sunday morning of Budd's ordination, she wrote that "somehow they managed to squeeze eleven hundred into the church. I can't imagine how they got them in! But Henry Budd's ordination was a great occasion."

By 1854, The Pas resembled a little village: trappers trapped muskrat, people set up sugar camps for maple syrup and hunted waterfowl and goose. Young men left in spring to work on the fur brigades to the Bay. Women and children cultivated gardens and operated fisheries. Most older converts were able to read and write in Cree syllabics. By 1857 there were 746 baptisms listed in the register and about 100 communicants. But Rev. Henry George, posted to The Pas in 1856, was unimpressed: "Abject poverty surrounds us here. The most opulent among them [the Indians] can only boast of his house, ox and horse together with a small patch of potatoes."

Budd was transferred to the mission at Fort à la Corne from 1857 to 1867. He hesitated to return to The Pas because of the rumours of the deterioration of the village and the relapse of the Indians there "back to their heathenish ways," he wrote in his journal. But back he went. Where he had once grown wheat and barley now lay exhausted land; half the Indian village had rotted or burned, and the villagers were living in tents with no livestock or gardens.

By 1870 he had rescued it from complete ruin. The farm now produced a surplus of food; three young men were being prepared for the ministry, and converts even proselytized among the local Indian bands.

"Into the Far North, which is just beyond"

In the spring of 1894, the surveyor Joseph Burr Tyrrell returned, on a repeated visit, to the Barren Lands, accompanied by a young Scottish sportsman, Robert Ferguson, an aide-de-camp of Governor-General Lord Aberdeen, who helped finance the expedition. Ferguson brought along a pair of carrier pigeons and two rifles.

Tyrrell hired three canoemen in Winnipeg and three more in Selkirk, then took a steamer to Grand Rapids and the mouth of the Saskatchewan River. On June 23, he launched the canoes and started up the river. The first hurdle was to get past the rapids. (The incident even made the national press.)

> *June 24. Sunday.*
> *As soon as we could get our canoes loaded we started to the Demicharge rapid. The birch and my canoe got up safely, but the third with Mr. Ferguson in it, and which Bell [a canoeist] was tracking, shot out into the rapid, and before anything*

could be done it filled and capsized and went down the rapid into Lake Cross, with many of its contents floating about. Ferguson and John Harper [canoeist] swam ashore. I at once sent up for one of the other canoes and as soon as it could be unloaded it came running down the rapids and out into the lake after the overturned canoe. Everything was brought ashore at a point when it was found that Ferguson's two rifles had gone, Bell's dunnage and blankets, 200 to 300 lbs of bacon, 40 lbs of sugar, while the tea and beans were thoroughly soaked. The carrier pigeons which were in a box tied on top of the canoe were drowned. It was a bright breezy day and we spread things out to dry till noon.

The party continued up river to Cedar Lake and the trading post where they were able to buy new guns. On June 27 they struggled against the heavy current. On June 28, they arrived at The Pas. For a surveyor, the most exciting thing on view was not the human settlement – if indeed there was one – but the "grey friable till" of the river bank.

Both Marjorie Wilkins Campbell and Lyn Harrington wrote of their impressions of The Pas, in books published in 1950 and 1951 respectively. Campbell wrote very energetically about the shops of The Pas that "outfit Indian trappers and big mining men and scientific expeditions into the Far North, which is just beyond" (evoking the adventures of the Tyrrell expeditions, perhaps). "Where the early traders and Indians hauled their heavy sledges great tractors today skiff up the snow and ice." She noted the "beady-eyed Cree youngsters," who raced around the Henry Kelsey monument in factory-issue blue jeans instead of deerskin, and the Indian canoes now fortified by outboard motors. "The future of The Pas is more important than the past."

Harrington agrees, though her visit is a more leisurely one, written up as the stroll about town that it was.

The Pas at first seemed small – but how it had grown in a week when we returned from Churchill! Now it seemed north. By then, it seemed 'way down south in the banana belt,' as the northerners said. By then, having seen the great marshes which will no doubt be drained for wheatland someday, the forests which sustain the woodworking industries at The Pas, the great hydro-electric power which the rivers of the north will one day supply, we could understand how some residents visualize their town as the future "Edmonton of Manitoba."...

The Pas has long been the distributing centre for northern Manitoba, the true "gateway to the north." Until 1930, all transportation was by winter road or summer canoe trail to the trading posts of the north, and The Pas was known as the place "where rail meets trail." In that year, the Hudson Bay Railway was officially opened. It is operated by the Canadian National Railways, and is the fulfilment of a dream long standing....

In the long northern summer evening, we strolled past the new Post Office, beyond the dome of the curling rink, down to the bank of the broad Saskatchewan. Opposite is the Indian village with its little steepled church. Near the bridge is a cairn commemorating Henry Kelsey's journey through this region. Kelsey was the first white man to gaze on the Canadian prairies and to miscall the bison of the plains, buffalo:

"Discoverer of the Canadian prairies. In memory of Henry Kelsey, Hudson's Bay Company fur trader and explorer; the first white man to travel inland from Hudson Bay to Eastern Saskatchewan and to see the Canadian prairies, 1690-1692. The first white person to record the existence of the musk-ox of the north, the buffalo herds and the grizzly bears of our plains."

Tomson Highway's novel *Kiss of the Fur Queen* is set in 1951 in northwestern Manitoba. Forty-three-year-old Abraham Okimasis of the Eemanapiteepitat Cree Indian reserve, caribou hunter, fur trapper, and fisherman, has just won the World Championship Sled Dog Race, the first Native musher to do so in its twenty-eight year history. He is as astonished as the crowd. Journalists move in on him as he lies exhausted at the finish line, their "large red moving mouths, prying, babbling in this language of the Englishman, hard, filled with sharp, jagged angles."

The setting is the loosely disguised Trappers' Festival in The Pas, a celebration of the coming spring that poet Birk Sproxton, also from northern Manitoba, described as "a drunken bash, a ripsnorter, a tear, an orgy."

One of the rewards awaiting Abraham for winning the dog sled race is a kiss from the winner of the festival's Fur Queen. The contestants have been poked and prodded and paraded around town (a version of The Pas), cut ribbons, sliced cakes, and given out prizes at the muskrat-skinning contest. Now, finally, the runners-up have been announced and the chairman of the judges' panel steps before the roaring crowd.

> Then the chairman of the judges' panel cleared his throat, thumped his chest, opened his mouth, and boomed into the microphone: "And the Fur Queen for the year 1951 is..." One could hear the ticking of watches, the buzzing of incandescent lights, the hum of loudspeakers. "Miss Julie Pembrook, Wolverine River, Manitoba. Miss Julie Pembrook!" The young woman burst into a blissful smile, stepped up to the chairman to receive her cash award and a bouquet of white roses. The radiant Miss Pembrook was draped not only with a white satin sash but with a floor length cape fashioned from the fur of the arctic fox, white as day. She had her head crowned with a fox-fur tiara ornamented with a filigree of gold and silver

beads, and was photographed a thousand times until all she could see was stars and showers of stars. And the crowd roared until the very ceiling of the building threatened to rise up and float towards the planet Venus.

In the thick of this raucous, festive throng, Abraham Okimasis stood, Cree gentleman from Eemanapiteepitat, Manitoba, caribou hunter without equal, grand champion of the world, unable to move, barely remembering to breathe....

Then Abraham Okimasis saw the sash, white, satin, draped across the upper body of a young woman so fair her skin looked chiselled out of arctic frost, her teeth pearls of ice, lips streaks of blood, eyes white flames in a pitch-black night, eyes that appeared to see nothing but the caribou hunter alone. And then the caribou hunter and the woman in white fur began floating towards each other, as if powerless to stay apart. And as the two moved close, Abraham Okimasis could decipher the message printed across her sash, syllable by syllable, letter by letter: "The Fur Queen, 1951."...

And then the Fur Queen's lips began descending. Down they came, fluttering, like a leaf from an autumn birch, until they came to rest on Abraham's left cheek. There.

After what seemed like years to Abraham Okimasis, she removed her lips from his cheek, expelling a jet of ice-cold vapour that mushroomed into a cloud. Her lips, her eyes, the gold and silver beads of her tiara sparkled one last time and then were swallowed by the billowing mist.

There was a time in The Pas when the town was clearly divided into two parts, one white and one Aboriginal, with the Saskatchewan River running between them. As the Aboriginal Justice Inquiry of Manitoba noted in 1999, "the division of the community was more than geographical in 1971," the year that nineteen-year-old Helen Betty Osborne, a Cree from Norway

House, was murdered by four white youths who were not brought to justice for another sixteen years. But when journalist John Stackhouse went to a hockey game in The Pas in November 2001, he discovered that healing had begun.

Less than a minute into game two of the provincial finals, the home team's star forward, Justin Tetrault, a Métis, takes a pass from captain Terence Tootoo, who is Inuit, and blasts it home. Before Mouse can flash the red goal light, the Gordon Lathlin Memorial Centre is shaking with the sound of air sirens, noise makers and the woodsy voices of 1,248 people from two communities that once were the most racially divided in Canada. To the sounds of Bachman Turner Overdrive – You Ain't Seen Nothing Yet *– the Crees, Métis, white and a few Inuit embrace in the stands, and on the ice.*

For the next two hours, the native-owned arena facing The Pas across the river will rock with delirium as the Opaskwayak Cree Nation Blizzard trounce the Winkler Flyers and build a commanding lead in their run for a third straight provincial championship – a feat not seen in Manitoba in nearly 30 years.

But in the racially mixed stands, most people know that the Blizzard's sudden dominance is about much more than hockey. In this isolated town and reserve, which straddle the Saskatchewan River 600 kilometres northwest of Winnipeg, the team has built a bridge that people once thought impossible.

It was near the arena site 30 years ago that a Cree woman named Helen Betty Osborne was murdered after being sexually assaulted by men from The Pas.

The horrible crime was followed by one of the darkest periods for race relations in modern Canadian history, as the entire population of The Pas joined in a notorious conspiracy of silence. For a decade, townspeople who knew the killers refused to identify them. Finally, one of the attackers, unable to bear his guilt any longer, went to the police.

Just a generation later, the native-owned Blizzard has used a mixed-race team and integrated home crowd to start a new chapter for both the town and reserve.

"I really believe it was the hockey club that bridged the divide," says Gary Hopper, mayor of The Pas, which is one of the Blizzard's top corporate sponsors. "When the team was announced, people bought season's tickets [he has two] and all of a sudden there was a white sitting beside a native, a total mix, and new friendships developing."

Amazingly, he says, "you would be hard pressed to find two communities that get along better."...

In his themed collection of poems, *Headframe*, Birk Sproxton drives with his friend Mark along the Saskatchewan River in a twentieth-century version – automobile, highway, motels – of the voyageur and trader travelling downstream to the Hudson's Bay Company posts on the Bay. There are familiar signposts along the way: the Pasquia Hills, Cumberland House, the journal of Robert Hood – naval officer, explorer, painter, and surveyor, who, in the spring of 1820, was in the area around Cumberland House to study the natural history and to record meteorological observations – and Carrot River. They are now driving from the Pasquia Hills to The Pas.

> We enter the flood plain and dikes sneak slowly out of the ground, worming flat to the river. "I was reading the map the wrong way," Mark says.
>
> The road changes from gravel to construction gumbo and then to asphalt. The plain so flat anything vertical draws the eye. Hundreds of blackbirds dip and reel behind tractor and

plough. We're watching the birds when a dog attacks from the ditch. I swerve and curse, nearly lose control. A fury to match Batoche mosquitoes.

In The Pas we edge through pedestrians and traffic. We've moved dramatically from a world of timber, through waterfowl and trapping country, across farmland, and into this. Mark sees a store sign, laughs, and copies it into his notebook vertically, the way it hangs on the store front.

Mining
Blasting
Trapping
Supplies
Sporting
Goods & (in larger letters)
FURNITURE

Three hundred years of European-Indian contact on a single piece of wood: trapping (still) in the centre of things, mining and blasting noisy on the northern limits, sporting goods and loud furniture here at the southern edge, The Pas, a playful and domesticated stepping (stopping) point, Kelsey's place of resonance.

In our turn we step across the Saskatchewan toward the mining world, and stop for gas at the shopping centre on the north shore. It is owned by a local Indian band and their prices are better than those in town. A Shell station operated by native people trading (mainly) with Canadians of European descent. (We're driving a Toyota, Ha.)

The smooth highway drive is mesmerizing, and puts the poet in a romantic, musing frame of mind, thinking about those other travellers of a couple of hundred years earlier, on the river.

*From: Alexander Henry
Tells a Trading Story*

I don't think that Kelsey or Chatique or Henry or Hood gave much of their energies to moving the paddle, slipping from side to side, stroke stroke stroke, slip, *stroke stroke stroke. I think they let the paddles pull the canoe and let themselves drift into labyrinths of thought and image, their moving forward (moving into, moving thru) driven by fingers of hunger in the gut, the remembered taste of lake trout, or the echo of the smell of a woman swinging thru the nostril hairs, beating time on hammer and anvil, riding the stirrup, stirring the blood to a drum beat,* slip *stroke stroke stroke*

And when they told of their travels and adventures, were the right words there, ready-made, to be bundled up for buying and selling?

(And which is the adventure: the going or the telling, the listening or the hearing? slip, stroke, stroke.

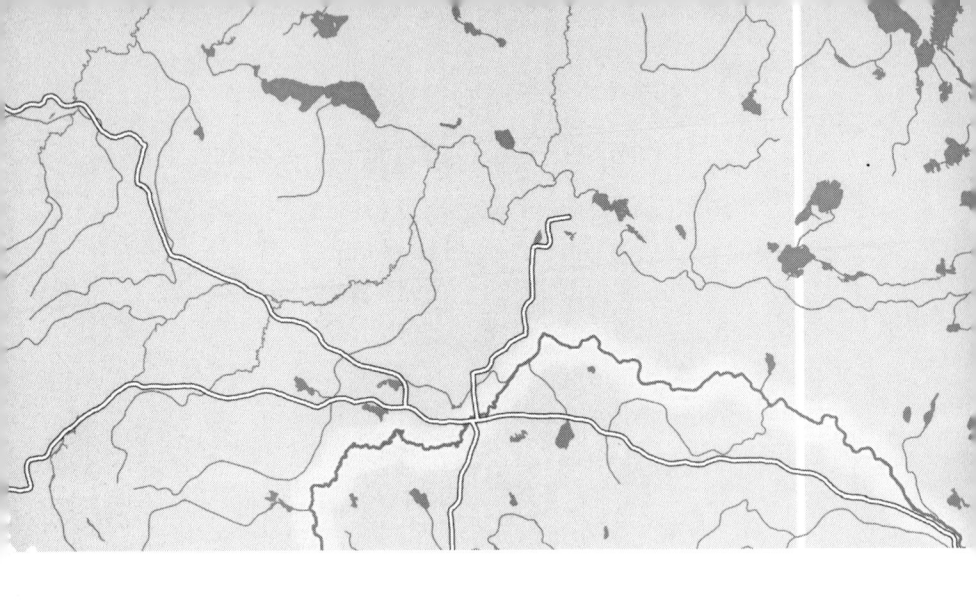

At daybreak the weather was clear, but we had a gale directly ahead. We renewed our search for a channel, and after a tedious spell of hauling the canoe over mud, into which the men more than once sunk up to the middle, we made an entrance, up which we proceeded. – Alexander Henry, *The Manuscript Journals*

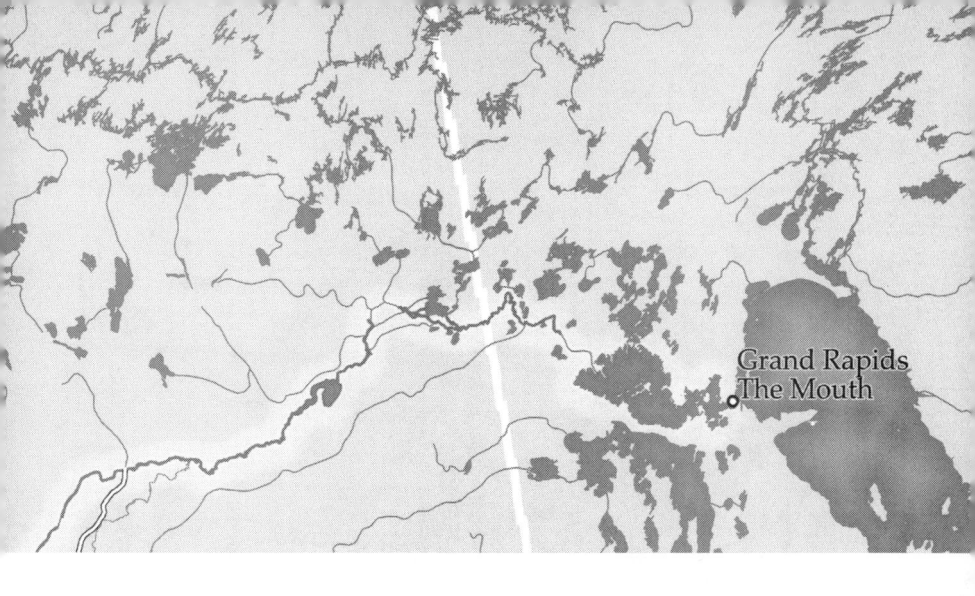

GRAND RAPIDS AND THE MOUTH OF THE SASKATCHEWAN
The Great Marsh

From the confluence of its north and south branches at The Forks (about 50 kilometres east of Prince Albert), the Saskatchewan River flows another 600 kilometres east through Tobin Lake and Cumberland Lake in Saskatchewan, and past The Pas in Manitoba to empty into Cedar Lake, having drained 340,000 square kilometres along the way. However, this is still not the end of the story, for its waters are considered to be carried through Cedar Lake finally to empty into Lake Winnipeg at Grand Rapids.

Grand Rapids, and the mouth of the river, are really at the beginning not the end of the narrative of the Saskatchewan River, for it is from this point (and upriver another 1939 kilometres to The Forks) that the fur trade was launched into the heart of the continent in the eighteenth century.

Come spring and icebreak on the river, the boatmen packed the canoes and York boats with three-tonne loads of pelts for the long haul down river to the supply stores of the company on the shore of Hudson Bay. Launching a York boat on to Saskatchewan River at Prince Albert, Saskatchewan, June 1907. J. Revillon, for Revillon Freres Company freighting.

The large canoe used by the North West Company on the river was manned by five or six paddlers and carried about 1,000 kilograms of cargo. The Hudson's Bay Company's York boat, manned by eight to fifteen Orkney oarsmen, was flat-bottomed and equipped with a sail, and could carry loads of three to four tons.

But first the voyageurs had to get through the rapids, a transportation bottleneck at the river's mouth.

The first post here was known as Fort Bourbon, built by Chevalier de La Vérendrye, son of the famous explorer, Pierre, in 1741. Many routes into the North and Northwest converged here – York boats and river steamers brought goods up from Fort Garry on the Red River and down from York Factory on Hudson Bay that would be shipped upriver to Edmonton House via Cumberland House and Fort Carlton – until the construction of the trans-Canada railway made the water route obsolete.

In 1877, the Hudson's Bay Company built a small tramway at Grand Rapids to "portage" furs and supplies from the steamers on Lake Winnipeg to boats on the Saskatchewan. This has been called the first railway constructed in western Canada.

Nowadays the Saskatchewan River serves a new purpose: a hydroelectric generating plant at its mouth began producing power for the provincial power grid in 1965. The reserve of the Chemawawin Band was flooded and the community relocated to the southern shore of Cedar Lake, 40 kilometres west of Grand Rapids, at the new townsite of Easterville.

Adventurer or trader, missionary or surveyor, first they had to get through the rapids, the Grand Rapids – 5 kilometres of wildly turbulent water – at the mouth of the river. After that, it was clear sailing, so to speak, right up to Fort Edmonton, it having been stated in the House of Commons, and cited by James Hector, that, "with this one exception you could take a vessel of considerable size up to the foot of the Rocky Mountains."

Alexander Henry rowed into the mouth of the *Saskatchewoine* on August 20, 1808 – or is it the *Saskatchewaine, Saskatchewine, Saskatchewane,* or *Saskatchewin?*, which are variations on French pronunciation of the Aboriginal name, *Kisiskatchewan, Kisiscachiwin,* or *Kejeechewon.* Editor Coues decides on the "present fixed form," the one that we now have, the *Saskatchewan.* In all cases, however, it means "swift flowing river." The early French explorers had their own name for it, derived from a place along the river, in such forms as Poskoiac, Pasquayah, and Pasquia. And, when it denotes its passage as the great thoroughfare of water into the interior, it is Rivière du Pas, Rivière aux Pas, and Rivière du Pass.

At sunrise that August morning in 1808, the wind had abated on the lake and the travellers shot a few ducks and gulls before hoisting sail "with a pleasant breeze aft." They will soon be at the rapids, formed, Coues tells us, by the passage of the river over a limestone plateau.

> The Saskatchewan is here a fine broad stream, which enters the lake with a swift current from S. to N. The lake shore to the N. and N.W. appears more elevated than that upon the S. We crossed to the W. side, and proceeded up river with poles to the foot of the first rapids, where we took towing-lines up the Grand rapids. Here we saw the vast number of pelicans that resort to the foot of those rapids, where I am told there is an abundance of fish of various kinds, particularly sturgeon. Loaded canoes generally discharge half their load, and make two trips, but as my canoe was light we went on without loss of time, and after a tedious walk along a rough, ugly shore, with loose stones, and perpendicular banks of clay, we arrived at Grand Rapid portage. The opposite [south] shore is almost a continuous high bank of limestone of different colors. Before the canoes arrived I went to see as much as I could of the falls or rapids that occasion this portage. I did not find them nearly so bad as I had been given to understand. There is no particular fall, but a succession of descents, especially on the S. Side, where I would not hesitate a moment to run down a canoe with half her cargo. On my return I found the canoes had arrived, and the people were busy carrying the baggage over the portage. This is upward of a mile long, but would be a very good road, were it not that the H.B.Co. from York Factory, with large boats, are in the habit of laying down a succession of logs from one end to the other for the purpose of rolling their boats over. This is a nuisance to our people, frequently causing accidents which endanger their lives. It was quite dark before we got everything over. We experienced much annoyance from mosquitoes, and had rain during the night.

The Saskatchewan River delta would bedevil generations of canoeists after Alexander Henry. The place where the Saskatchewan finally discharges into Lake Winnipeg does not seem to have altered much in historic times, but the delta is constantly changing, as its channels appear and disappear in mud flats and muskeg that barely emerge above water level and shift after every storm and flood. It took Henry and his party two days to find the main channel.

Nevertheless, on August 22, 1808, Alexander Henry entered the delta from Cedar Lake, sliding his canoe through "nothing but an extensive marsh covered with reeds and long grass." His editor adds that "our author flounders through this swamp," but at first all seems fine sailing, "as the wind continued fair." However, as the sun set, the wind increased, "and we had all our canoes could bear."

> *When it became quite dark we found ourselves astray, unable to discover the entrance of any one of the numerous channels of the Saskatchewan which empty into this lake. We repeatedly ran aground upon mud banks, and could see no dry land on which to camp. Having paddled and dragged our canoe about until my men were quite harassed, I ran her in among the rushes for the night. Here we were sheltered from the wind, which continued to blow hard. I sounded and found eight feet of water. Soon after we had taken our berths for the night a thunderstorm from the W. made our bad situation worse.*

On the 1858 expedition to the Assiniboine and Saskatchewan rivers with geologist Henry Youle Hind, surveyor John Arnot Fleming wrote his own narrative of their return to the Red River settlement in Manitoba from Fort à la Corne. It was a journey that concluded dramatically in the run of the rapids before spewing out into the "wonderful calm" of the lake.

> *In running the rapid we followed as closely as possible the instructions given to us by our old guide on the Plains (John Spence), who had often piloted the old North-West Company's North canoes down its entire length. In attempting, according to his directions, to cross from the north to the south side of the*

rapid in order to get into what was reported to be the best channel for a small canoe, such was the fierceness of the current, and the turbulence of the great surges and breakers in the middle, that we were nearly engulfed; and although every nerve was strained we were swept down with impetuous velocity, and did not get near the other side till we were about three quarters of a mile below our starting point. We were then impelled with astonishing swiftness along the south side of the torrent, often in dangerous proximity to the rugged wall of rocks bounding the channel, and now and then whizzing past – almost grazing – sharp rocky points jutting out into the river against which the thundering waters seethed and foamed in their fury. During the descent the voyageurs exerted themselves to the utmost of their strength, and evinced an admirable degree of coolness and dexterity....

We entered Lake Winnipeg at sunset, and camped not far from the mouth of the Saskatchewan, upon a narrow spit of gravel, separated from the wooded shores by a marsh. The night was clear and beautiful, and the lake wonderfully calm. From our bivouac, where we lay with cramped limbs outstretched on the shingle-beach, could be seen the great headland "Kitchi-nashi," vanishing away to the south-east in the far distant horizon. A view very extensive and beautiful, but which betokened many hours of paddling and tracking out of the direct course to Red River. To the east and north the only limit to our gaze was the dim horizon of the great lake which lay tranquilly outspread before us like an unruffled sea.

"The great lone land"

In January 1871, William Francis Butler stood on the banks of the Saskatchewan River at Cumberland House and mused on the fact that "five hundred miles lay between me and Red River" – his destination – "five hundred miles of marsh and frozen lakes, the delta of the Saskatchewan and the great Lakes Winnipegoosis [sic] and Manitoba." He had just made the acquaintance of the first genuine train of sled dogs he had seen on his long journey to the Rocky Mountains and back – "I had suffered so long from the wretched condition and description of the dogs of the Hudson's Bay Company" – and was so impressed that he purchased them at once.

On January 31 he set out with "this fine train of dogs" accompanied by Bear, a Swampy Indian with his own team, whom he would later "award" as voyageur, snowshoer, and camp-maker "second to none." It was a journey he would reflect on as the riverine rite of passage through the vast, ennobling interior.

> *During five days our course lay through vast expanses of stiff frozen reeds, whose corn-like stalks rattled harshly against the parchment sides of the cariole as the dog-trains wound along through their snow-covered roots. Bleak and dreary beyond expression stretched this region of frozen swamp for fully 100 miles. The cold remained all the time at about the same degree – 20° below zero. The camps were generally poor and miserable ones. Stunted willow is the chief timber of the region, and fortunate did we deem ourselves when at nightfall a low line of willows would rise above the sea of reeds to bid us seek its shelter for the night. The snow became deeper as we proceeded. At the Pasquia three feet lay level over the country, and the dogs sank deep as they toiled along. Through this great marsh the Saskatchewan winds in tortuous course, its flooded level in summer scarce lower than the alluvial shores that line it. The bends made by the river would have been too long to follow, so we held a straight track through the marsh, cutting the points as we travelled. It was difficult to imagine that this many-channelled, marsh-lined river could be the same noble stream whose mountain-*

> birth I had beheld far away in the Rocky Mountains, and whose central course had lain for so many miles through the bold precipitous bank of the Western prairies....
>
> Glad was I then, on the night of the 7th, to behold the wooded shores of the Cedar Lake rising out of the reeds of the great marsh, and to know that by another sunset I would have reached the Winnipegoosis [sic] and looked my last upon the valley of the Saskatchewan....
>
> He who has once tasted the unworded freedom of the Western wilds must ever feel a sense of constraint within the boundaries of civilized life. The Russian is not the only man who has the Tartar close underneath his skin. That Indian idea of the earth being free to all men catches quick and lasting hold of the imagination – the mind widens out to grasp the reality of the lone space and cannot shrink again to suit the requirements of fenced divisions. There is a strange fascination in the idea "Wheresoever my horse wanders there is my home;" stronger perhaps is that thought than any allurement of wealth, or power, or possession given us by life. Nor can aftertime ever wholly remove it; midst the smoke and hum of cities, midst the prayer of churches, in street or salon, it needs but little cause to recall again to the wanderer the image of the immense meadows where, far away at the portals of the setting sun, lies the Great Lone Land.

William Francis Butler missed the excitement of the Grand Rapids because he travelled in the winter over frozen terrain; but the intrepid journalist Agnes Laut, a century after John Fleming and Henry Youle Hind, relived the fury of the raging water in her touring canoe – an experience she recounts with characteristic exuberance and relish.

It was early September. They had paddled past Indian camps on Cedar Lake and the white-log store of the Hudson's Bay

Company with its red door while a crimson sun set the lake on fire. "The wind lulls at last," she remembered, "the first time, I think, since we left Edmonton five weeks ago." The willow bushes are turning gold, the air is tangy with chill, but they still camp out, under a sky she likens to a Turner painting, "all bronze and gold mist with a blood-red sun." Midday the next day they swirled out to the river again, the canoe bouncing about "giving prelude of what was to come in Grand Rapids."

> *Where the waters of half a continent become hemmed in between rock walls not a third of a mile wide with such steep descent over huge boulders and rocky islets that it could not be any steeper without being a cataract – I can promise you that things are doing in the river. We heard the far wh-u-sh; then the wild roar; then the full-throated shout of triumphant waters! You think your blood will not run any faster at that sound after having run more rapids than you can count? Try it! We sat up from our sluggish easy postures. Then the river began to round and rise and boil in oily eddies and the canoe to bounce forward in leaps without any lift on our part – then a race-horse plunge; and we are in the middle of furious tumult! The Indian rises at the stern and leans eagerly forward. Even the cool Sexsmith admits, "This is a place where the river really does things – isn't it?" But the Indian is paddling like a concentrated fury. Sexsmith drops to the bottom of the canoe to lower weight and prevent rolling. Then we shoot forward into a vortex of whirling sheaves of water.*
>
> *"She-strong-she-*ver*'-strong rapid," shouts the Indian as we swirl past one rock and try to catch the current that will whirl us past the next. "Pull-pull-pull-a strong paddle," and we rise to a leap of wild waters, have plunged into the trough, and are climbing again before some one can remark "Say, I don't like ever sidling to rapids."*

There is a rock ahead about the size of a small house, where the waters are breaking, aquiver and white with rage. The Indian had risen again. "Stop," he yells, "don't paddle! Let her go!" but he, himself, is steering furiously as we graze past out to the bouncing waves! So we run the Big Rapids for about a mile, and then ride a third rapid in a long easy swell, and swerve in to the north or left side where a tramway of three miles leads past the last and worst of Grand Rapids. Only a riverman who knows this last rapid as other men know their dining-room will conduct parties down. As we did not care to risk our expensive canoe, I sent the Indian overland to the Hudson's Bay manager asking for the tram-car to convey our kit across to the lake.

A walk of three miles over punky logs along that very foot trail which the fur brigades used to follow of old brought us suddenly to an opening on the high cliff commanding the Big Chute. It is a wild scene – the wildest of any rapids I know in America. The river bed is scored and torn to tatters with rage. Huge rocks split the torrents and throw them back in furious turmoil. These are the rocks where so many countless craft have come to grief when the crews failed of strength or nerve for the big lift past the undertow. Great rockets of spray rise above black pools with deafening roar.

Gary and Joanie McGuffin

In 1983, Joanie and Gary McGuffin, two youthful, self-confessed Canadian adventurers, set out by canoe from the Gulf of St. Lawrence to the Bering Sea, a 13,200-kilometre journey that would begin and end in a salt sea. It made practical sense to travel from east to northwest, over two seasons, so that the upstream and "big lake" paddling would be undertaken in the longer ice-

Grand Rapids: "The Saskatchewan River once plunged to its journey's end through a limestone gorge descending almost 60 feet in one three-mile section."

free season, putting them into The Pas halfway along their route by autumn. The draw toward northern Saskatchewan was rooted in Gary's father's own youthful expedition toward Lake Athabasca.

As far as Gary and Joanie McGuffin knew, no one had paddled from as far east to as far west in an open canoe. In preparation, they read the diaries and journals of Alexander Mackenzie, J. W. Tyrrell, Samuel Hearne, and David Thompson. Half their route crossed the same waterways the North West Company traders plied between Montreal and Lake Athabasca.

On the Lake Winnipeg-Saskatchewan River waterway, they made a visit to Grand Rapids, as had generations of travellers and adventurers before them. "Here," they write, "the Saskatchewan River once plunged to its journey's end through a limestone gorge descending almost 60 feet in one three-mile section." No more.

The McGuffins got out of their canoe to have a look.

Thirty feet below us lay the Grand Rapids riverbed; the turbulent rapids reduced to a mere trickle and the thunder of white water silenced forever. In the early 1960s Manitoba Hydro harnessed Grand Rapids for hydroelectric power. The power dam was constructed to receive the water flow through turbine generators while a control dam was built to stop the water flow through the original gorge. The headpond formed behind the dam is one of the 10 largest man-made lakes in the world.

Before striking out across the enormous forebay area of Cross and Cedar Lakes, we decided to have a closer look at the operation of the Grand Rapids generating station. A brochure was thrust into our hands by one of the operation's supervisors. It featured a stylized picture of the Manitoba watershed and described every stretch of moving water in the province, including the Nelson and Churchill rivers.

"We're not even half done yet!" the supervisor boasted....

Water power is always taken at a cost to the natural environment. In central Manitoba, where the topography provides no natural barriers against a dam's reservoir, a vast lowland prairie region had been wiped out by flooding. A high price was paid for the construction of the Grand Rapids dam. The flooding destroyed thousands of acres of wildlife and their habitat and the livelihood of the local native people.

Mrs. Huff, a resident of Grand Rapids, remembered what it was like before the river was dammed. The sound of the water thundering through the gorge was an essential part of the community. She referred to that day when Manitoba Hydro first cut off the Saskatchewan's flow through the gorge as an unforgettable time. The great obstacle at the convergence of the fur trade routes to the northwest had been completely obliterated....

It seemed a strange world we paddled through on Cross and Cedar lakes, with their forests of dead timber and thou-

sands of stumps and deadheads. Hundreds of weird shapes in burnished silver wood curved and weaved like writhing snakes. Round stumps resembled black bears and tall slender branches looked like cranes. Some even gave the illusion of men fishing. Solid land seemed to be non-existent. Every island was just a fragile construction of driftwood piled up by the wind and waves....

We followed the Cedar Lake shoreline westward. Soon we found that the distinctive landforms marked on our map failed to correspond to the surroundings. The effects of the flooding were becoming quite apparent. Moreover, it was very disconcerting to discover that our chart mapped out the area as it had been before the completion of the dam, using a purple broken line to approximate the position of the new landmarks. Therefore, the chart was highly unreliable for such a low-lying area where it took very little water-level fluctuation to alter the entire landscape. We had the map spread out between us on the deck of the canoe. As we debated the best plan of action, Gary suddenly looked up to see a church spire piercing through the upper limbs of the forest cover close by. We felt certain that this was the original site of Easterville before the dam's construction. Keeping our eyes on the spire, we paddled toward the marshy land, left the canoe and made our way through thick grasses and underbrush to the higher ground.

A church bell, cracked in half, lay in the middle of the clearing as if representing the broken spirits of those for whom it once chimed. A sign hung over the church door proclaiming, "This is none other than the house of God and the gateway to heaven." We stepped into the gloomy interior. Deep silence. The rows of pews waited for a congregation that would never come again.

Two centuries after Mackenzie's birchbark canoes had passed by his home on the banks of the Ottawa River, Maxwell Finkelstein found himself "staring up the river, feeling the river pulling me..."

On May 7, 1997, on a cold, blustery spring day, I carry my canoe, a Verlen Kruger designed craft appropriately named Loon, to the Ottawa River. Here I began my journey, retracing the route of Mackenzie across the continent, with a stuffed toy bear named Sir Alex tied securely to the bow as my lookout and his diaries at hand. My plan – to paddle 3,000 kilometres to Cumberland House, at the centre of the continent, by the end of July. The following year, I would begin on the Pacific Coast and paddle east to Fort Chipewyan in Alberta. The third and final leg would be across Alberta and northern Saskatchewan to Cumberland House. In total the trip would take more than six months and cover more than 7,000 kilometres and 135 portages. A most amazing trip.

July 14: It's been pouring rain all night... Rained 3" the night before. What kind of stupid weather is this for July? I've had it. You go out for a pee, and the tent fills up with mosquitoes.... As I look out of the tent, the vestibule is dripping water drops and mosquitoes. They hang there like stalactites, water drop, mosquito, water drop, mosquito.... No parking space left empty. There is no sound but the hiss of rain on nylon and water, and the whine of mosquitoes.... I'm in a BAD MOOD....

Today, Cedar Lake, its water level raised by the dam at Grand Rapids, is a vast swamp, sixty miles long, and too wide to see across. "Ghost" forests of dead, silver tree trunks define the old lake's shores....

My challenge is to find the mouth of the Saskatchewan River, somewhere in the middle of Cedar Lake. For thousands of years, the muddy Saskatchewan River meandered through this flat land, depositing sediments along its banks, until the banks became the highest land. When the dam was built, the water rose over the river banks, spreading out over the land. The river now enters the new, expanded Cedar Lake somewhere in its middle, still flowing through now submerged banks. If you miss the mouth, you could paddle twenty miles or more, and end up in the tangle of dead trees that rims the reservoir. To make things even more difficult, large patches of rushes grow in the middle of the lake, obscuring the view from a canoe. I don't really know what I am looking for - some clue, some anomaly. I paddle in the general direction of the old river mouth, and see a lone weathered tree trunk. I paddle to it, and see another, and another, and if I squint, I can imagine that these line up to follow a submerged meandering riverbank. I follow the tree trunks, like joining the dots of a puzzle, until they end at a clump of willows. I puzzle about where to go next, when I notice that the water beneath me is muddier than before, and I am drifting backwards. I have found the river, or rather, it has found me.

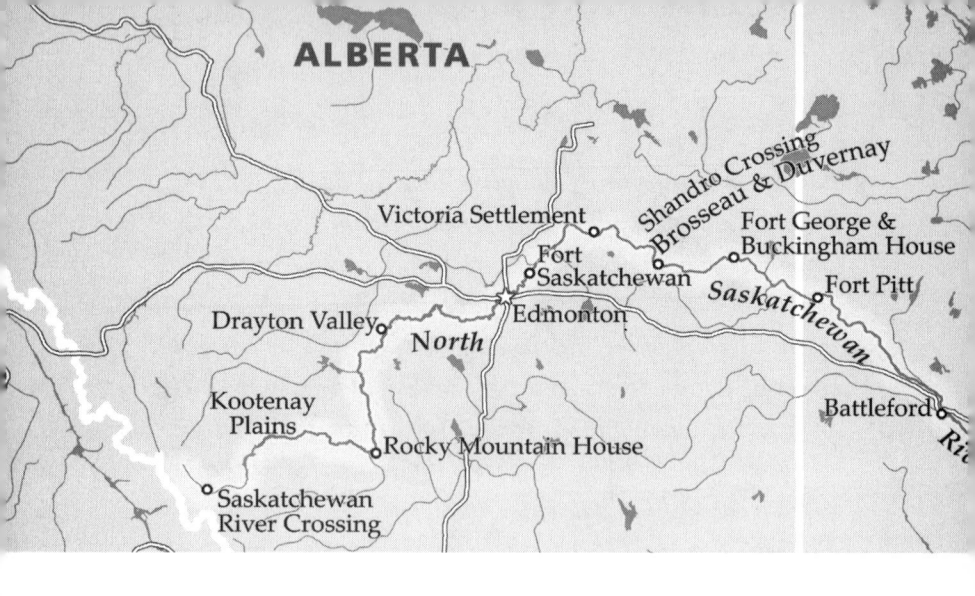

"[The river] is an environment where the sturgeon, creatures from prehistory, swim just below the buzz of motorboats, where mineshafts from the days of coal power crumble under the erosion of its banks.... It's a crime scene, a make-out spot, a playground, a habitat, a form of transportation. A view. We wouldn't be here without it." – Editorial, *SEE Magazine*, July 3 – July 9/03.

CONCLUSION
What Is A River For?

In July 2004, Calgary-based writer and journalist Andrew Nikiforuk went hiking in the Rockies to have a look at one of the more historic and much photographed glaciers, Peyto. "Only after crossing a log bridge, scrambling up a moraine, climbing for another kilometre and entering a broad alpine bowl did I finally spy it: a gnarly and unhealthy block of ice not much more than a kilometre long and gushing like an open fire hydrant."

Peyto Glacier is melting faster than it can accumulate snow, each year losing some 3.5 million cubic metres of water, roughly the amount the city of Edmonton consumes in a day. With summers getting warmer and winters getting shorter, 70 per cent of Peyto's ice mass is already gone. Peyto now collects only about one-sixth of the snowfall it received annually from 1955 to 1975. "Before long," Nikiforuk warned, "we'll be talking about our glaciers, and the mighty rivers they once fed, in the past tense."

Robert Rundle, laboriously making his way upstream to Fort Edmonton in 1840, whipped out his Bible on entering the muscular main channel of the Saskatchewan and read Isaiah 60: "Arise, Jerusalem, rise, clothed in light; Your light is come and the glory of the Lord shines over you." Night time view of downtown Edmonton, Alberta, with the North Saskatchewan River, 1980.

According to some rough estimates, Canada houses about 44 per cent of earth's glaciers, including the Peyto, the Robson, and the Saskatchewan. These have now wasted away to such a degree that "they have spit out debris that includes trees 3,000 to 8,000 years old," and their meltwaters flush out long-banned and deeply-buried chemicals such as PCBs and DDT.

Ecologists of our water systems note that lake levels are dropping, wetlands are drying, and ground water is declining. Politicians propose damming more and more rivers to store up water for the drought that is sure to come, apparently not a good idea: reservoirs behind dams expose even more water to evaporation while thirsty urban populations grow, and industrial agriculture and the energy sector compete for strained water sources. The shrinking glaciers could stop supplying cities with water in the next thirty to fifty years. Competition among the three provinces that depend on the Saskatchewan River for their needs will become fierce. The master agreement on apportionment of water in the Saskatchewan-Nelson watershed is already being tested as the water that is supposed to be flowing into Manitoba is being diverted into the industrial cattle and crop irrigation systems of Saskatchewan and Alberta.

The major rivers of the western prairies are now reduced to 20 to 70 per cent of their historic flows by the pressure of human activity. Today's river water carries herbicides, pesticides, oils, animal wastes, fertilizers, detergents, PCBs, pharmaceuticals, and hormones, along with bacteria and protozoans that are increasingly resistant to chlorination. In June, 1998, grade eleven biology students from Edmonton rafted from Dawson Park to the Gold Bar Wastewater Treatment Plant, where they tested the water downstream from the plant's outflow. They found it contained phosphates (found in some detergents) and ammonium nitrates (in urine) but were nevertheless impressed the river wasn't quite the "dirty, brown toilet water" they had expected it to be.

The human footprint on the river is enormous and approaching the catastrophic. But that isn't the only story. In the Canadian Council for Geographic Education's teaching resource on the Internet, we are reminded that, in human geological terms, the communities of the Canadian plains have been the source of political freedoms and innovations in health care and co-operative enterprise. Think of the Saskatchewan River, then, as a cultural as well as agricultural and geological zone: here be prairie populists and socialists, medicare visionaries, and Wheat Pool radicals. And now there are "water vigilantes": environmental think-tanks, "watershed alliances" that monitor fish tissues for chemical residues, river basin "partners" who plant seedlings and monitor local stream conditions, public forums or "community cafés" that solicit information on water use and water flow through the Saskatchewan River aquatic ecosystem.

In the 1993 film by Wayne Schmalz, *Saskatchewan,* he narrates that "thousands of people continue to live and work along the Saskatchewan and yet there is no central mythology associated with it that binds them together. For many, the river is simply a barrier to be crossed, a watery line to cross over and forget." But we have always had poets amongst us, who have generated mythologies, or at least metaphors. For example, a descendent of the voyageurs tells Schmalz that, for his people, "the river was a road but a road that wasn't man-made, it was a pathway, it was an artery, a place that you followed and didn't determine where it went." The river as continental circulatory system? Even dammed and polluted and prettified, the Saskatchewan River acts out its own dramatic cycles of the primal and natural: it floods its banks, it erodes its trench, it dries up on its own bed.

Of course, the river hasn't really been following its own course since the heyday of dam-building in the 1960s and 1970s. One of them, the Bighorn in Alberta, partially flooded the Kootenay Plain, homeland of the Stoney Indians and a paradise of chinook-sweetened meadowland for which all explorers and traders prayed in gratitude, stumbling out of the bush.

Perhaps in unconscious revenge against the industrial exploitation of the waterways, we have probed a deeper meaning by imagining our ideal relationship with the "untamed" river as adventure, nostalgia, romance of the rugged, a process that began with the first urban canoeist or hiker who had no reason to be there. Metaphors of transportation and passage produce mystic currents that "will take you where all things at last must come together," in Glen Sorestad's "Rivers," or, like the River Styx of

Greek mythology, to your death. If you get in a canoe and ride it, wherever it's going, you're going with it.

What Is a River For?

The river flows both ways
where it reverses, unexplorably shifts
[...]
Until still points of spinning
nothing
nothing turn and wheel away
Time vanishes, in the flow of metaphor.

Jon Whyte, "Homage, Henry Kelsey"

What is a river for? In historic times, it has been primarily an economic instrument of human interests, whether among First Nations before European contact – the Cree, previously a forest people, arrived on the plains via the Saskatchewan River, bearing trade goods for exchange with the Gros Ventre and Blackfoot – or after, between them and the Euro-Canadian bosses of the fur trade. For those who actually laboured on the river, the water represented the full spectrum of energies from mind-numbing tedium to deadly maelstrom that swallowed them whole. The river was also the only means of efficient transportation and communication along the east-west grid of the continent. In those days, the river always flowed two ways, upstream to the furs, downstream to the fort. (Even today there are Métis communities along the North Saskatchewan who say they are "going east" when they go out shopping.) In the literature associated with this period, the river is still a force of Nature independent of human will upon it; humans adapted to it, and shared the rhythms of its dramatic cycle. It could be awesome in its primal forcefulness: Reverend Robert Rundle, laboriously making his way upstream to Fort Edmonton in 1840, whipped out his Bible on entering the muscular main channel of the Saskatchewan and read *Isaiah 60:* "Arise, Jerusalem, rise, clothed in light; Your light is come and the glory of the Lord shines over you."

The Australian John Foster Fraser, author of *Canada As It Is,* stands in downtown Edmonton in 1905, and fancies he stands at a portentous border between a city growing up behind his back – "There are six thousand people in Edmonton; they have electric cars along their main streets" – and a journey north "to grim death," or at least to those gaunt men lingering at the end of the fur trade, "stalk[ing] the wild and frozen lands searching for skins." It has come to this.

All this changes with the coming of the telegraph and railway when, quite suddenly, the rivers are deserted of their traffic except for a brief period of steamboats and recreational paddlewheelers. Bridges become extensions of the railway tracks, and a whole literature of the drama of the perilous river crossing disappears (it will reappear in the age of tourism). In fact, the river all but disappears from human interest in the new age of agriculture and then urbanization – "the river steams / a touch of hell / but it's only the power station / pouring waste energy into the water," sardonically writes Peter Stevens in "On The Edge."

But there is another consistent metaphor – river as communiqué, linking us up – that is also, in this digital age, as literal as it is metaphoric. Harold Innis, the pre-eminent historian of the fur trade, began with his observation in 1956, in *The Fur Trade in Canada,* that "a system of communication" was established among the trading posts and supply depots of the fur companies, citing David Thompson's *Narrative:* "There is always a Canoe with three steady men and a native woman waiting the arrival of the annual Ship from England to carry the Letters and Instructions of the company to the interior trading houses." The east-west waterways of "the trade" etched the outlines of a future nation: the "distinctive economy" of the fur trade had laid down the communications grid that incorporated as a single coherent unit the east-west orientation of the British and French colonies distinct from the colonies that would become the United States.

Map-making played an interesting role in laying out this communications "grid": in the case of Native cartography, records of journeys and the shape of tribal territory might be drawn on the skins of elk, beaver, bison, or deer as the primary means of "transferring intelligence" from one generation to the next; in the case of European exploratory maps, following lines of longitude and latitude, they were "declarations of land ownership." A considerable amount of "translation" was required as explorers, ignorant of territory deeply familiar to the Native populations, "could gain information only by finding European equivalents for the map structure and topographical details which the Natives had provided," writes Professor Barbara Belyea.

Nowadays, when the post-exploration era of national dreams held in common, of metaphors of shared revelation, yields to a time of fractious difference, poets see the challenge differently. Not even the ambition of conservationists contains everything we want, for the ceremonial and sacred places of the First Nations, such as their mountains and rivers, have become destinations of eco-tourism, "protected" even from the Aboriginal celebrants themselves. No, the best we can hope for is to talk it over. The writer and philosopher B. W. Powe boldly asserts in *A Canada of Light* (1997): "The old Canada is ending.... In the rampage of what seem to be terminal disagreements and divisions, rising confusions and intolerance, we can be certain only of this: our time and place have been electrified.... I perceive communication to be the value of Canada." For this to be true, no one needs a real river. Still, according to Hugh MacLennan, Canadians lost their soul when they left the rivers.

But these ideas are not what's on my mind when I stand at the window and rejoice, at spring break-up, at the liberated surge of water that has gushed out of the mountains and into this embrace of the loamy, bushy banks at Edmonton. I am with writer Hugh MacLennan in 1961 at the Columbia Icefield: "...and when you stand on the little bridge over the North Fork and look at that lithe, frigid stream, not glacial-green but milky from limestone, so narrow in August that a broad-jumper could clear it, you can have a strange sensation when you think how far this water has to go."

It has got to me, and then it rushes on.

We stop on its bridges and banks, staring down into the streaming current of murky water racing east, mesmerized by that quality a river has if we stand looking at it in one spot: a thing that is passing us, going somewhere else, leaving us and not coming back. Wherever it's going, we're not going with it. We may be lost in contemplation but it does not stop its run to the sea. That's what rivers do. That's what this river is for.

Historical Biographies

HOWARD ADAMS (1926-2001) – Métis scholar and activist Howard Adams was born in St. Louis, Saskatchewan. His Métis identity, which lay at the root of his intellectual and political radicalism, was reinforced by family stories of great-grandfather Maxime Lepine and great-uncle Ambroise Lepine, who stood with Métis leader Louis Riel during the North-West Rebellion. In his 1975 book, *Prison of Grass: Canada from the native point of view,* Adams dedicated the work to Maxime, "a guerrilla warrior who sacrificed his life in the struggle against imperialism." Nevertheless, Adams joined the RCMP briefly, before moving on to university education and a teaching certificate.

In 1995 he published *A Tortured People: The Politics of Colonization.* He was awarded the National Aboriginal Achievement Award.

REV. EDWARD AHENAKEW (1885-1961) – Edward Ahenakew's grandfather and great-uncles had hunted and trapped for Fort Carlton post. Edward was born on the Sandy Lake Indian Reserve, educated in Saskatchewan mission schools, and then at theological colleges in Toronto and Saskatoon. As an Anglican clergyman and eloquent speaker and writer in Cree and English, Ahenakew travelled and spoke to meetings on reserves in his Saskatchewan diocese and at church synods across Canada. He edited a monthly newsletter written in Cree syllabics and regularly published Cree "Trickster tales" in *American Folklore* magazine. Much of his work was published posthumously in *The Beaver* and *Saskatchewan History.*

His best known work is the collection, *Voices of the Plains Cree,* an account of tales related to Ahenakew by Chief Thunderchild in 1923.

Shaken by the toll that the 1918-19 flu epidemic had taken on the reserves, Ahenakew began studying to be a medical doctor when he himself fell ill, and was sent by the diocese to recover his health on Thunderchild's Reserve. The entry in his journal for February 17, 1923, begins: "Made arrangements with the Chief to tell me Indian traditions." A sympathetic review of the book at the time of publication described Thunderchild as a man who looked back at "the fierce and vanished freedom he enjoyed in his youth" when he was one of the "River People," the Cree who lived along the North Saskatchewan River.

REVEREND HENRY BUDD (C. 1812-1875) – A Hudson's Bay Company clerk, farmer, teacher, and eloquent orator in Cree, Henry Budd was also the first Native Canadian to be ordained in the Anglican Church in North America.

Orphaned as a child, Budd was educated at the HBC's Norway House where he was soon "capable of reading the New Testament and repeating the Church of England Catechism correctly." After clerking and farming, he was persuaded to teach at a parish school in Red River in 1837. It was explicit Anglican Church policy to encourage Native participation in mission work. In 1840, spurred perhaps by a rumour that the Roman Catholic Church intended to "fix a priest" at Cumberland House that same year, Budd was sent to Cumberland House District to begin a new school and mission for the Indians, and then down the Saskatchewan River to W'passkwayaw or Paskoyac (The Pas). He was ordained an Anglican priest there in 1853. "The most solemn vows that man can make to God on earth are now upon me," he recorded in his journal, "and the eyes of my countrymen are daily upon me."

MARJORIE WILKINS CAMPBELL (1901-1986) – An immigrant with her parents to the Qu'Appelle Valley in Saskatchewan in 1904, Campbell developed a deep interest in early Canadian history. She wrote historical fiction, juvenile literature, and biographies, and contributed to a number of magazines. But it was her nonfiction book *The Saskatchewan* that won her literary acclaim and the Governor-General's Award for creative nonfiction in 1950. Later books, fiction and nonfiction, focussed on the history of the fur trade, probably her favourite subject, among them *The Nor'Westers* and *McGillivray, Lord of the North West*. She became a Member of the Order of Canada in 1978.

BLISS CARMAN (1861-1929) – The son of United Empire Loyalists who settled in New Brunswick, William Bliss Carman was educated at the Universities of New Brunswick, Edinburgh, and Harvard, before settling into a comfortable literary life in New York City, where he edited literary journals and the *Oxford Book of American Verse* (1927) as well as publishing volumes of his own poetry. After 1909, he lived in Canaan, Connecticut, where he died, but was returned home to be buried in Fredericton.

ELLIOTT COUES (1842-1899) – A medical doctor, Coues was also an ornithologist (he collected birds in Labrador for the Smithsonian Institute in Washington, D.C., and wrote *Key to North American Birds* in 1872), as an army surgeon during the American Civil War, a naturalist on United States government surveys, including the U.S. northern boundary commission that surveyed the line along the forty-ninth parallel from the Lake of the Woods to the Rocky Mountains, and as editor of twelve volumes of some of the most celebrated travel narratives of the North American West.

PETER ERASMUS (1833-1931) – Born in the Red River settlement of Manitoba to a Danish farmer father and a Cree mother, the prodigiously capable Erasmus was educated by the Anglican church and moved to The Pas in 1851 to assist his uncle, Rev. Henry Budd, as a schoolteacher in the mission. Next he worked as a teacher and missionary among the Aboriginals around Fort à la Corne. He then agreed to work as guide and surveyor with James Hector of the Palliser Expedition in 1858-59 in the passes of the Rockies. (Hector named a mountain after him in the North Saskatchewan River Valley.) He helped build the Methodist mission at Smoking Lake, where he served as an interpreter, guide, builder, and freighter for Rev. Thomas Woolsey, then moved with the McDougalls – George,

Elizabeth, and John – to the mission at Victoria. In 1876 he acted at Forts Pitt and Carlton as chief interpreter for the Plains Cree in their negotiation of Treaty 6. For years he worked for the Canadian government's Department of Indian Affairs as a farming instructor and teacher and labourer on reserves, still trapping and fishing, hunting and trading, for as long as he could. Just before his death he dictated his memoirs to Henry Thompson, a Métis journalist, narrating a life that spanned the days of the buffalo hunt on the open plains of Rupert's Land to urban congestion in the prairie provinces.

LYN HARRINGTON (1911-1991) – A prolific freelance writer of magazine articles, an indefatigable worker on behalf of writers' organizations, and a knowledgeable traveller, Lyn Harrington and her photographer husband, Richard, travelled through much of Canada as well as abroad, resulting in books such as *How People Live in Canada, Greece and the Greeks,* and *How People Live in China,* many of them for young adults.

FLORENCE PAGE JAQUES (1890-1972) – Jaques and her husband, Francis Lee Jaques, nature artist, wrote and illustrated eight books together, including the early classic *Canoe Country* (1938), about their honeymoon canoe trip through the boundary waters of Minnesota and Ontario, and *Snowshoe Country* (1944), about northern Minnesota. They became celebrated public champions of the Boundary Waters region, water and woods, and its traditional inhabitants, trappers and lumberjacks. Among Florence Jaques's fans were the members of the Minnesota Women's Press, who assured her readers that "whether you're an active or vicarious woodswoman, you can count on Jaques to bring you into the forest with her...."

PAUL KANE (1810-1871) – Although Paul Kane asserted repeatedly that he was born in Toronto, his biographers have no doubt he was actually born in Ireland and came to Toronto as a child with his immigrant parents in 1819. He had some education and art lessons but really learned "on the job" as a decorative sign and furniture painter. For five years he travelled in the American Midwest painting portraits. According to his passport, he then shipped out of New Orleans to Marseille in 1841, and travelled around Italy, sketching. His meeting with the American artist George Catlin in London was fortuitous: Catlin was exhibiting his paintings of Indians from the American prairies and foothills of the Rockies, and arguing that it was the artist's duty to record the faces and customs of the Aboriginals of the West for posterity. In 1845, back in Canada, Paul Kane set off alone to travel from Toronto to the Great Lakes en route for the Pacific coast, determined at least to sketch Aboriginal portraits before these First Nations were, he feared, rendered extinct by the coming White settlement.

He was granted access to the Hudson's Bay Company's posts and their officials by HBC Superintendent Sir George Simpson himself. In May 1846 he reached Fort William at the head of the Lakes, and from there, travelling with the company's fur brigades, he headed westward for the Pacific, which he would reach in December, by canoe and foot, horseback and snowshoe and sled. He kept a travel diary and sketch book, recording in both his careful observations of Native everyday life, from buffalo hunts to encampments to women spinning and weaving. A version of these was published in 1859 as *Wanderings of an Artist among the Indians of North America.* According to the Dictionary of Canadian Biography, "No other pictorial record of the early Canadian northwest even approaches the wealth or magnitude of that made by Kane."

EDWARD WILSON (TED) KEMP (1924-1977) – The son of a United Church minister who served in several small Alberta towns, Ted Kemp was a highly lauded teacher in Edmonton public schools and at the University of Alberta's Department of Philosophy, and was one of the first academic staff at the new Grant MacEwan College in Edmonton in 1971. He was always an adventuresome thinker and drawn to the outdoors.

JAMES G. MACGREGOR (1905-1989) – Born a Scotsman and educated an electrical engineer, James G. MacGregor worked faithfully for twenty-one years with Canadian Utilities Ltd., all the while writing about western Canadian history, a subject about which he felt passionate. He retired in 1970 and turned to writing full time about Alberta history. An indefatigable researcher as well as popularizer, he wrote twenty books, several of them best-sellers. He served a long term on the editorial board of the *Alberta Historical Review* as well as governor of the Glenbow Institute in Calgary. In 1973 he was named a member of the Order of Canada. Literary historian George Melnyk considers his biographies about Father Lacombe, John Rowand, and Senator Hardisty "yet to be surpassed."

HUGH MACLENNAN (1907-1990) – Over a fifty-year-long professional writing career, MacLennan wrote seven novels, three works of nonfiction, and three collections of essays, all of which established him as one of Canada's most important writers in the twentieth century, and earned him five Governor General's Literary Awards. He was born in Glace Bay, Nova Scotia, then moved as a boy to Halifax. Educated at Dalhousie University and at Oxford and Princeton, he taught in the English Department of McGill University in Montreal from 1951 to 1980. Internationally acclaimed, he was one of the postwar generation of writers in English Canada who helped shape a Canadian literature distinctive from the world of British and American writing. The renowned American critic Edmund Wilson recognized this as early as 1960. Writing of MacLennan's essays, he described "a point of view surprisingly and agreeably different from anything else...in English..., a Canadian way of looking at things...a self-confident detachment in regard to the rest of the world."

ELIZABETH MACPHERSON (1937-2001) – Elizabeth emigrated to Canada from Budapest, Hungary with her parents as a young girl. She met her husband, Andrew, at McGill University, where she was studying biology, and together they performed Arctic field studies. The Macphersons moved to Edmonton in 1970 and Elizabeth became a guide and researcher at the Provincial Museum of Alberta and in 1988 began work at the Musée Héritage Museum in St. Albert. As assistant curator, she developed a strong personal and professional interest in the genealogy of Alberta's Métis and authored *The Sun Traveller*, a history of the Calihoo family, in 1998.

ELI MANDEL (1922-1992) – Eli Mandel was born in Estevan, Saskatchewan, served overseas with the Canadian Army Medical Corps, received a university education in Saskatoon and Toronto, and taught English at the University of Alberta and York University from 1961 to 1986. Besides his poetry – *Idiot Joy* won the Governor-General's prize for poetry in 1967 – Mandel made outstanding contributions to literary scholarship.

EDWARD MCCOURT (1907-1971) – An Irishman raised on an Alberta homestead and later a Rhodes Scholar, Edward McCourt was professor of English at the University of Saskatchewan in Saskatoon (1944-1971), where he encouraged a generation of students to strike out as writers as well as scholars. As an editor and writer of fiction, he advocated passionately for the Canadian West in such classics as *Music at the Close* (a novel about the Depression era) and *The Canadian West in Fiction* (the first critical study of the literature of the prairies).

JOHN CHANTLER MCDOUGALL (1842-1917) – Rev George McDougall's mission work among the First Nations of the Canadian northwest was a pioneering effort of the Christian ministry there. His son, John McDougall, an ordained minister of the Methodist church, set up a mission at Pigeon Lake, Alberta, under his father's tutelage, followed by missions among the Stony, Cree and Blackfoot people in Morley, southern Alberta. A prolific writer, he wrote of his experiences with keen observation and obvious respect for the Native peoples among whom he worked – fluent in

Cree, he was an interpreter and mediator at the Treaty Six and Seven negotiations, for instance – and hoped that the Christian missions would buffer them somewhat from the drastic encounters with ever-encroaching white enterprise: smallpox epidemics, whiskey trading, hunger, and the arrival of the NWMP.

FRANK MITCHELL (1892-1974) – Frank Mitchell was the son of John A. Mitchell, who had been a partner with Frank Oliver in the *Edmonton Bulletin* and later owned land in Victoria Settlement. John Mitchell worked as Indian agent before opening a general store, grist mill, and a farm implement dealership in 1899. An HBC post until 1883, the store stocked merchandise bought in Edmonton and brought down river by scow. With the influx of immigrants after 1900, Victoria/Pakan revived as a commercial and service centre, a community where families could make a good living operating a general store or livery stable or saw mill.

Young Mitchell was schooled in Pakan and served as a councillor for the municipal district of Smoky Lake in the 1920s. Recognizing the historical importance of Victoria settlement and the need to preserve its memory, he ran a private museum in Pakan that housed his own collection.

PETER REAM (1925-2004) – Founder of the Fort Saskatchewan Historical Society and an ordained minister in the United Church, English-born Peter Ream "will long be recognized as one of the great figures in Fort Saskatchewan history.... He was the first to see that this is a community worth writing about and to do something about that. Without him, the site of the original fort that is the heart of our city might easily be buried under condominiums.... He said he could see history disappearing as he watched, and felt compelled to gather as much as possible right away. That's why he wrote *The Fort on the Saskatchewan* within a year of his arrival here, a book that expanded from 155 pages to 591 as he updated it." (*Sturgeon Creek Post*, 3 Nov. 2004)

JON WHYTE (1941-1992) – Born in Banff, Alberta, where in fact he spent most of his life, Jon Whyte made it his literary business to explore it: its geography, its history, its mythology. Variously a bookseller, editor, book designer, arts journalist, film-maker, local historian, environmentalist, museumologist, and above all poet, he experimented with several different "languages" in his ambition to re-envision the western Canadian landscape. Deeply influenced by his aunt and uncle, the painters Peter and Catherine Whyte, who also lived in Banff, he wrote and edited books of art and photography.

"There's no question," writes one of his editors, Harry Vandervlist, "he became a guiding spirit in Banff from the late 1960s to the 1990s, when it began to shed the last of its Edwardian tourist-village isolation and turn itself into a meaningful centre for artists."

An early version of his poem "Homage, Henry Kelsey" appeared in 1971, the final version in 1981.

Acknowledgements

I am indebted to the Writer-in-Residence program at the University of Alberta, which provided me the time and money to work on a substantial part of *Reading the River,* and to the unfailing helpfulness and patience of the staff of the English Department, especially Kris Calhoun and Marcie Whitecotton-Carrol.

The Alberta Foundation for the Arts provided funding for part of the research. Rick Boychuk, editor of *Canadian Geographic,* encouraged and published an early version of the idea for "Reading the River." I thank Steven and Mary Ann Tymchuk for their expert guidework to their homeplaces on the Saskatchewan, and Rick Kunelius for leading the way along Parker Ridge. The generous assistance of Brenda Niskala in Regina and Marian Hebb in Toronto in the matter of locating copyright holders kept me as sane as possible in the circumstances.

Without Roberta Coulter's attentive and patient work as editor of the manuscript, *Reading the River* would not have found its shape. And thanks to Darcia Dahl, keyboard whiz who was a reader too. – *Myrna Kostash*

Text Acknowledgements

HOWARD ADAMS. Excerpt reprinted with permission from *Prison of Grass: Canada from the Native Point of View.* Copyright © 1975. Howard Adams. Published by Fifth House Ltd., Calgary, Canada

THE REVEREND EDWARD AHENAKEW. *Voices of the Plains Cree.* (Toronto: McCelland & Steward, 1973). Reprinted by permission of the editor, Ruth Buck.

DOUG BARBOUR. "Saskatchewan Drive." Unpublished. Reprinted by permission of the author.

TED BARRIS. Excerpt from *Fire Canoe: Prairie Steamboat Days Revisited.* (Toronto: McClelland & Stewart, 1977). Reprinted by permission of the author.

WADE BELL. Excerpt from *The North Saskatchewan River Book*. (Toronto: Coach House Press, 1976). Used by permission of the author.
GEORGE BOWERING. "The Oil" from *Touch: Selected Poems 1960-1970*. (Toronto: McClelland and Stewart, 1971). Used by permission of the author.
THE REVEREND HENRY BUDD. Excerpt from *the diary of the Reverend Henry Budd*. (Winnipeg:, Hignell Printers. 1974).
MARJORIE WILKINS CAMPBELL. Excerpt from *The Saskatchewan* (Toronto: Clarke, Irwin, 1950).
BLISS CARMAN. "David Thompson" from *Bliss Carman's Poems* (Toronto: McClelland and Stewart, 1931).
AGNES MACKENZIE CARRIERE. Excerpt from "Agnes Carriere, Grandmother." (Regina: *New Breed* magazine, July/August 2002). Reprinted by permission of the Gabriel Dumont Institute.
TONY CASHMAN. Excerpt from *Edmonton: Stories from River City*. (Edmonton: University of Alberta Press, 2002). Reprinted by permission of the publisher.
PAM CHAMBERLAIN. Excerpt from *North of the River*. Unpublished. Reprinted by permission of the author.
PETER CHRISTENSEN. "River Dance" from *Rig Talk*. (Saskatoon: Thistledown Press, 1981). Reprinted by permission of the author.
ELLIOT COUES, Ed. *The Manuscript Journals of Alexander Henry and of David Thompson 1799 - 1814*. (Minneapolis: Ross & Haines, 1897).
MEL DAGG. Excerpt from *The Women on the Bridge*. (Saskatoon: Thistledown Press, 1992). Reprinted by permission of the publisher.
REECE DEMCHUK. Excerpt from hand-written notes. Unpublished. Reprinted by permission of the author.
HUGH DEMPSEY. Excerpt from *The Rundle Journals 1840-1848,* including the introduction by Gerald Hutchinson. (Calgary: Historical Society of Alberta, 1977). Reprinted by permission of the authors.
PETER ERASMUS, as told to Henry Thompson. Excerpts reprinted with permission from *Buffalo Days and Nights*. Copyright © 1999. The Glenbow Museum. Published by Fifth House Ltd., Calgary, Canada
MAXWELL W. FINKELSTEIN. Excerpt from *Canoeing a Continent: On the Trail of Alexander Mackenzie* (Natural Heritage Books, 2002). Reprinted by permission of the publisher.
_____. Excerpt from *Water, Earth and Sky: Canoeing a Continent in the Wake of Alexander Mackenzie: Ottawa to Bella Coola*. Published online at http://www.chrs.ca/Stories/Story05_e.htm.
ROMAN FODCHUK. Exerpt from "Blessing the Waters." From *Zhorna*. (Calgary: University of Calgary Press, forthcoming). Reprinted by permission of the author.
MYRNA GARANIS. Excerpt from *Gracing the Space* (Unpublished, 2004). Reprinted by permission of the author.

DARRIN HAGEN. Excerpt from *The Edmonton Queen (not a riverboat story)*. (Edmonton: Slipstream Books, 1997). Reprinted by permission of the publisher.

LYN HANCOCK & MARION DOWLER. Excerpt from *Tell Me, Grandmother*. (Toronto: McLelland & Stewart, 1985). Used by permission of the authors.

LYN HARRINGTON. Excerpt from *Manitoba Roundabout*. (Toronto: Ryerson Press, 1951). Reprinted by permission of the estate of Lyn Harrington.

GAIL HELGASON. Excerpt from *Swimming Into Darkness*. (Regina: Coteau Books, 2001). Reprinted by permission of the publisher.

TOMSON HIGHWAY. Extracted from *The Kiss of the Fur Queen* by Tomson Highway. Copyright © Tomson Highway 1988. Reprinted by permission of Doubleday Canada and the author.

WALTER HILDEBRANDT. "Fort Battleford's History," from *Heading Out: The New Saskatchewan Poets*. (Regina: Coteau, 1986), Reprinted by permission of the author.

DAVE HOWELL. "Crossroads at Rossdale" from the *Edmonton Journal*, April 4, 2004. Reprinted by permission of the publisher.

BARBARA HUCK & DOUG WHITEWAY. Excerpt from *In Search of Ancient Alberta*. (Winnipeg: Heartland Associates, 1998). Reprinted by permission of the publisher.

LIONEL HUGHES, Excerpt from "From the Ferry to the Bridge to the Twentieth Century." *Saskatchewan Naturally Magazine*, Vol 1, #2. Reprinted by permission of the publisher.

MARY ANN HUSHLAK. "Safe." Unpublished. Reprinted by permission of the author.

FLORENCE PAGE JAQUES, Excerpt from *Canadian Spring* (New York: Harper, 1947)

PAUL KANE. "Wanderings of an Artist," from *Paul Kane's Frontier*. (Toronto: U of T Press,1971)

TED KEMP. Excerpt from "Tender Feet: Raft Down the Rushing North Saskatchewan and Learn." *Rod and Gun*, September 1957. Reprinted by permission of the Estate of Edward Wilson Kemp.

MARIE AND JOHN KOCH. Translated excerpt from Nordegg's German letters, from *To the Town that Bears Your Name*. (Edmonton: Brightest Pebble Publishing, 1995). Reprinted by permission of the publisher.

JOHN LENT. "In the Rear-View Mirror of the Finning Cat" from *The Face in the Garden*. (Saskatoon: Thistledown Press, 1990). Reprinted by permission of the publisher.

JAMES G. MACGREGOR. Excerpt from *Blankets and Beads: A History of the Saskatchewan River*. (Edmonton: Institute of Applied Art, 1949).

———. Excerpt reprinted with permission from *Peter Fidler: Canada's Forgotten Explorer*. Copyright © 1998. Estate of J.G. MacGregor. Published by Fifth House Ltd., Calgary, Canada

———. Excerpt from *John Rowand: Czar of the Prairies*. (Saskatoon: Western Producer Prairie Books, 1978).

IAN MACLAREN. Excerpt from "Do the Aspen Still Tremble? Cultural Memory and Place" from *Museums Review,* Fall 1995. Reprinted by permission of the author.

HUGH MACLENNAN. Excerpts from *Seven Rivers of Canada.* (Toronto: Macmillan, 1961).

ELIZABETH MACPHERSON. Excerpt from *The Sun Traveller.* (St. Albert, Alta.: Musee Heritage Museum, 1998, reprinted from the *Edmonton Bulletin,* February 25, 1888. Reprinted by permission of the Provincial Archives of Alberta.

ALICE MAJOR "Contemplatio" from *Malahat Review,* 2001. Reprinted by permission of the author.

ADELE MANDRYK. Excerpt from "Can the Deepest Mysteries of Creation Be Found in Edmonton's River Valley?" *Express News,* University of Alberta, 7 August 2005. Reprinted by permission of the author.

ELI MANDEL. "From the North Saskatchewan," from *The Other Harmony: The Collected Poetry of Eli Mandel.* (Regina: Coteau Books, 2001). Reprinted by permission of the publisher.

JOYCE MCCART, PETER MCCART. Excerpt reprinted with permission from *On the Road with David Thompson.* Copyright © 2000 Joyce McCart and Peter McCart. Published by Fifth House Ltd., Calgary, Canada

EDWARD MCCOURT. Excerpts from *Saskatchewan* (Toronto: Macmillan Publishing, 1968).

KEN MCGOOGAN. Excerpt from *Ancient Mariner:The Amazing Adventures of Samuel Hearne, the Sailor Who Walked to the Arctic Ocean,* A Phyllis Bruce Book, published by HarperCollinsPublishing Ltd. Copyright © 2003 by Ken McGoogan. All rights reserves. Reprinted by permission of the publisher.

GARY AND JOANIE MCGUFFIN. Excerpt from *Where Rivers Run.* © GaryandJoanieMcGuffin.com (Toronto: The Boston Mills Press, 1988). Reprinted by permission of the authors.

FRANK MITCHELL. Excerpt from *Pioneering in the Pakan District.* (Self-published, 1972). Reprinted by permission of the estate of Frank Mitchell.

MARK MORRIS. *Drayton Valley Gaze.* Unpublished. Reprinted by permission of the author.

JACK NISBET. Excerpt from *Sources of the River: Tracking David Thompson Across North America.* (Seattle: Sasquatch Books, 1994). Reprinted by permission of the publisher.

HARRY PINIUTA. Excerpt from *Land of Pain, Land of Promise: First Person Accounts by Ukrainian Pioneers 1891-1914.* (Saskatoon: Western Producer Prairie Books, Saskatoon 1978).

ROBERT PRUDEN. Excerpt from *Yakking the River.* Unpublished. Reprinted by permission of the author.

LLOYD RATZLAFF. Excerpt from *The Crow Who Tampered With Time*. (Saskatoon: Thistledown Press, 2002); Reprinted by permission of the publisher.

PETER REAM. Excerpt from *The Fort on the Saskatchewan*. (Self-published, 1974). Reprinted by permission of the estate of Peter Ream.

BRIAN O.K. REEVES. 'Sacred Geography: First Nations of the Yellowstone to Yukon' from *A Sense of Place*. (http://www.y2y.net/science/conservation/sensey2y.pdf: Yellowstone to Yukon Conservation Initiative, 1998). Reprinted by permission of the author.

BRUCE RICE. "Enough," from *Descent Into Lima*. (Regina: Coteau Books, 1996). Reprinted by permission of the author.

MARION SMITH: Excerpt from *Koo-Koo-Sint : David Thompson in Western Canada*. (Calgary: Red Deer Press, 1975). Reprinted by permission of the publisher.

JOHN SNOW. Excerpts reprinted with permission from *These Mountains are Our Sacred Places*. Copyright © 1977. John Snow. Published by Fifth House Ltd., Calgary, Canada.

GLEN SORESTAD. 'Rivers' from *Blood and Bone, Ice and Stone*. (Saskatoon: Thistledown Press, 2005). Reprinted by permission of the publisher.

———. "Windsong" from *What is Already Known*. (Saskatoon: Thistledown Press, 1995). Reprinted by permission of the publisher.

BIRK SPROXTON. Excerpt from *Headframe*. (Winnipeg: Turnstone Press). Reprinted by permission of the publisher.

JOHN STACKHOUSE. "The Healing Power of Hockey," from the *Globe and Mail*, Nov 7, 2001. Reprinted by permission of the author.

FRED STENSON. Excerpts from *The Trade*. Copyright © 2000 by Fred Stenson. Published by Douglas & McIntyre Ltd. Reprinted by permission of the publisher.

JAMES R. STEVENS. Excerpt from *Sacred Legends*. (Ottawa: Penumbra Press, 2003). Reprinted by permission of the publisher.

BLAIR STONECHILD & BILL WAISER. Excerpt reprinted with permission from *Loyal Till Death: Indians and the North-West Rebellion*. Copyright 1997. Blair Stonechild and Bill Waiser. Published by Fifth House Ltd, Calgary, Canada

PETER SVARICH. Excerpt from *Memoirs: 1877-1904*, translated by William Kostash. (Edmonton: Ukrainian Pioneers Association of Alberta, 1999).Reprinted by permission of Mary Kostash.

ARITHA VAN HERK. Excerpts from *Places far From Ellesmere*. (Calgary: Red Deer Press, 1990). Reprinted by permission of the publisher.

JON WHYTE. "Homage, Henry Kelsey" from *Jon Whyte: Mind Over Mountains*. (Calgary: Red Deer Press, 2000). Reprinted by permission of the publisher.

———. Excerpt from *Indians in the Rockies*. (Banff: Altitude Publishing, 1985).

RUDY WIEBE. Extracted from *The Temptations of Big Bear* by Rudy Wiebe. Copyright © 1973 by Rudy Wiebe. Reprinted by permission of Knopf Canada.

Photograph Acknowledgements

p. 2, Whyte Museum of the Canadian Rockies, V263, Byron Harmon (Banff, AB).
p. 8, "Kootenay Plains and North Saskatchewan River Alberta, Canada." © Daryl Benson / Masterfile.
p. 14, Map courtesy of *Canadian Geographic Magazine*.
p. 21 or 22 or 23, Courtesy of Myrna Kostash.
p. 25, Glenbow Archives NA-3148-1.
p. 27, Whyte Museum of the Canadian Rockies, V653, Vaux family (Philadelphia, USA).
p. 30, Glenbow Archives NA-2657-32.
p. 34, Permission granted by Anne (McMullen) Belliveau, Nordegg and Area Historian.
p. 36, Glenbow Archives NA-1263-9.
p. 41, Glenbow Archives NA-1263-25.
p. 50, Glenbow Archives NA-577-2.
p. 57, Glenbow Archives NA-642-1.
p. 61, Glenbow Archives NA-614-11.
p. 63, Glenbow Archives NA-2657-32.
p. 76, Glenbow Archives NA-2657-21.
p. 84, Glenbow Archives NA-3993-8.
p. 88, Glenbow Archives NA-1258-26.
p. 91, Glenbow Archives NA-1408-4.
p. 101, Glenbow Archives NA3190-1.
p. 109, Glenbow Archives NA-2750-33.
p. 111, Glenbow Archives NC-6-6210.
p. 112, Glenbow Archives NC-6-1438.
p. 112, Glenbow Archives NC-6-1432.
p. 115, Glenbow Archives NA-709-1.
p. 122, Glenbow Archives NC-6-519.
p. 124, Glenbow Archives ND-3-5833C.
p. 128, Glenbow Archives NC-6-1107.
p. 138, Glenbow Archives NA-1529-7.
p. 144, Glenbow Archives ND-3-3757.
p. 150, Royal Alberta Museum.
p. 162, Glenbow Archives NA-3764-1.
p. 173, Glenbow Archives NA-1654-1.
p. 190, Glenbow Archives NA-1906-6.
p. 206, Glenbow Archives NA-1138-3.
p. 218, Courtesy of Athanasious Garanis.
p. 224, © Robin Karpan.
p. 226, With permission of the Royal Ontario Museum © ROM.
p. 242, Glenbow Archives NA-2022-9.
p. 244, Glenbow Archives NA-2589-10.
p. 254, © Robin Karpan.
p. 264, © Robin Karpan.
p. 272, Glenbow Archives NA-361-25.
p. 273, Glenbow Archives NA-303-237.
p. 279, Archives of Manitoba N21180.
p. 284, Glenbow Archives PA-2218-393.
p. 286, Saskatchewan Archives Board (SAB) S-B9787.
p. 292, Glenbow Archives NA-2186-44.
p. 312, Glenbow Archives NA-1338-45.
p. 320, Canada. Dept. of Interior / Library and Archives Canada / PA-041575.
p. 328, Glenbow Archives NA-4205-1.

PHOTO: RICHARD GISHLER

MYRNA KOSTASH is one of Canada's best-known non-fiction writers, with seven critically acclaimed books to her credit, including the classic *All of Baba's Children*, as well as *Bloodlines: A Journey Into Eastern Europe*, and the deeply personal *The Doomed Bridegroom*. Besides writing for many magazines, she has written for theatre cabaret, radio drama, and television documentary, and has published work in numerous anthologies, such as Coteau Books' *Going Some Place*.

She has worked as a writer-in-residence in Regina, Saskatoon, Minneapolis, the University of Alberta, and at the Whyte Museum in Banff; and as the Ashley Fellow at Trent University; and has lectured throughout Canada. Alberta-born and raised, Myrna continues to live and work in Edmonton.

DUANE BURTON lives in Edmonton where she works as a researcher, video producer, and social worker. She is a student of teachings from the Native Oral Tradition. Currently she is working on the Standoff Reserve's video project *Blackfoot Ways of Knowing* and the Prairie Child Welfare Consortium's project *Making Our Hearts Sing: An Exploration of Aboriginal Child Welfare*.

OKANAGAN REGIONAL LIBRARY
3 3132 02554 3887